The
Reference Shelf®

Revisiting Gender

The Reference Shelf
Volume 86 • Number 2
H. W. Wilson
A Division of EBSCO Information Services
Ipswich, Massachusetts
2014

GREY HOUSE PUBLISHING

The Reference Shelf

The books in this series contain reprints of articles, excerpts from books, addresses on cur-rent issues, and studies of social trends in the United States and other countries. There are six separately bound numbers in each volume, all of which are usually published in the same calendar year. Numbers one through five are each devoted to a single subject, provid-ing background information and discussion from various points of view and concluding with an index and comprehensive bibliography that lists books, pamphlets, and articles on the subject. The final number of each volume is a collection of recent speeches. Books in the series may be purchased individually or on subscription.

Library of Congress Cataloging-in-Publication Data

Revisiting gender / [compiled by H. W. Wilson].
    pages : illustrations ; cm. -- (The reference shelf ; volume 86, number 2)
    Includes bibliographical references and index.
    ISBN: 978-1-61925-433-6 (v. 86, no. 2)
    ISBN: 978-1-61925-261-5 (volume set)
    1. Sex role--United States. 2. Women--Education--United States. 3. Women in tech-nology--United States. 4. Women in the professions--United States. 5. Women--Political activity--United States. 6. Women--United States--Social conditions. I. H.W. Wilson Company. II. Series: Reference shelf ; v. 86, no. 2.
HQ1421 .R48 2014
305.42/0973

Cover: Sheryl Sandberg (© The Washington Post/Getty Images)

The Reference Shelf, 2014, published by Grey House Publishing, Inc., Amenia, NY, under exclusive license from EBSCO Information Services, Inc.

Printed in the United States of America

Contents

3

Women, Men, and Political Life

4

Media and the Sexes

5

Gender Roles in America

Preface

Gender in the United States

Throughout the twentieth century, American women increasingly broke free from gender stereotypes, leaving behind traditional roles in the home and taking to the public sphere. Women pursued higher education in greater numbers, sought careers in traditionally male-dominated technology and science fields, and strived for executive positions in major corporations. In the early twenty-first century, female leaders in education, politics, business, and media serve as role models for young girls and provide additional opportunities for female participation and leadership in all areas of society. However, this growth brings unique challenges, and much work remains to be done in order to understand why women continue to be underrepresented in many of these areas.

Women in STEM

As women increasingly enter the workforce and build careers outside the home, concern grows over whether a gender gap exists in education, and if so, what can be done to close the gap. In particular, the lack of female professionals in STEM (science, technology, engineering, and math) fields raises questions about why women do not pursue these fields at the same rate as men. One controversial explanation is that women have a lower aptitude for logical and analytical problem solving than men; on the other hand, some suggest that stereotypes, cultural conditioning, and the environment within many US public school systems discourage women from pursuing these fields regardless of aptitude.

Some educators favor providing single-sex education, on the grounds that girls will be more likely to pursue—and succeed in—traditionally male subjects in an all-girl classroom environment. However, a study published in 2014 in the American Psychological Association's *Psychological Bulletin* analyzed forty-five years of data collected from 1.6 million students in twenty-one countries, and found the advantages of single-sex education to be trivial or nonexistent. So the debate about alleged gender bias in the classroom continues.

Despite the potential challenges, women increasingly pursue careers in STEM fields: as of 2009, about 24 percent of individuals employed in STEM fields were women. The percentage of women in STEM-related higher education also increased over time, and as of 2013, women earn 41 percent of the PhD degrees in STEM fields. However, despite their increasing qualifications, women still only make up 28 percent of tenure-track faculty in those same fields, raising questions as to why. Studies conducted by the American Institute of Physics and the *Guardian* newspaper showed that women who pursue doctorate degrees in physics and chemistry left research and academia at a much higher rate than men with the same education level, although the reasons for this are still unclear.

Addressing the gender gap in STEM education is also significant because of its potential relationship to the wage gap between men and women. STEM fields tend to have the highest-paying jobs, but these fields are largely male-dominated (as much as 80 to 90 percent men); by contrast, traditionally female-dominated careers such as teaching and counseling are routinely among the lowest-paying jobs. Women who work in STEM fields earn on average 33 percent more than women in other fields, and STEM fields have a smaller pay gap for equal work based on gender.

However, it is unclear how to encourage girls to pursue STEM careers effectively, and how to keep women in these fields once they arrive. A White House report issued in June 2013 emphasized the importance of providing girls and young women with highly visible and successful role models in STEM fields, as well as increasing access to educational opportunities through internships, funding, and mentoring. But until we understand why girls choose to avoid STEM careers—and why so many women who pursue them ultimately leave—it will be difficult to establish these types of opportunities in any lasting way.

Women in Politics

While female representation in politics has yet to match the population at large, women increasingly occupy seats in federal and state legislative bodies. As of 2014, in the US House of Representatives, women hold 18.2 of the seats (79 of 435); in the US Senate, women hold 20 percent of the seats (20 of 100). Nationwide, women occupy 24.2 percent (1,784 of 7,383) of state legislative seats.

Within the judicial branch, women hold three of the nine seats on the US Supreme Court: Justices Ruth Bader Ginsberg, Sonia Sotomayor, and Elena Kagan. And women occupy seven cabinet and cabinet-level positions within the executive branch, including Secretary of the Interior Sally Jewell, Secretary of Commerce Penny Pritzker, and Secretary of Health and Human Services Kathleen Sebelius. Women occupy other notable executive positions as well, including Senior Advisor Valerie Jarrett and Director of the US Secret Service Julia Pierson.

The growing number of female representatives in federal and state government is an important step toward ensuring that women's rights and perspectives receive proper coverage and attention. They also provide strong role models for young girls who aspire to shape public policy and assume leadership roles in their communities.

Women in Corporate America

In addition to being underrepresented in STEM fields, women also make up a very small percentage of top-level executives in major corporations. As of 2014, women hold 4.6 percent of the chief executive officer positions in Fortune 500 companies—this means twenty-three female CEOs out of five hundred. These include Mary Barra of General Motors, Meg Whitman of Hewlett-Packard, Virginia Rometty of IBM, Indra K. Nooyi of PepsiCo, Marillyn Hewson of Lockheed Martin, and Ellen J. Kullman of DuPont.

However, the picture is changing rapidly: prior to 2011, there were only nine women in such positions, and growth had been nearly flat for at least a decade. Women are also rising to other high-level executive positions within major companies, such as Sheryl Sandberg, formerly of Google, and since 2008, chief operating officer of Facebook. Additionally, about 17 percent of the board members of Fortune 500 companies are women.

The increased visibility of women in high-ranking positions within major corporations raises a number of questions. Some wonder if aspiring female executives need to more closely match their male counterparts in behavior in order to be promoted into executive positions; and if so, is this necessarily a positive development? In 2013, Sandberg published the book *Lean In: Women, Work, and the Will to Lead*, in which she shares personal anecdotes and discusses the traits she believes lead her and fellow female executives to success in business. Sandberg's approach seems to be a hybrid in which she observes that some stereotypically male traits like strong self-esteem are necessary elements, but counters that more stereotypically female notions such as work/life balance do not preclude success. Perhaps unsurprisingly, she encountered criticism from both sides.

As more women take on higher-ranking positions, companies wonder how this will affect corporate culture. Traditionally—and perhaps stereotypically—male CEOs measure a company's success purely based on the financial bottom line, while female CEOs are more attuned to employee contentment and work/life balance. Former General Electric CEO Jack Welch seemed to reinforce this stereotype during his speech at the *Wall Street Journal's* Women in the Economy conference in 2012. Welch opined that success in business is about focused performance, and that mentoring and women's employee groups should be avoided, as they encourage women to adopt a "victim" attitude within the workplace. While female executives largely agreed with his advice that taking on risks and challenging assignments is a good way to establish worthiness as an executive, they balked at his failure to grasp the impact that gender bias can have in the boardroom—even in simple matters, such as how the same idea is received differently depending on whether the person presenting it is a man or a woman.

Women in the Media

Women's roles in society can also be shaped by their portrayal in the media. The Women's Media Center, founded by Jane Fonda, Robin Morgan, and Gloria Steinem, issued a report in 2013 on women in the US media, investigating trends such as the positions women hold in major media organizations, and the frequency of consultation and citation of female news contributors. The report noted that women were underrepresented in media benchmarks such as front-page bylines at top newspapers during coverage of the 2012 presidential election (where they were outnumbered by men three to one). Women made up 30 percent of television news directors—a slight increase from previous years—although the overall employment of women in television news remained flat, and women made up only about 25 percent of guests on Sunday television talk shows. On the bright side, the percentage of women employed as news directors in radio increased slightly, as did the overall percentage of female employees in both public radio and at large commercial stations.

This underrepresentation can affect how women are portrayed in the media, which in turn can influence how society views women more generally. Significant news issues, including issues that directly affect women, such as abortion and contraception, are still covered largely by male reporters (around 70 percent). And since men hold most of the news director positions, they retain control over what news is reported and who is given the assignment.

However, women such as Oprah Winfrey and Martha Stewart are changing this picture. Although they both started in stereotypically female television roles by hosting talk shows and cooking shows, they eventually established multimillion-dollar media empires that include magazines, television channels, and books. By establishing their own media outlets, they provide an opportunity for women to change the way they are represented in the media without relying on support from traditionally male-dominated outlets.

Women in Culture and Society

The issues addressed above are all part of the overarching issue of attitudes toward women in American culture generally. Traditionally, women's roles in housekeeping and child-rearing relegated them to the private sphere, while men dominated the public sphere in work, politics, and media. This shifted significantly during the twentieth century, as some of the women who took over men's jobs during World Wars I and II decided to keep their new careers and the independence that came with them.

However, the image of the home as the woman's domain persists. Female professionals may face discrimination in the workplace due to the perception that women put their families before the company. And indeed, women who work outside the home do report that they are tasked with family responsibilities more often than their male spouses, even if they are the primary breadwinner. And perhaps some men feel threatened by increased competition in the workforce or are unsure whether and how having more women in key roles might affect their own career progression; change is never easy, to be sure.

But as more women enter the traditionally male arenas of higher education, STEM careers, politics, executive positions, and media ownership, public perception changes and momentum builds. Women are increasingly pursuing STEM fields—both professionally and in higher education—and mentoring girls who express interest in these fields. The US government and private companies provide opportunities for girls and women to explore these careers by offering resources such as job opportunities, research funding, and mentorship. Female CEOs and top-level executives show young women that it is possible to succeed in big business, and their increased presence provides more comfortable environments for women to pursue their career goals free from harassment and stereotypes. And finally, female media moguls provide more opportunities for women to shape how they are portrayed in the media, what news is reported, and whose perspective is heard.

—Tracey DiLascio

Bibliography

Bussey, John. "How Women Can Get Ahead: Advice from Female CEOs." *Wall Street Journal*. Dow Jones, 18 May 2012. Web. 12 Feb. 2014.

"Current Numbers of Women Officeholders." *Center for American Women and Politics*. Rutgers, 2014. Web. 12 Feb. 2014.

Henderson, Nia-Malika. "Obama, Democrats Put Spotlight on Gender Pay Gap. Will It Matter?" *Washington Post*. Washington Post, 29 Jan. 2014. Web. 12 Feb. 2014.

Ivie, Rachel, and Casey Langer Tesfaye. "Women in Physics: A Tale of Limits." *Physics Today*. American Inst. of Physics, Feb. 2012. Web. 12 Feb. 2014.

Klein, Rebecca. "Single-Sex Education Does Not Improve Girls' Self-Esteem, Math Achievement: Study." *Huffington Post*. TheHuffingtonPost.com, 5 Feb. 2014. Web. 6 Feb. 2014.

Klos, Diana Mitsu. "The Status of Women in the US Media 2013." *Women's Media Center*. Women's Media Center, 2013. Web. 12 Feb. 2014.

Luscombe, Belinda. "GM's New Boss Is a Woman, but the CEO Gender Gap Is Still Gaping." *Time*. Time, 10 Dec. 2013. Web. 12 Feb. 2014.

Pahlke, Erin, Janet Shibley Hyde, and Carlie M. Allison. "The Effects of Single-Sex Compared with Coeducational Schooling on Students' Performance and Attitudes: A Meta-Analysis." *Psychological Bulletin*. American Psychological Assoc., 3 Feb. 2014. Web. 12 Feb. 2014.

"Women and Girls in Science, Technology, Engineering, and Math (STEM)." *WhiteHouse.gov*. Executive Office of the President, June 2013. Web. 12 Feb. 2014.

1

The Balance in Education

Stephanie Godding of the Renaissance School works on a solar cell project during the Women in Engineering and Computing Career Day at the University of Massachusetts.

The Gender Gap in Education and Employment

In 2011, the US Census Bureau announced that in 2010, among working Americans aged twenty-five and older, more women had bachelor's degrees than men (37 versus 35 percent)—reflecting a history since the 1990s of American women enrolling in college at a greater rate than men. As of 2013, the World Economic Forum reported that the United States ranked first (tied with twenty-four other countries) out of a sample of 136 nations in terms of gender equality in education, and yet the same report indicates that the United States ranks twenty-third in overall gender equality, just behind the African nation of Burundi.

While women have made significant gains, they continue to lag behind men in professional achievement and are underrepresented in key occupations, including the STEM fields (science, technology, engineering, and mathematics). The gap between education and professional achievement is one of the current frontiers in the ongoing struggle to achieve gender equality. To investigate this complex issue, researchers are taking an in-depth look at each stage of education and reevaluating seminal issues—including the benefits and detriments of coeducation and the formation of gender stereotypes—to discover the best way to address educational disparities in the present and future.

Shifting Balance in Education

America's first public school was established in 1635 near Boston, Massachusetts, but women were not permitted to attend public schools for more than a century. Boston public primary schools began admitting women in 1789 and, in the 1820s, opened public secondary schools to female students. In 1789, the literacy rate for American women was only half that of men. After women were admitted to the public school system, literacy rates quickly grew, and by the 1870s, women students surpassed their male counterparts in literacy and academic achievement at the primary and secondary levels.

Efforts to promote educational equality commingled with the women's suffrage movement and the struggle to achieve employment equality. Landmark legal victories, such as ratification of the Nineteenth Amendment in 1920, passage of the Civil Rights Act of 1964, and the Title IX amendment of 1972, which officially prohibits gender bias in higher education, have helped to level the playing field in terms of educational opportunity. By 1980, women outpaced men in undergraduate enrollment, though they still lagged behind in degree completion.

In 2011, the Census Bureau reported that 36 percent of women aged twenty-five to twenty-nine obtained bachelor's degrees or higher, compared to 28 percent of men.

In the wake of these developments, researchers are attempting to determine how the changing demographics of education will affect the future of American society. In addition, educators are still attempting to address continuing gender gaps in education and the disparity between female educational achievement and later career success.

Gender and Learning

In the twenty-first century, there has been a growing effort to discover why men are falling behind in education. Some theorists argue that the education system has become increasingly "feminized" through the adoption of teaching methods that favor women over men. Increasingly, theoretical gender-based differences in learning have been used as an argument to promote same-gender schooling or specific single-gender programs within public schools.

Recent MRI studies have shown that male and female brains develop differently, and that these differences may affect cognitive learning. Gender differences in neurology have become a primary argument for gender-specific education. However, neurologists argue that the complexity of brain development makes it difficult to differentiate between the effects of biology and environmental influence. For instance, a 2008 study published in *Scientific American* found that neuronal structures used in social cognition appear to correlate with a child's biological sex but also with the development of "feminine" personality characteristics that appear in both male and female children.

Dr. Leonard Sax, director of the National Association for Single Sex Education, has been one of the most outspoken supporters of creating single-sex options in public education. Sax believes that single-sex institutions and programs can address innate and learned behavioral characteristics that differ according to gender and argues that the current model, with a focus on homework and independent study, is not the best way to educate male students. Supporters also argue that single-sex education frees both sexes from engaging in gender roles aimed at the opposite sex and therefore allows students to concentrate on their education.

However, in a 2011 study published in *Science*, researchers presented evidence that single-sex education may contribute to the development of institutional sexism and argued that current research does not validate the claim that single-sex education is more effective for learning. While limited studies indicate improved academic performance in single-sex schools, critics argue that these same pilot programs also feature innovations such as smaller class size and modern teaching methods that might be responsible for improved student performance. A 2010 study in *Child Development* suggests that children as young as three display an increased tendency to accept gender stereotypes when separated into single-sex classrooms.

In a 2006 report for the think tank Education Sector, analyst Sarah Mead questions the need to better address the educational needs of male students, and cites statistics indicating that both male and female academic performance has improved, though female students are improving at a faster rate. Some critics of single-sex education believe that research is needed to determine the psychological mechanisms underlying differences in learning styles, which could then be used to create learn-ing style–based, rather than gender-based, educational programs.

Educational Completion

A 2012 study by the American Sociological Association indicates that the gender gap in college dropout rates may be related to the continuing gulf between male and female earning potential. The study shows that men who drop out of college to enter the labor market initially earn about the same as recent male college gradu-ates; however, women who drop out earn an average of $6,500 less than recent female college graduates. Because men have better job opportunities in entry-level positions, more men may opt for immediate earning rather than accruing debt by attending college. However, longitudinal studies show that the male earning advan-tage is not lasting, and that by middle age, men with college degrees earn signifi-cantly more than those who did not finish college.

Women also enroll in college at a higher rate than men, and this phenomenon may be related to ongoing gender norms in American society. Men may be encour-aged to begin working at an earlier age, while education may be preferred for women until they reach marriage or childrearing age. This phenomenon may also be related to the fact that many "untrained" labor positions and careers based on professional apprenticeship are in fields dominated by men.

In the 2013 book *The Rise of Women: The Growing Gender Gap in Education and What It Means for American Schools*, authors Thomas DiPrete and Claudia Buch-mann suggest that the social construction of masculinity may also play a role in discouraging male interest in education. Men involved in alternative school activi-ties, such as art, music, theater, and foreign languages, display a higher interest in education, and yet men are less likely to pursue alternative interests because of gen-der stereotypes that label these activities as non-masculine. The authors argue that schools need to move beyond gender stereotypes by treating students as individuals with individual learning styles.

Achievement after Graduation

According to 2013 data presented by the Pew Foundation, the wage gap between women and men is narrowing. In 2013, women earned 84 percent of what men earned for the same occupations, as compared with 64 percent in 1980. The study also indicated that the current generation of women reaching working age will earn, on average, approximately 93 percent as much as men, marking the first generation in American history to achieve near-parity in income.

The narrowing of the wage gap is related to higher levels of education among women, an overall increase in women's salaries over the last thirty years, and a 4 per-cent reduction in male salaries between 1980 and 2012. In 2012, Census Bureau statistics indicated that women comprised 47 percent of the American workforce. Women have also advanced in managerial positions, with 14 percent of women working in management or administration in 2012, an increase of 6 percent since

1980. Comparatively, only 4.2 percent of managers of the nation's Fortune 500 companies are women, indicating that women have made far less progress in breaking into the nation's more elite economic environments.

The wage gap differs according to industry, with women's salaries ranging from 69 to 94 percent of men's. Women continue to earn less in fields dominated by men, such as business and commerce, where women earn an average of 74 percent of men's salaries in the same fields. Women also have continued difficulties reaching parity within academic research and higher education. According to the National Science Foundation, women hold 19 percent of full professorship positions in the United States and lag significantly behind male colleagues in terms of publishing in academic journals. National Academy of Sciences data from 2007 also indicates that women in academia earn as much as 30 percent less, on average, than men in the same fields and are less likely to be promoted to leadership positions within American universities.

The achievement gap between men and women in STEM fields is related to lower levels of interest among female students at the primary and secondary levels and to gender-role stereotypes that discourage women from entering STEM fields. A 2011 report from the US Department of Commerce indicated that female involvement in STEM fields has not increased since 2000 and that women account for less than 30 percent of STEM jobs as a whole. Potential solutions that have been proposed to address this issue include creating female-oriented science and technology programs beginning at the K–12 level and training teachers and parents to discourage gender role stereotypes that equate men with occupations like computer science and engineering. The Women in STEM program, initiated by the administration of President Barack Obama, has resulted in a series of informational websites and advertisements aimed at attracting young women to STEM fields.

Creating Balance

While female participation in education represents a major step toward gender equality, it is still necessary to facilitate female success in traditionally male-dominated fields in an effort to foster occupational balance that mirrors the nation's increasing educational balance. Even as women approach occupational parity with men, women who choose to have children suffer from more substantial earning and advancement setbacks than men who have families, and this dynamic continues to prevent the establishment of gender equality.

While a variety of policy and institutional changes have been proposed to address current imbalances in education, the general consensus across fields is that further research is needed to investigate the relationship among gender, education, and future success. Further, it may be necessary for educators and psychologists to create programs that work by addressing individual personality types rather than gender models in efforts to promote education that allows the greatest number of students to succeed within and beyond education.

—Micah Issitt

Bibliography

DiPrete, Thomas A., and Claudia Buchmann. *The Rise of Women: The Growing Gender Gap in Education and What It Means for American Schools.* New York: Russell Sage, 2013. Print.

Dwyer, Rachel E., Randy Hodson, and Laura McCloud. "Gender, Debt, and Dropping Out of College." *Gender and Society* 27.1 (2013): 30–55. Print.

Eliot, Lise. "Girl Brain, Boy Brain?" *Scientific American.* Scientific American, 8 Sept. 2009. Web. 7 Feb. 2014.

Hillman, Lacey J., and Lynn S. Liben. "Differing Levels of Gender Salience in Preschool Classrooms: Effects on Children's Gender Attitudes and Intergroup Bias." *Child Development* 81.6 (2010): 1787–98. Print.

Lewin, Tamar. "Single-Sex Education Is Assailed in Report." *New York Times.* New York Times, 22 Sept. 2011. Web. 7 Feb. 2014.

Mead, Sara. "The Truth about Boys and Girls." *Education Sector.* Education Sector, 2006. Web. 7 Feb. 2014.

"More Working Women Than Men Have College Degrees, Census Bureau Reports." *US Census Bureau.* US Census Bureau, 26 Apr. 2011. Web. 7 Feb. 2014.

"On Pay Gap, Millennial Women Near Parity—For Now: Despite Gains, Many See Roadblocks Ahead." *Pew Research Social and Demographic Trends.* Pew Research Center, 11 Dec. 2013. Web. 7 Feb. 2014.

"Science and Gender." *Nature Immunology* 11.2 (2009): 99. Print.

Wilson, Robin, "Scholarly Publishing's Gender Gap." *Chronicle of Higher Education.* Chronicle of Higher Education, 22 Oct. 2012. Web. 7 Feb. 2014.

An Educator's Primer on the Gender War

By David Sadker
Phi Beta Kappan, February 1, 2011

Several recent books, a seemingly endless series of television and radio talk shows, and a number of newspaper columns have painted a disturbing picture of schools mired in a surreptitious war on boys. In such books as *The War Against Boys* (Sommers 2000) and *Ceasefire!* (Young 1999), readers are introduced to education using war metaphors and are informed that boys are daily casualties of zealous efforts to help girls. These "schools-at-war" authors also call for more "boy-friendly" education, including increased testing, frequent classroom competitions, and the inclusion of war poetry in the curriculum—all measures intended to counter feminist influences. They also argue that sections of Title IX, the law that prohibits sex discrimination in education, be rescinded. Teachers are informed that giving extra attention to boys in classrooms and building up school libraries that are dominated by books about male characters are useful strategies to improve boys' academic performance. As one book warns, "It's a bad time to be a boy in America."

After over a quarter century of researching life in schools, I must admit that at first I thought this "gender war" was a satire, a creative way to alert people to the difficulties of creating fair schools that work for all children. Certainly boys (like girls) confront gender stereotypes and challenges, and teachers and parents must work hard every day to make schools work for all children. But these recent books and talk shows were not intended as satire; they purported to present a serious picture of schools in which girls ruled and boys were their victims.

The irony of girls waging a war on boys reminded me of a "Seinfeld" episode that featured "Bizarro World." For those of you not versed in the culture of Bizarro World, it is a Superman comics theme in which everything is opposite: up is down, in is out, and good is bad. When the popular sitcom featured an episode on Bizarro World, Kramer became polite and discovered that doors were to be knocked on, not stormed through. George went from nerdiness to cool, from dysfunctional to popular; he was rewarded with two well-adjusted parents. Elaine's self-absorption was transformed into compassion, a change that would probably lead to a hitch in the Peace Corps and stardom in her own "Seinfeld" spin-off, "Elaine in Africa." In this topsy-turvy transformation, the entire "Seinfeld" gang became well-adjusted, with their ethical compasses recalibrated to do the right thing. What would schools be like, I thought, if such Bizarro World changes came to pass? What would school look like if "misguided feminists" were actually engaged in a "war against boys"? And then I thought, what if girls really did rule?

(Camera fade-in)

The statue of the great woman dominates the front lawn of suburban Alice Paul High School. *(Alice Paul, of course, led the courageous fight for women to be recognized as citizens, and her efforts contributed to passage of the 19th Amendment.)* By 2003, Alice Paul, Susan B. Anthony, and Hillary Rodham Clinton have become the most common names for America's schools.

The statute of Alice Paul at the entrance of the school has become a student talis-woman. Students rub Alice's big toe before taking the SAT or on the eve of a critical soccer match with their cross-town rivals, the Stanton Suffragettes. Although Alice Paul died in 1977, she remains a real presence on campus.

Once inside Alice Paul High School, images of famous women are everywhere. Pictures of Jeannette Rankin, Mary MacLeod Bethune, Margaret Sanger, Carry Nation, and Mia Hamm gaze down on students as they go to their classes, constant reminders of the power and accomplishments of women. There are few if any pictures of men, as if in confirmation of the old adage, "It's a woman's world." Trophy cases overflow with artifacts trumpeting women's role in ending child labor, reforming schools, eliminating domestic violence, confronting alcoholism, and battling for healthcare reform. It is the same story in the technology and math wing of Alice Paul High, where the influence of such computer pioneers as Ada Loveless and Grace Hopper can be seen everywhere.

Few images of males can be found anywhere in the hallways—or in the textbooks. The typical history text devotes less than 5% of its content to the contributions of men, a percentage that actually shrinks in math and science texts. Other than the one or two "unusual men" who find their way into the curriculum, students learn that their world was constructed almost exclusively by and for women.

Not everyone is happy with female-dominated bulletin boards and textbooks, as school principal Anna Feminie knows all too well. *(Most school principals are, of course, female, since they seem better equipped to manage demanding parents and a predominantly male faculty.)* From time to time, a few vociferous parents of boys complain about the lack of male images. But Anna has been in her job for five years now, and she knows just how to handle angry parents. She makes a big show of Men's History Month. Almost magically, every March, a new crop of male figures materializes. Anna understands that Men's History Month is nothing more than a nod to political correctness. Luckily, most parents and faculty agree with Anna and feel more comfortable with the well-known female names and images from their own student days. But all that may be changing with the increased emphasis on standardized state tests. New history standards put the traditional female front and center once again, and perhaps the end of Men's History Month is in sight. And if that should come to pass, it would be just fine with principal Anna Feminie.

By 8 a.m., hallway noise is at a peak as students exchange last-minute comments before the late bell sounds. Crowds of girls rule the school's "prime real estate": main stairwells, cafeteria entrance, and the senior locker bay. In groups, the girls can be even more intimidating. Individual boys carefully weave their way around these "girl areas," looking down to avoid unwanted stares and snares. The strategy is less than effective. Sometimes, the boys are forced to pretend that they do not hear those louder-than-a-whisper *offensive comments. At other times, the boys rapidly sidestep the outstretched arms of some of the more aggressive girls who are trying to impress their friends. Boys at Alice Paul travel in bands for safety, like convoys at sea. They smile a lot and speak a little. Although they do not quite understand it all, they know that they are at some risk, even in their own school, and taking precautions has become second nature.*

Girls dominate in classrooms as well. They shout out answers, and teachers accept their behavior as "natural," part of their more aggressive biological makeup. Not true for the boys. When boys call out, they are likely to be reminded to "raise your hand." Even when girls do not shout out, teachers call on them more often than on boys, reward them more, help them more, and criticize them more. With girls as the center of classroom attention, boys seem content to sit quietly on the sidelines: Low profiles are safe profiles.

Most boys take to their quiet, second-class role with incredible grace. They enroll in the programs more suitable for their nature: the humanities and social sciences courses, as well as the typical and predictable vocational programs. Few boys are assigned to costly special education programs. While educating boys is relatively inexpensive, there are rewards associated with lower career goals, docility, and conformity. Every quarter, boys are rewarded with higher grades on report cards. Boys are also more likely to be listed on the honor roll and chosen to be the school valedictorian. Teachers appreciate boys who do their work on time, cause few disruptions, demand less in class, rarely complain, and do not need special education.

While these higher report card grades are comforting, low test scores are disturbing. When the SAT and other competitive tests roll around, boys' scores lag behind girls on both math and verbal tests. On virtually every high-stakes test that matters, including the Advanced Placement tests and later the Graduate Record Exam, girls outscore boys. Few adults wonder why boys' high report card grades are not reflected in these very important test scores.

While the athletic field offers a change of venue, it is basically the same story. At Alice Paul, boys' football, baseball, and basketball do not hold a candle to girls' field hockey and soccer. The student newspaper is filled with the exploits of the Alice Paul Amazons, as the female athletes are called. The Gentleman Amazons draw smaller crowds and less coverage in the school paper. Funding for just one of the girls' teams can equal the entire male athletic budget. Although some parents have tried to bolster male sports, coaches, parents, and the influential state athletic association have thwarted their efforts.

Female domination of athletics is accompanied by the ringing of a cash register. A few female athletes not only have won college scholarships but also have moved into the multimillion-dollar ranks of the professionals. Amazon booster clubs have been generous to Alice Paul, funding the new athletic field, the state-of-the-art girls' training facility, and a number of athletic scholarships. The Alice Paul Amazons ignite school spirit and have won several state championships. No one was surprised five years ago when the former girls' field hockey coach, Anna Feminie, was chosen as the new principal.

If Alice Paul were alive today, she would be proud of her Amazons. Alice Paul women dominate corporate boardrooms and government offices, and many are leaders

promoting social reform around the globe. And Alice herself would be no less proud of the men who graduate from her school, true partners with women at work and at home.
(Camera fade-out)

The description of the fictional Alice Paul High School is a true reflection of hundreds of studies of school life, with one obvious modification (after all, it is Bizarro World): The genders have been reversed. The idea that "girls rule" in school is not only silly, it is intentionally deceptive. So, why all the recent commotion about "a war on boys"?

Certainly boys do not always fit comfortably into the school culture, but this has little to do with girls—and a lot to do with how we conduct school. In fact, both girls and boys confront different school challenges, and they respond in different ways. Girls are more likely to react to problems in a quieter and less disruptive fashion, while boys are more likely to act out—or drop out. Males of color in particular drop out of high school more often and enroll in college less frequently than either minority females or white males. Decades of studies, books, and reports have documented the school difficulties of boys generally and of boys of color in particular.

The new twist in the current debate is the scapegoating of the feminist movement. And for those who were never very comfortable with the feminist movement, these new books and their ultraconservative spokespeople have an allure. Many mainstream media fixate on the audience appeal of a "Mars versus Venus" scenario, portraying boys as hapless victims of "male-hating feminists." Even educators and parents who do not blame females for the problems boys experience still buy into the argument that girls are "ahead" in school.

But, for people to believe that "girls are responsible for boys' problems," they must repress historical realities: These problems predated the women's movement. Boys' reading difficulties, for example, existed long before modern feminism was even a twinkle in Betty Friedan's eye, and the dropout rate has actually decreased since the publication of *The Feminine Mystique*. Ironically, it was female teachers who fought hard to remove corporal punishment, while promoting new instructional strategies that moved teachers beyond lecture and recitation. Women educators led the movement for more humane classrooms, and the current attack on feminism has the potential of hurting boys as well as girls.

The truth is that *both* boys and girls exhibit different strengths and have different needs, and gender stereotypes shortchange all of us. So, where are we in terms of the progress made for both girls and boys in school today? And what challenges still remain? The following "Report Card" takes us beyond the phony gender war and offers a succinct update of salient research findings.

A Report Card on the Costs of Gender Bias

Grades and Tests

Females. Females receive better grades from elementary school through college, but not everyone sees this as good news. Some believe that this may be one of the "rewards" girls receive for more quiet and conforming classroom behavior (Sadker and Sadker 1995).

Female test scores in several areas have improved dramatically in recent years. The performance of females on science and math achievement tests has improved, and girls now take more Advanced Placement tests than boys. Yet they lag behind males on a number of important tests, scoring lower on both the verbal and mathematics sections of the SAT, the Advanced Placement exams, and the Graduate Record Exam (NCES 1999, 2000a: 149; Coley 2001; ACT 1999; ETS 2000: 8)

Males. Males (and students from low-income families) not only receive lower grades, but they are also more likely to be grade repeaters. Many believe that school norms and culture conflict with many male behavior patterns (Sadker and Sadker 2001: 130). The National Assessment of Educational Progress and many other exams indicate that males perform significantly below females in writing and reading achievement (Sadker and Sadker 2001: 130, 136).

Academic Enrollment

Females. Female enrollment in science and mathematics courses has increased dramatically in recent years. Girls are more likely to take biology and chemistry as well as trigonometry and Algebra II. However, boys still dominate physics, calculus, and more advanced courses, and boys are more likely to take all three core science courses—biology, chemistry, and physics (AAUW 1998).

College programs are highly segregated, with women earning between 75% and 90% of the degrees in education, nursing, home economics, library science, psychology, and social work. Women trail men in Ph.D.s (just 40% are awarded to women) and in professional degrees (42% to women). And women are in the minority at seven of eight Ivy League schools (NCES 2000a: 290; 1999 data gathered from university admissions offices of Brown, Columbia, Cornell, Dartmouth, Harvard, Princeton, the University of Pennsylvania, and Yale).

Computer science and technology reflect increasing gender disparities. Boys not only enroll in more such courses, but they also enroll in the more advanced courses. Girls are more likely to be found in word-processing classes and clerical support programs. Girls are also less likely to use computers outside school, and girls from all ethnic groups rate themselves considerably lower than boys on technological ability. Current software products are more likely to reinforce these gender stereotypes than to reduce them (AAUW 1998: 54–55).

Males. Males have a higher high school dropout rate than females (13% to 10%), and they trail females in extracurricular participation, including school government, literary activities, and the performing arts (NCES 2000a: 127).

Men are the minority (44%) of students enrolled in both undergraduate and graduate institutions, and they lag behind women in degree attainment at the associate (39%), bachelor's (44%), and master's (44%) levels. Although white males and females attend college in fairly equal proportions, black and Hispanic males are particularly underrepresented at all levels of education (NCES 2000a: 290).

Gender segregation continues to limit the academic and career majors of all students. Male college students account for only 12% of elementary education majors, 11% of special education majors, 12% of library science majors, and 14% of those majoring in social work (NCES 2000a: 290).

Academic Interactions and Special Programs

Females. Females have fewer academic contacts with instructors in class. They are less likely to be called on by name, are asked fewer complex and abstract questions, receive less praise or constructive feedback, and are given less direction on how to do things for themselves. In short, girls are more likely to be invisible members of classrooms (Good and Findley 1985: 271–294; Jones and Wheatley 1990; Morse and Handley 1985; Sadker and Sadker 1984, 1995: 42–46).

In elementary school, girls are identified for gifted programs more often than boys; however, by high school, fewer girls remain in gifted programs, particularly fewer black and Hispanic girls. Gender segregation is also evident in the low number of gifted girls found in math and science programs (OCR 1999; AAUW 1998).

Males. Boys receive more teacher attention than females, including more negative attention. They are disciplined more harshly, more publicly, and more frequently than girls, even when they violate the same rules. Parents of male elementary school students (24%) are contacted more frequently about their child's behavior or schoolwork than parents of female students (12%), and boys constitute 71% of school suspensions ("Adolescent Boys" 1999; NCES 2000b: 32).

Males account for two-thirds of all students served in special education. The disproportionate representation of males in special education is highest in the categories of emotional disturbance (78% male), learning disability (68% male), and mental retardation (58% male) (OCR 1999: 1).

Health and Athletics

Females. About one million U.S. teenagers get pregnant each year, a higher percentage than in other Western nations. Fifty percent of adolescent girls believe that they are overweight, and 13% are diagnosed with anorexia, bulimia, or binge-eating disorder (Zoli 1999; CDCP 2000: 607).

Girls who play sports enjoy a variety of health benefits, including lower rates of pregnancy, drug use, and depression. But despite these benefits, only 50% of girls are enrolled in high school physical education classes. Women today coach only 44% of women's college teams and only 2% of men's teams, while men serve as athletic directors for over 80% of women's programs (Women's Sport Facts 2002: 6; NCAA 2000).

Males. Males are more likely than females to succumb to serious disease and be victims of accidents or violence. The average life expectancy of men is about six years shorter than that of women (CDCP 1999).

Boys are the majority (60%) of high school athletes. Male athletes in NCAA Division I programs graduate at a lower rate than female athletes (52% versus 68%) (Women's Sport Facts 2002: 2).

Career Preparation, Family, and Parenting

Females. Women dominate lower-paying careers. Over 90% of secretaries, receptionists, bookkeepers, registered nurses, and hairdressers/cosmetologists are female, and, on average, a female college graduate earns $4,000 less annually than a male college graduate. Nearly two out of three working women today do not have a pension plan (NCES 2000b: 8487; AFL/CIO 1997; BLS 1999: 1–11).

More than 45% of families headed by women live in poverty. For black women, that figure rises to 55%, and it goes to 60% for Hispanic women. Even when both parents are present, women are still expected to assume the majority of the household responsibilities (U.S. Bureau of the Census 1998; Stier and Lewin-Epstein 2000).

Males. Men make up 99% of corporate chief executive officers in America's 500 largest companies but account for only 16% of all elementary school teachers and 7% of nurses (although this last figure is an increase from 1% of nurses in 1972) (BLS 1999: 1–11).

Women and men express different views of fatherhood. Men emphasize the need for the father to earn a good income and to provide solutions to family problems. Women, on the other hand, stress the need for fathers to assist in caring for children and in responding to the emotional needs of the family. These differing perceptions of fatherhood increase family strain and anxiety (Kimmel 2000; August 1986).

Even this brief overview of gender differences does little more than confirm commonsense observations: Neither boys nor girls "rule in school." Sometimes, even progress can mask problems. While a great deal has been written about females attending college in greater numbers than males, this fact has at least as much to do with color as with gender. The disparity between males and females in college enrollment is shaped in large part by the serious dearth of males of color in postsecondary programs. Moreover, attendance figures provide only one indicator; enrollments in specific college majors tell a different story.

As a result of striking gender segregation in college programs, women and men follow very different career paths, with very different economic consequences. Although most students are female, the college culture is still strongly influenced by male leaders. Four out of five full professors are males, more male professors (72%) are awarded tenure than female professors (52%), and, for the last 30 years, full-time male professors have consistently earned more than their female peers (NCES 2000a: 264). Even at the elementary and secondary levels, schools continue to be managed by male principals and superintendents. If feminists are waging a "war on boys," as some proclaim, they are being led by male generals.

It is not surprising that many educators are confused about gender issues. Both information and misinformation abound. There is little doubt that boys and school are not now—nor have they ever been—a match made in heaven. But this is a far cry from concluding that a gender war is being waged against them or that girls now "rule" in school, as one recent magazine cover proclaimed.

In the midst of the adult controversy, we can easily overlook the obvious, like asking children how they see the issue. Students consistently report that girls get easier treatment in school, are the better students, and are less likely to get into trouble. Yet school lessons are not always life lessons. When researcher Cynthia Mee asked middle school students about boys and girls, both had more positive things to say about being a boy than being a girl. When, in another study, more than a thousand Michigan elementary school students were asked to describe what life would be like if they were born a member of the opposite sex, over 40% of the girls saw advantages to being a boy, ranging from better jobs to more respect. Ninety-five percent of the boys saw no advantage to being female, and a number of boys in this 1991 study indicated they would consider suicide rather than live life as a female. While some adults may choose to argue that females are the advantaged gender, girls and boys often see the world before them quite differently (Mee 1995; Office for Sex Equity in Education 1990).

The success of the backlash movement has taught us a great many lessons. It has reminded us of the slow pace of social change and of the power of political ideologues to set the agenda for education.

How ironic that the gender debate, once thought to be synonymous with females, now hinges on how well boys are doing in school. And in the end, reframing gender equity to include boys may prove to be a very positive development. For now, it is up to America's educators to duck the barrage from the gender-war crowd and to continue their efforts to make schools fairer and more humane environments for all our students.

Bibliography

ACT. *National Score Report*. Iowa City, Iowa: ACT, 1999.

"Adolescent Boys: Statistics and Trends." 1999. From www.maec.org/boys.html.

American Association of University Women (AAUW). *Gender Gaps: Where Schools Still Fail Our Children*. Washington, D.C.: American Association of University Women, 1998.

American Federation of Labor/Congress of Industrial Organizations (AFL/CIO). "Fact Sheet: Working Women: Equal Pay." Washington, D.C.: AFL/CIO, 1997.

August, Eugene. *Men's Studies*. Littleton, Colo.: Libraries Unlimited, 1986.

Bureau of Labor Statistics (BLS). *Employed Persons by Detailed Occupation, Sex, Race, and Hispanic Origin*. Washington, D.C.: U.S. Department of Labor, 1999: 1–11.

Centers for Disease Control and Prevention (CDCP). "United States Life Tables, 1997." *National Vital Statistics Reports* 47 (1999): 1–40.

Centers for Disease Control and Prevention (CDCP). "National and State-Specific Pregnancy Rates Among Adolescents—United States." *National Vital Statistics Reports* 49 (2000).

Coley, Richard T. *Differences in the Gender Gap: Comparisons Across Racial/Ethnic Groups in Education and Work*. Princeton, N.J.: ETS, 2001.

Educational Testing Service (ETS). *Sex, Race, Ethnicity, and Performance on the GRE General Test, 1999–2000*. Princeton, N.J.: ETS, 2000.

Good, Thomas L., and M.J. Findley. "Sex Role Expectations and Achievement." In *Teacher Expectations*, ed. Jerome B. Dusek. Hillsdale, N.J.: Erlbaum, 1985: 271–294.

Jones, M. Gail, and Jack Wheatley. "Gender Differences in Student-Teacher Inter-actions." *Journal of Research in Science Teaching* 27 (1990): 861–874.

Kimmel, Michael. "The Gendered Family." In *Gendered Lives*, ed. Michael Kimmel: 111–149. New York: Oxford University Press, 2000.

Mee, Cynthia S. *Middle School Voices on Gender Identity*. Newton, Mass.: Women's Education Equity Act Publishing Center, March 1995.

Morse, Linda, and Herbert Handley. "Listening to Adolescents: Gender Differences in Science Classroom Interaction." In *Gender Influences in Classroom Interaction*, ed. Louise Wilkinson and Cora Marrett. New York: Academic Press, 1985.

National Center for Education Statistics (NCES). *Condition of Education*, 1999. Washington, D.C.: U.S. Department of Education, 1999.

National Center for Education Statistics (NCES). *Digest of Education Statistics*, 1999. Washington, D.C.: U.S. Department of Education, 2000. a

National Center for Education Statistics (NCES). *Trends in Educational Equity for Girls and Women*. Washington, D.C.: U.S. Department of Education, 2000. b

National Collegiate Athletic Association (NCAA). "Women in Intercollegiate Sport." *NCAA News*, May 22, 2000.

Office for Civil Rights (OCR). *Elementary and Secondary School Compliance Reports*. Washington, D.C.: U.S. Department of Education, 1999.

Office for Sex Equity in Education. *The Influence of Gender-Role Socialization on Student Perceptions: A Report Based on Data Collected from Michigan Public School Students*. Lansing, Mich.: Michigan State Board of Education, Office for Sex Equity in Education, 1990.

Sadker, David, and Myra Sadker. "Gender Bias: From Colonial America to Today's Classrooms." *In Multicultural Education: Issues and Perspectives*, ed. James Banks and Cherry McGee Banks: 130. New York: Wiley, 2001.

Sadker, Myra, and David Sadker. "Promoting Effectiveness in Classroom Instruction: Year 3 Final Report." ERIC ED 257819, March 1984.

Sadker, Myra, and David Sadker. *Failing at Fairness: How American Schools Cheat Girls*. New York: Touchstone Press, 1995.

Sommers, Christina H. *The War Against Boys: How Misguided Feminism Is Harming Our Young Men*. New York: Simon & Schuster, 2000.

Stier, Haya J., and Noah Lewin-Epstein. "Women's Part-Time Employment and Gender Inequality in the Family." *Journal of Family Issues* 21 (2000): 390–410.

U.S. Bureau of the Census. "Poverty in the United States: 1998." Current Population Reports, Series P-60–198. Washington, D.C.: U.S. Bureau of the Census, 1998.

Women's Sport Facts, July 15, 2002.

Young, Cathy. *Ceasefire! Why Women and Men Must Join Forces to Achieve True Equity*. New York: Free Press, 1999.

Zoli, M.H. "Centers for Eating Disorders Try to Reprogram Girls' Self-Image." *American News Service*, April 25, 1999, article no. 850.

Are Gender Stereotypes Taught in School?

Female Elementary School Teachers May Project a Fear of Math onto Their Female Students, Causing Them to Do Poorly in the Subject, According to a New Study.

By KeriLee Horan
District Administration, April 2010

Female elementary school teachers may project a fear of math onto their female students, causing them to do poorly in the subject, according to a new study, "Female Teachers' Math Anxiety Impacts Girls' Math Achievement," published by the University of Chicago on January 25, 2010. With over 90 percent of elementary school teachers being female, this finding has brought attention to gender roles within elementary education and could have administrators seeking additional professional development for teachers anxious about math.

Sian Beilock, associate professor of psychology at the University of Chicago, conducted this study in a large, public, urban Midwestern school district and surveyed 17 teachers, 52 male students and 65 female students in first- and second-grade classrooms over the course of one academic year. A series of tests revealed all the teachers involved had a significant level of anxiety while doing math, and as a result, while teaching it in the classroom.

Students participated in an activity designed to assess their subconscious gender role beliefs. They were read two gender-neutral stories, one about a high-achieving math student and the other about a strong reading student, and were then asked to draw the students. Researchers were interested in what gender the respective students were depicted as. At the beginning of the year, there was no strong correlation; when the test was redistributed to the same students at the end of the year, many female students drew a male student as being good at math and a female student being good at reading. These girls had the lowest math scores in the class.

"I think this shows we need to make sure we're preparing early-grade teachers with what they need," says Beilock. "It's not only about skills, but also positive attitudes and not being gender specific in who teachers think is better in math."

Hank Kepner, president of the National Council of Teachers of Math (NCTM), thinks this study could force districts to look more critically at how math is approached in the classroom. "We have to be sure that teachers have a chance to work

17

together, to come up with common lessons, talk through curriculum as a group, maybe with a math teacher leader, and to challenge themselves as adults."

While the study sheds light on certain trends within elementary education, it opens the door to future questions. The study did not address the role of male teachers in the classroom and their role in reinforcing gender stereotypes. Because children are more likely to emulate teachers of the same gender, the study speculates it is more likely that male teachers who have an anxiety toward reading may project that onto young boys. "If it is simply the case that highly math-anxious teachers are worse math teachers, then one would expect to see a relation between teacher anxiety and the math achievement of both boys and girls," the study notes.

"We need training around biases," says Kepner. "We can take videos of teachers in their classrooms, watching for tone, how you say something, everything down to your facial expressions."

"The point I'm most interested in is that we need to make sure we're preparing our teachers to effectively teach and portray positive attitudes in the classroom," Beilock says. She hopes the study draws attention to the need for the next generation of elementary school teachers to be aware of their potential to negatively influence students and reinforce gender roles at such a formative age.

Feminization of Schools

If Young Boys Are Being Left Behind, What Targeted Teaching Strategies Can Lead Them to Reach Their Potential?

By Janet D. Mulvey
School Administrator, September 1, 2009

The evidence is clear: America's boys are being left behind by current practices in the classroom. Statistically, they are performing less well than they were 10 years ago. Boys are dropping out of high schools in significant numbers, failing to complete college degrees and behaving more violently.

We should pay close attention to the statistics that track these trends, seriously regard the research, and immediately incorporate changes in our elementary and secondary schools that will bring boys back into an environment that motivates them to learn to the fullest.

The 21st century is becoming the era of the woman. The feminization of our schools and other learning organizations has placed females in a role of increasing achievement while leaving behind their male counterparts. Women have begun to use their own strengths in leadership to excel in corporate industry and at higher education institutions competing with men. The natural tendencies of women to work in teams, build consensus and communicate openly are encouraged and reinforced in our schools from kindergarten through the high school years.

Enrollment of boys in colleges and universities nationwide is declining, and many institutions now worry seriously about the widening gender gap on their campuses, estimated nationally at 56 percent girls versus 44 percent boys in a 2006 U.S. Census Bureau report. Even in the hard sciences and engineering, where males traditionally have dominated, the margin is narrowing. Recent data compiled by the U.S. Department of Education indicate college-bound females are more apt than males both to complete college-preparatory courses in secondary school and to finish their college degrees.

In their November 2004 Educational Leadership article, "With Boys and Girls in Mind," Michael Gurian and Kathy Stevens report that boys account for 70 percent of the D's and F's in schools. Boys also account for two-thirds of disability diagnoses and represent 90 percent of discipline referrals. Alarmingly, the Organisation for Economic Co-operation and Development, reporting on a three-year study of knowledge and skills of males and females in 35 industrialized nations, including the United States, found "girls outperformed boys in every country."

Just a decade ago, concerns that elementary and secondary schools were not addressing the needs of girls in the fields of math and science became a national discourse. New strategies and targeted programs favored the more cooperative and noncompetitive style of teaching and learning that better suited girls' learning needs. The results are proving to be most beneficial to girls, but concern about boys is beginning to emerge.

Early Readiness

Mandates placed on young elementary students affect their readiness to process and achieve grade-level expectations. Kindergarten at age 5 has become the year that formal reading and writing instruction now begins.

Boys who are two years behind girls in their readiness for formal reading and writing instruction now are asked to master skills in these subjects even earlier. Girls are ready to sit and are more passive in their behaviors and cooperative in their learning styles. Boys at age 5 are impulsive, less mature and physiologically less able to acquire the skills necessary for the reading and writing process.

Advances in brain imaging have shown differences between the sexes in brain development, leading to identifiable differences in learning strengths and styles between boys and girls. The area connecting the left and right hemispheres of the brain is 25 percent larger in girls than in boys. This strength allows girls to remember details, make connections with those details, and pay better attention to lessons and directions at an earlier age.

The language areas of the brain also develop sooner, resulting in better language acquisition and vocabularies among girls. Boys, whose physiological brain development is two years behind and who are less mature than girls, have a difficult time with the early demands of classroom instruction.

Instead of being able to build with blocks, handle manipulatives and remain fairly active in kindergarten classes, boys are expected to sit on the carpet, listen to stories and write their letters in coherent form. The lack of ability to explore and design with their natural spatial capabilities not only frustrates but discourages them right from the beginning of their school careers.

Thus the problem for boys begins early on and influences their feeling about school. The problems in learning in the early years affect many boys through their middle and high school years, leading to achievement gaps between the genders.

Classroom Culture

Enter almost any elementary school classroom or, in some cases, prekindergarten room and notice the neat tables with crayons, large-lined writing paper, oversized pencils with finger grips and lots of picture books. Buried in the back corners of the rooms are the blocks, interlocking logs and other materials that engage the young male minds in creative and imaginative play. The location of these materials immediately sets the tone that designates what is most important in the classroom and school.

Take the example as illustrated by psychologist Michael Thompson in his documentary film *Raising Cain*. Thompson observes and consults with researchers and educators to investigate the dissonances that are present for young boys in the classroom. The story of a kindergarten teacher who scribes the tales told by her 5-year-old pupils reveals the imaginations and inner emotions of both boys and girls. The stories then are read aloud to the class by the teacher for discussion.

The film shows a young boy's dictated story that results in the death of one of the characters—something that occurs in many of his dictations.

When the girls object to the ending, the class discusses how it could be changed to satisfy the class. Consensus is reached that the death of the characters is not an acceptable ending. The young boy then becomes unable to create or relate any stories to his teacher and withdraws from the story circle. This rejection of his ideas and creations by the class has an impact that stifles his motivation and results in his withdrawal from the schooling process.

Changing Practices

Several years ago an experiment involving a single-gender math class was conducted at the elementary school in Van Cortlandtville, N.Y., where I served as principal for 13 years. Concerned that the 6th-grade girls were being overwhelmed by the natural, rambunctious and aggressive behaviors of the boys, we experimented with single-gender classes in math. Strong female and male teachers were assigned to the groups with cohesive lesson plans and consistent objectives for both classes.

Through consistent assessment, observation and analysis, we found both groups did extremely well and on the average scored equally on the assessments. What began as a program to benefit girls in math in fact benefited both genders. The girls approached the subject through a more exploratory process and verbal analysis in a cooperative style, while the boys were allowed to use their more competitive and abstract styles without distraction and correction for impulsiveness.

Because our schools have become more feminized, where many boys are not meeting their potential to achieve, we put in place strategies to ensure both genders receive the best opportunities for an education that meets their needs and desires. Girls' more natural tendencies for language are motivated by literature to read and write. Boys often find the writing process tortuous and have difficulty developing stories from books and classroom activities.

Ndidi Evans, primary school teacher at St. Johns Upper Holloway School in London, England, explained in a case study developed by the Islington Learning Team her inspiration for engaging young boys in the writing process. Evans struggled to motivate the boys in her class to write. Frustrations—theirs and hers—became apparent.

She began to observe boys' behaviors outside the classroom. Watching them use imaginative play with superheroes as their characters, she asked them to express in words what the characters were doing. She exposed the boys to Discover Story, a place in Stratford, England, where they could make their stories come alive. In the classroom, she gave them materials to recreate their characters and the boys eventually began to respond with picture stories. This engagement and excitement in creating stories led to dictation and finally inventive and traditional writing.

Possible Solutions

The evidence seems apparent that boys are being left behind. What is it we can do to continue supporting girls while beginning to help boys re-engage in learning?

- **EXAMINE PRE-SERVICE AND IN-SERVICE DEVELOPMENT COURSES.** Undergraduate, graduate and professional development courses offered by colleges, universities and school districts have emphasized the cooperative and consensus-building learning styles in their methodology classes. Group planning and projects, literacy concentration in all classes, and a noncompetitive format are the lessons for the day.

  Classroom teachers at all grade levels need to understand the learning preferences for both sexes. Brain research, learning styles, developmental readiness and statistical analysis on success rates should be an integral part of the curriculum for current and future teachers.

- **IMPLEMENT SINGLE-SEX CLASSROOMS IN PUBLIC SCHOOLS.** Families currently can select a single-sex private or parochial school. Why shouldn't they be offered the opportunity for single-sex classrooms within the regular public schools? In public schools, single-sex classrooms for some subjects, in fact, may motivate both sexes to engage in the type of learning that benefits their gender- and brain-based styles.

- **COMBINE COOPERATIVE AND COMPETITIVE LEARNING STRATEGIES.** In classrooms where both boys and girls participate, combine both the cooperative learning strategies that now exist with a more abstract and competitive plan of action, and then allow choice for participation for both sexes. Allow for imaginative play to motivate and create opportunities for expression. Differentiation for learning levels is practiced in classrooms, so why not learning styles?

- **DELAY FORMAL READING AND WRITING INSTRUCTION UNTIL BOYS ARE READY DEVELOPMENTALLY.** Delayed initiation for boys into the formal reading and writing process may decrease the feeling of failure at the early stages. Brain-based research indicates that the part of the brain for memory and language acquisition is not only 20 percent larger in girls but also develops earlier in girls than in boys. Give the boys an opportunity to use their exploratory and spatial strengths early on, to build confidence and positive feeling toward school and learning, with the reading and writing instruction coming when they are ready.

- **ADJUST MIDDLE SCHOOL INSTRUCTION IN MATH AND SCIENCE TO THE LEARNING PREFERENCES OF THE SEXES.** Subjects such as science and math that seem to be in the middle of the controversy, especially at the middle and high schools levels, can be taught according to the learning preferences of the male student (more individualized and competitive) and the female student (more cooperative and specific).

- **INCLUDE WRITTEN-ANALYTICAL FORMATS FOR GIRLS WHILE ALLOWING BOYS TO USE SPATIAL (ABSTRACT) FORMATS TO GET TO THE ANSWER.** Assessments and evaluations that measure the mastery of the subjects should be designed so boys and girls can demonstrate their levels of attainment either through the verbal and written analytical format favored by girls or the more straightforward and abstract format favored by boys. Authentic assessments from projects and hands-on activities may inspire and engage male students.

- **LOBBY AND EDUCATE LEGISLATORS.** Help state and federal lawmakers create a new vision of America's schooling by providing poignant and understandable data on where we are failing our boys in particular. Assist them in replacing the No Child Left Behind Act with its irresponsible mandate of testing young children and labeling them failures before they have had a chance to succeed. Encourage legislators to study systems in other countries that delay the age of entry into formal education until the age of 7 and that outperform us in almost every area.

The Need to Address Equal Educational Opportunities for Women and Girls

By Ariela Migdal, Emily J. Martin , Mie Lewis, Lenora M. Lapidus
Human Rights, Summer 2008

While all students are vulnerable to assaults on their rights, girls and women face a distinct set of challenges. This article examines three trends illustrating obstacles to an equal education for girls and women. The first section addresses the current popularity of sex-segregated programs in public schools, in which boys and girls are taught differently in curricula based on gender stereotypes that traditionally have been used to limit girls' opportunities. The next section discusses the growing use of a federal educational equity statute as a tool to combat colleges' inadequate response to sexual violence on campus. Finally, the last section exposes the inadequate and unequal education provided to society's most marginalized girls—those imprisoned in youth correctional facilities.

The New Push for Sex-segregated Schools

> Our society is not based on your gender, and the schools are supposed to prepare us for when we enter the real world. How does separating students by sex prepare us for society when society is not segregated that way?
>
> Nikki Anthony, 9th grade, *Coming to Washington to Talk about Equality* (posted May 20, 2008)

Today, more and more public school districts separate girls from boys. According to the National Association for Single-Sex Public Education (NASSPE), a leading proponent of sex-segregated programs, while only four sex-segregated public schools existed in the country a decade ago, today there are approximately four hundred. A sex segregation movement is successfully pushing to increase this number, recently amending laws in Michigan, Wisconsin, Delaware, and Florida to foster the creation of sex-segregated programs in public schools. This trend is accelerating in the wake of the federal Department of Education's (DOE) 2006 revision of a long-standing regulation to permit sex-segregated classes in coeducational schools receiving federal funding.

An increasingly popular rationale for separating boys and girls in school is the notion that boys' and girls' brains are so different that they cannot both succeed in the same classroom. Two influential proponents of this theory are the writers Leonard Sax and Michael Gurian. Sax is a psychologist and the director of NASSPE; Gurian is a counselor and corporate consultant with a graduate degree in creative writing, as well as founder of the Gurian Institute, which conducts trainings on brain differences between the sexes. Both Sax and the Gurian Institute are in the business of training teachers from public school districts across the country. Many of those teaching single-sex classes rely on their theories and methods.

While Sax and Gurian concede that not all boys or all girls are the same, they attempt to prove that, as the title of one of Gurian's books proclaims, *Boys and Girls Learn Differently!*, and they argue that teachers should treat boys and girls differently as a result. For example, Sax claims that teachers should smile at girls and look them in the eye but must not look boys directly in the eye or smile at them. Leonard Sax, *Why Gender Matters: What Parents and Teachers Need to Know About the Emerging Science of Sex Differences* (2005). He claims that boys do well under stress, while girls do badly. As a result, according to Sax, girls should never be given time limits on tests and should be encouraged to take their shoes off in class because this helps them relax and think. Id. at 88–92. Sax also claims that girls will do better in school if they are allowed to bring blankets from home to cuddle in during class time. See Carol E. Tracy & Terry Fromson, "Single-Sex Schools Don't Work," Philadelphia Daily News, at 21 (Feb. 3, 2006) (describing Leonard Sax training for public school teachers in Philadelphia). Sax argues that any boy who likes to read, does not enjoy contact sports, and does not have a lot of close male friends should be firmly disciplined, required to spend time with "normal males," and made to play sports. SAX, supra, at 218–28. Gurian propounds similar theories, including that boys are better than girls in math because their bodies receive daily surges of testosterone, while girls have equivalent mathematics skills only during the few days in their menstrual cycle when they have an estrogen surge. Michael Gurian, *The Boys and Girls Learn Differently Action Guide for Teachers* 100 (2003).

These theories have a real world impact in schools. David Chadwell, a member of the board of directors of NASSPE, directs the Office of Single-Gender Initiatives in the South Carolina Department of Education. South Carolina has more sex-segregated schools and classes than any other state in the country, a trend Chadwell encourages by publicizing sample lesson plans emphasizing physical activity, competition, and technology in classes for boys and friendship, team building, decorating assignments and projects, and stress reduction in classes for girls.

Most proponents of single-sex education argue that segregation leads to greater academic achievement. Yet no compelling, consistent evidence supports this conclusion. Some studies find that students in coeducational schools do better than students in single-sex schools. Other studies find the opposite. The bulk of studies show no difference between the two in terms of student achievement. In fact, in 2005 the DOE published an extensive review of existing studies and characterized the data as "equivocal." US Department of Education, *Single Sex versus Coeducational Schooling: A Systematic Review* at x (2005). In other words, it found no clear evidence showing that, in general, students are more likely to succeed in single-sex schools. Id.

Few cases have yet challenged sex segregation in public elementary and secondary schools, probably because, until recently, such segregation was rare in the thirty-six years since the passage of Title IX of the Education Amendments of 1972, 20 U.S.C. §§ 1681–1688, the federal law prohibiting sex discrimination in federally funded education. With narrow exceptions for activities such as father–son activities and beauty pageants, Title IX states, "No person in the United States shall, on the basis of sex, be excluded from participation in, be denied the benefits of, or be subjected to discrimination under any education program or activity receiving Federal financial assistance." 20 U.S.C. § 1681(a). For more than thirty years, DOE regulations implementing Title IX had interpreted the statute to prohibit coeducational schools from segregating students by sex in almost all circumstances, with exceptions for sex education and contact sports. 34 C.F.R. § 106.34 (2005). (Because Title IX includes an exception for admissions to elementary and secondary schools, 20 U.S.C.A. § 1681(a)(1) (2007), it generally has not been understood to prohibit single-sex schools, as opposed to classrooms, although the Equal Protection Clause limits school districts' ability to create such programs. In addition, current Title IX regulations require that—with some important exceptions for charter schools—if a district operates a single-sex school, it must provide a substantially equal educational opportunity to the excluded sex. 34 C.F.R. § 106.34(c).)

In 2006, however, the DOE revised its Title IX regulations to permit coeducational schools to offer sex-segregated classes. 34 C.F.R. § 106.34 (2007); see also 71 Fed. Reg. 62,530 (Oct. 25, 2006). The new regulations allow a school to create sex-segregated classes or extracurricular activities either to provide "diverse" educational options to students or to address what the school has judged to be students' particular educational needs. 34 C.F.R. § 106.34(b)(i). The regulations make clear, however, that participation in a sex-segregated class must be completely voluntary and explain that participation is not completely voluntary unless a "substantially equal" coeducational class is offered in the same subject. Id. § 106.34(b)(iii), (iv).

The DOE's regulatory change, however, does not affect other laws limiting sex segregation in public schools. First, other federal agencies funding educational programs and activities have regulations prohibiting sex-segregated classes; thus, for example, school districts that receive U.S. Department of Agriculture funding for school lunch programs are presumably bound by its regulations prohibiting sex segregation. 7 C.F.R. § 15a.34. Second, the U.S. Supreme Court has made clear that at least some single-sex programs violate the Equal Protection Clause of the U.S. Constitution, striking down both the Virginia Military Institute's men-only policy and Mississippi University for Women's women-only policy as unconstitutionally discriminatory. *United States v. Virginia*, 518 U.S. 515 (1996); *Mississippi University for Women v. Hogan*, 458 U.S. 718 (1982). The Court warned that public schools attempting to justify sex-segregated programs shoulder a heavy burden of persuasion and made clear that generalizations about average differences in the pedagogical needs of women and men do not justify excluding members of one sex from a unique educational opportunity. Virginia, 518 U.S. at 525, 533. Third, the federal Equal Educational Opportunities Act prohibits assigning students to single-sex schools. 20 U.S.C.A. § 1703© (2007).

Based on conflicts between the 2006 DOE regulations and the requirements of Title IX and the Constitution, the American Civil Liberties Union has recently challenged the validity of these regulations in federal court; the legality of the regulations likely will be litigated in coming months. Despite the continuing uncertainty of the legal status of single-sex programs in public schools, many school districts nationwide have read the new Title IX regulations as a green light to segregate. As a result, more and more programs are being crafted throughout the country based on the notion that boys and girls require very different kinds of education—a theory that by definition will introduce sharp sex-based inequalities to the public schools.

Sexual Assault on Campus

During the mediation, [University of Washington student] S.S. expressed her desire that Alexander [a football player who allegedly raped her] be suspended from participation in several football games. Alexander denied S.S.'s rape allegation and threatened that he would leave the U W if he were suspended from any football games. Tuite [an athletics administrator] refused to consider suspending Alexander, stating that the media "would ask why he was not playing."

S.S. v. Alexander, 177 P.3d 724 (Wash. App. 2008).

Title IX has long been known as the federal law that guarantees equal access for girls and women in education, including equal opportunity to participate in athletics and higher education. In the past decade, however, Title IX has also become known as a tool for guaranteeing equal access to education in another way: by holding schools and colleges accountable for discrimination against female students who are sexually harassed or assaulted. When Tiffany Williams, a student at the University of Georgia, was gang-raped by campus football and basketball players, she became more than a rape victim. Williams, who dropped out of the university after the rape, brought a Title IX lawsuit against her former school. She alleged that the university's basketball coach, athletic director, and president recruited and admitted one of the men despite knowing that he had been kicked out of other schools because of sexual harassment, and that the university had failed to train its students on its sexual assault policies. The U.S. Court of Appeals for the Eleventh Circuit agreed that Williams had stated a claim that the University of Georgia and its athletics association were deliberately indifferent to the alleged discrimination. *Williams v. Board of Regents of the University of Georgia*, 477 F.3d 1282(11th Cir. 2007).

Such lawsuits have become increasingly common since the Supreme Court held that schools receiving federal funding can be held liable for discrimination arising out of teacher-student or student-student sexual harassment. In *Gebser v. Lago Vista Independent School District*, 524 U.S. 274 (1998), the Court held that schools receiving federal funding may be held liable for a teacher's sexual harassment of a student where the school knows of the harassment and responds to it with deliberate indifference. The next year, in *Davis v. Monroe County Board of Education*, 526 U.S. 629 (1999), the Court held that schools receiving federal funding may be liable for damages for student-on-student sexual harassment if the victim can show that the school acted "with deliberate indifference to known acts of harassment in its programs or activities." Id. at 633. The harassment must be severe enough to effectively bar the victim's access to equal education. These protections emerge from Title IX's guarantee that no person may be "subjected to discrimination under any educational program or activity receiving federal" funds on the basis of sex. 20 U.S.C. § 1681(a).

Since *Gebser and Davis,* many cases have highlighted the problems that victims of sexual violence face when they come forward. In one case, a former University of Washington student alleging that she was raped by a well-known football player claimed that athletics administrators at the university responded to her complaints by suggesting that she leave her job as an assistant equipment manager with the football team. *S.S. v. Alexander*, supra. A state court found that the victim had provided enough evidence for a jury to hear her Title IX claims. Other cases similarly emphasize colleges' responsibility to respond to victims and put effective policies and response measures in place, rather than sweeping sexual violence under the rug and turning a blind eye to sexual harassment and assault. See, e.g., *Simpson v. University of Colorado Boulder*, 500 F.3d 1170 (10th Cir. 2007) (sending to jury the question of whether the university was deliberately indifferent to a risk of sexual assault in its football recruiting program).

The message for schools and universities is clear: campus rape can violate victims' federally guaranteed rights to equal access to education. Human rights organizations have recognized that sexual violence violates women's right to be free from sex discrimination under such human rights conventions as the International Covenant on Civil and Political Rights (ICCPR) (ratified by the United States in 1992), the Convention on the Elimination of All Forms of Racial Discrimination (CERD) (ratified by the United States in 1994) and the Convention on the Elimination of All Forms of Discrimination Against Women (CEDAW) (signed by the United States in 1980 but not yet ratified), as well as the American Declaration on the Rights and Duties of Man (adopted in 1948). Now, appeals courts around the country are increasingly willing to hold colleges accountable under domestic law for failures to ensure that female students are not subject to discrimination in the form of sexual violence or harassment. While Title IX does not require schools to prevent every incident of sexual violence committed by a student or faculty member, it does require schools to avoid denying and covering up sexual violence where it occurs.

Girls in Conflict with the Law

> School was a setup. They teach you all this kindergarten or easy work. You'll come back in the world and not be able to survive in regular schools. Part of school was crochet! Come on, we're fourteen, fifteen, sixteen years old, that should not be part of our

curriculum. I think it was every day, a significant amount of time was crochet, beading, or making blankets to sell.

American Civil Liberties Union & Human Rights Watch, Custody and Control: Conditions of Confinement in New York's Juvenile Prisons for Girls 82 (2006) (excerpt from an interview with a formerly incarcerated teenage girl).

Girls represent a small but growing proportion of children entering the juvenile justice system. A disproportionate number of these girls are African American and Latina; most are poor. Along with difficult family lives and gaps in the social safety net, the failure of schools in many communities to nurture girls' intellectual development is one factor responsible for girls' delinquency. This failure is especially significant in light of research suggesting that, for girls in particular, academic engagement can mitigate the effects of abuses like sexual assault, leading to less aggressive and antisocial behavior, and therefore to a lower likelihood of juvenile justice involvement.

International human rights instruments, including the Convention on the Rights of the Child (CRC) (signed by the United States in 1995 but not yet ratified), art. 3 ¶ 3 & art. 37, and the United Nations Standard Minimum Rules for the Administration of Juvenile Justice (Beijing Rules) (adopted in 1985 by General Assembly Resolution 40/33), contain numerous provisions protecting girls in the juvenile justice system. The standards regulate the adjudicative process for youths, as well as conditions of confinement in youth prisons. With respect to education, human rights norms guarantee incarcerated children the right to services, including education and vocational training, with the goal of helping them achieve "socially constructive and productive roles in society." Beijing Rules, ¶¶ 26.1, 26.2. Human rights standards, such as those established by the United Nations Rules for the Protection of Juveniles Deprived of their Liberty (adopted in 1990 by General Assembly Resolution 45/113), ¶ 77, also stress the provision of quality education in youth prisons so that children may continue to pursue their education without difficulty upon release. Other multilateral international agreements such as the International Covenant on Civil and Political Rights (ratified by the United States in 1992); CRC, CERD, CEDAW, and the American Declaration on the Rights and Duties of Man, for example, also contain multiple provisions prohibiting discrimination based on sex more generally.

Nevertheless, once enmeshed in the juvenile justice system, both girls and boys suffer violations of these basic rights. Among the problems facing children regardless of gender are interruptions in schooling during court processing and incarceration. Once locked up, children are starved of basic educational resources. Budgetary constraints can make books, computers, and other tools scarce, and the remote, rural location of many youth prisons leaves teaching vacancies unfilled. In addition, incarcerated children are often steered away from high school coursework and toward the General Education Diploma because juvenile justice agencies find general education preparation easier and less expensive to administer than a high school curriculum. Children's schooling is also sacrificed to exaggerated security concerns;

for example, children may be barred from taking school materials out of classrooms or having more than a small number of books in their cells.

In addition to these shared deprivations, girls bear an extra, gender-linked burden of educational deprivation. Because the number of girls locked up is much smaller than the number of boys, the girls confined within a single building or wing of a youth prison are often of different ages, grade levels, and degrees of educational aptitude. A single custody unit may confine an intellectually precocious sixteen-year-old who aspires to attend college alongside a twelve-year-old who can barely read. Because there are not enough girls at the same educational level, such girls, despite their widely divergent academic needs, may be crowded into a single classroom. In such circumstances, the single classroom teacher often takes a "lowest common denominator" approach to instruction, frustrating older and more academically talented girls. Or educational staff may abandon classroom instruction, whether entirely or in part, in favor of self-directed study. When this happens, girls are denied the human connection crucial to learning. Moreover, many incarcerated girls are unprepared to pursue self-study and, when left sitting alone with a book or worksheet, learn little or nothing. *Custody and Control*, supra at 81–82.

Although the future economic independence of incarcerated girls depends on their ability to find and keep a job, vocational and career training for girls in prison is seldom adequate. Many youth prisons provide little or no such training. In those that do, the range and quality of the training offered to incarcerated girls embody archaic gender stereotypes and do not measure up to the training offered to boys. Courses commonly offered to girls include cooking, hairdressing, and clerical work, or even crocheting and other economically valueless crafts. Boys, in contrast, may be offered classes in automobile repair, building trades such as carpentry and plumbing, and other fields that are both stereotypically male and far more lucrative than traditionally female vocations. The juvenile justice system thereby helps perpetuate the cycle of economic dependence and vulnerability suffered by women and girls, especially those from economically and racially marginalized communities.

Conclusion

The trend toward sex-segregated educational programs and the inadequate educational programs for girls in the juvenile justice system are two examples of ways in which girls are deprived of equal educational opportunities, in part because of pernicious and outdated gender stereotypes about what and how it is appropriate for girls to learn. Similarly, girls and women continue to be deprived of educational opportunities as a result of sexual violence and institutional indifference to that violence on the part of schools—an indifference that is, itself, rooted in stereotypes about the seriousness of sexual harassment and violence. Gender biases in all three scenarios operate to deprive girls and women of the equal educational opportunities to which they are entitled under both domestic law and internationally recognized human rights norms.

Gender Versus Sex: What's the Difference?

By John Carl
Montessori Life, Spring 2012

As a parent, sociologist, and educator, I often seem to see the world differently from others. While some see a public policy debate as a football game between winners and losers, I see it as a vital way to create a good society. While some see education as a means to an end, I see it as a goal in and of itself. Some see gender equality growing in society because of the obvious changes in women's roles. However, I question this perception of increasing equality, as gender roles appear to me to remain strongly tied to traditional practices.

My youngest daughter attended an excellent preschool program. It was widely known for its open atmosphere, its racial and ethnic diversity and its fair-minded attitude toward teaching young children. At this bastion of equality gender differences still existed. Each year on Mother's Day the children held a Mother's Day Tea Party at which they sang to their mothers a song of love and tenderness. The event ended with the children presenting their mothers with a long-stemmed rose and a kiss on the cheek, reciting, "In all the world, there is no other to take the place of my dear mother."

Contrast this with Father's Day. For that holiday, the school held a hot dog cookout on the playground. The fathers did the cooking and played with their children. For the presentation, the children sang a ditty called "Roadkill Charlie," a fun little song about a man who cooks and serves dead opossum. While singing the song, the children tossed hand-painted T-shirts with "DAD" on them to their fathers.

When I suggested to the director of the school that fathers might prefer a touching poem and/or song in lieu of an invitation to eat roadkill, she laughed, saying, "Dads don't want that. Mommies are special." This progressive, well-intentioned person was unknowingly reinforcing gender stereotypes. Such are the ills of thinking of gender differences in the United States. You find yourself often raising points of view that others don't seem to be able to see.

Gender and sex are not the same thing. Gender is defined as the personal traits and position in society connected with being a male or female. For instance, wearing high heels is associated with the female gender, while wearing combat boots is associated with the male gender. Gender is different from sex because sex refers strictly to the biological makeup of a male or a female. Clearly boys and girls have different biology, but that does not necessarily mean that biology creates personality. The simple correlations of boys to aggression and girls to verbal expression are not the whole story. Correlation is not cause, though it may be tempting to think that these simple correlations support the idea that gender-based behavior emanates from biological sex (Kennelly Merz & Lorber, 2001). As a sociologist, I would suggest that a more important factor than biology is socialization.

I am not a house husband, but I do my share of cooking, shopping, and chores around the house. When my daughter was born, I was in graduate school, so I spent a lot of time bathing, feeding, and caring for her. At one point, my father suggested that I was "doing too much with her." He said, "She's a girl, and fathers need to be careful about that kind of stuff." I can only surmise that he feared she might develop some nontraditional ideas about gender because her father was so involved. Personally, I hoped she would become nontraditional in her understanding of gender roles.

In their classic book, *The Second Shift* (2003), Arlie Hochschild and Anne Machung contend that the women's liberation movement may have actually created additional burdens for women because many of these women have entered the working world while at the same time coming home to a second shift of work at the end of the day. Interestingly, the authors find that most women think this distribution of labor is fair. Why? I would surmise that at some level, the gender construction (how we get ideas about gender) these women were taught told them that this was their role. But gender is not a set of traits or roles; "it is the product of social doings of some sort" (West and Zimmerman, 1987). Sociologists West and Zimmerman suggest that gender is developed in two ways. Not only do we "do gender," or participate in its construction, but we also have gender done to us as members of society. When little girls are told their fathers do not want tenderness from them, they are both doing gender to themselves and their dads, and having gender done to them.

Theorist Janet Chafetz argues that "doing gender" not only "(re)produces gender difference, it (re)produces gender inequality" (1997). This is quite clear in verbal exchanges between men and women. Deborah Tannen's *You Just Don't Understand: Women and Men in Conversation* suggests that through our conversations we pass on "different, asymmetrical assumptions about men and women" (2007). In other words, the way we talk about men and women is different and frequently reproduces gender stereotypes, like "Mommies are special." Chafetz argues that it does seem true that men and women communicate in different ways. Men tend to dominate conversations, while women might struggle to follow some undefined rule dictated to them by men. Women use "verbal and body language in ways that weaken their ability to assert themselves," which supports the notion that they are somehow less powerful than men. This is learned early in life, when girls take a backseat to boys while they wait in line for the swingset or help the teacher clean the room during recess. Girls quickly learn that women who do not behave in this way, who "do gender" inappropriately, are often rejected by both men and women (Chafetz, 1997). Doing gender means that boys and girls are likely to follow prescribed behavior that they think is appropriate for their gender.

When my daughter's preschool teacher suggested that children should give their mommies flowers and their daddies Tshirts because that is what each group would expect, she was really teaching the children to "do" gender. The message was: Pay attention, children—cherish your mother because your father doesn't need your affection. I would suspect that no other man at that event thought he had been slighted, as I did. Was that because I am educated on the matter, or merely because I was jealous I didn't get a flower?

Perhaps the answer is rooted in my own sense of male gender or "gender identity." Childhood is the prime time for development of gender identity. Children learn what behavior is "appropriate" for each gender and how to fit in with others who are like us. At my daughter's preschool, there was a tire swing hanging from a tree. On a parent visiting day, my daughter asked me to help her ride on the swing. While we stood in line, I noticed she was the only little girl waiting. She noticed this too and asked, "Is it okay for me to do this?" Do we teach children gendered identities that can set them up for problems later in life?

Sociologist Michael Messner (2000) looked at the differences between two soccer teams and how boys and girls behaved. He observed the all-boy Sea Monsters and the all-girl Barbie Girls. Gender construction occurred at the first practice, even before the season started. As the Barbie Girls met, they began to dance and sing around a float with a miniature Barbie doll on it. The girls were color-coordinated, in team uniforms perfect for "Barbie Girls." Meanwhile, the Sea Monsters were rather disheveled. The boys saw the girls dancing and singing and quickly invaded, resulting in a game of chase, which stopped the dance and resulted in chaos in both groups. The parents who saw this happening suggested that little boys and little girls are two different species—boys aggressive and girls sweet.

As the season went on, Messner pointed out that most parents failed to recognize the similarities between the girls and boys. For example, all children cried when injured and seemed more interested in postgame snacks than the game itself. Frequently, boys and girls could be seen in the middle of a game watching birds, looking at clouds, or generally not paying attention to the game itself. Messner argues that adults have no problem seeing differences in boys and girls, in part because it is what we expect to see. Gender is being done to them. However, we fail to see similarities because they do not fit into our preconstructed notions of gender. In other words, we have trouble seeing the similarities between boys and girls because we approach them as different in the first place.

Nowhere are gender differences more pronounced than on television. If you want to understand how popular culture views gender, look no further than reality shows. Shows like *The Bachelor* teach us that men pick women, and women must "sell" themselves to attract men. What are the lessons for gender in this show or its counterpart, *The Bachelorette*? The icons for beauty and manhood present themselves to the public as ideal types for the display of gender. In the show *Bridalplasty*, brides-to-be compete to win free plastic surgery to become "perfect brides." Can you imagine men doing this? What do these images teach our children about gender?

In Dr. M. Gigi Durham's *The Lolita Effect: The Media Sexualization of Young Girls and What We Can Do About It* (2008), she articulates how girls are socialized into gender. They are taught to "do gender" through five myths. Durham calls these myths the "Lolita Effect" and suggests that they ultimately work to undermine girls' self-confidence while condoning female objectification. According to her, popular media teach girls that:

1. Girls do not choose boys; boys choose girls, and only the sexy ones;

2. There is only one kind of sexy: slender, curvy, and white;

3. Girls should work hard to be that type of sexy;

4. The younger the girl, the sexier she is;

5. Sexual violence can be attractive. If you think about the way movies and television shows, even those directed at children, depict gender, you will see how frequently such a message is given to girls.

Consider the Disney Channel. In most of its shows, stereotypical myths are directed to young people. When Miley Cyrus puts on her blonde wig to become teen sensation Hannah Montana, she instantly illustrates for girls that physical transformations can change you from awkward girl to teen idol. Disney movies are filled with "princesses," such as Ariel, Cinderella, or Sleeping Beauty, all giving clear messages to children: girls must be pretty if they want to get boys. The gender lessons for such films are clear: strong boys save pretty girls. While this message may seem to provide a harmless fantasy for children, it clearly defines gender for them. Are these really the messages we want to give all children? What does the child who feels weak or unattractive learn from such messages?

What can educators do about the reality of gender differences? What have we done? The research on how teachers interact with boys and girls and how that may or may not affect those children is diverse. For example, it appears that in general teachers do not view gender differences in ability in children unless those children are performing poorly. This is particularly true for boys and girls and math. Teachers do not view math performance based on differences in gender for strong students, but for poorly performing students they often do. Their gender biases tend to support the notion that girls are not good in math, and so their behavior toward boys and girls who are underperforming is different (Tiedemann, 2002).

We also know that demographics influence how students and teachers interact. In short, teachers respond more positively to students from the same or similar backgrounds as themselves. Such interaction influences student outcomes. And since most teachers of young children are women, it makes sense that they would see young girls favorably. Could this play a role in the development of children? If a student perceives that a teacher has an interest in her, that student is more likely to be successful (Dee, 2005).

A few years ago, my daughter began second grade very excited but came home the first day feeling down. When I asked why she was so upset, she said it was because she had "a boy for a teacher." In fact, the "girl teacher" she had expected to have had recently quit and the school had hired a man to take her place. What does my daughter's disappointment reflect? Indeed, what might such gender distribution teach boys and girls about education?

Is it possible that the distribution of teachers in the educational system is unconsciously teaching a generation of children to "do gender" in a way that stresses the importance of education to girls and boys differently? Is this changing? Perhaps a look back can help. Historically, men and women have received vastly different educations. Oberlin College was the first college to offer coeducational enrollment in 1837, but even so, women students were encouraged to study "feminine" concentrations, such as nursing and teaching. Men at Oberlin focused on fields that involved either vocational or intellectual skills, such as engineering. While these differences are no longer forced on specific genders, there still remains a clear educational divide between men and women nationally ("Colleges for Women").

Women now earn the majority of associate's and bachelor's degrees in the US. Further, women earn slightly more than half of all master's and professional degrees and about 40 percent of doctoral degrees (Jacobs, 1999). Although this is a major improvement for women, it also reflects a slight decrease in higher education attainment for men. In addition, women still seem to make gendered choices when settling on major courses of study in college, as they receive the majority of art, music, and social science degrees, while men receive the majority of engineering, chemistry, and medical degrees. Clearly, we are still "doing gender" in education today.

Mark Twain wrote, "Education consists mainly in what we have unlearned" (Tripp, 1987). If that is true, then each of us seems to have some unlearning to do. Gender roles and expectations consist not only of what we do, but what is done to us. As a little league coach for a girls' soccer team, I frequently had to teach the girls to attack the ball aggressively. I never saw a boys' coach do the same drills. Why? In part because, with every Mother's Day Tea Party and every self-fulfilling math prophecy, we teach our children what we expect of them and how we expect them to react to us. Clearly, and with few exceptions, the media seems intent on reinforcing gender stereotypes, some of which can lead girls in particular to seeing themselves as little more than sex objects, left hoping to be the next bride chosen to win plastic surgery so she can be "perfect." Surely we can do better than this.

Bibliography

Chafetz, J. S. (1997). Feminist theory and sociology: Underutilized contributions for mainstream theory. *Annual Review of Sociology*, 23: 97–120.

"Colleges for Women," National Women's History Museum, www.nmwh.org/exhibits/education/1800s_6.htm. Retrieved August 18, 2008.

Dee, T. (May 2005). A teacher like me: Does race, ethnicity, or gender matter? *The American Economic Review*, Vol. 95, No. 2, Papers and Proceedings of the One Hundred Seventeenth Annual Meeting of the American Economic Association, 30 Philadelphia, PA. January 7–9, 2005. pp. 158–165.

Durham, M. G. (2008). *The Lolita Effect: The Media Sexualization of Young Girls and What We Can Do About It*. Woodstock, NY: The Overlook Press.

Hochschild, A., & Machung, A. (2003). *The Second Shift*. New York: Penguin.

Jacobs, J. (1999). Gender and the stratification of colleges. *The Journal of Higher Education*, 70(2): 161–187.

Kennelly, I., Merz, S. N. & Lorber, J. (2001). What is gender? *American Sociological Review*, 66(4): 598–605.

Messner, M. A. (2000). Barbie girls versus sea monsters: Children constructing gender. *Gender and Society*, 14(6): 765–784.

Tannen, D. (2007). *You Just Don't Understand: Women and Men in Conversation*. New York: HarperCollins Publishers.

Tiedemann, J. (2002). Teachers' gender stereotypes as determinants of teacher perceptions in elementary school mathematics. *Educational Studies in Mathematics*, Vol. 50, No. 1, pp. 49–62.

Tripp, R. T. (1987). *International Thesaurus of Quotations*. New York: Harper and Row, p. 279.

West, C., & Zimmerman, D. H. (1987). Doing gender. *Gender and Society*, 1(2): 125–151.

For Women on Campuses, Access Doesn't Equal Success

By MaryAnn Baenninger
The Chronicle of Higher Education, October 2, 2011

The influence of gender is lurking on our campuses—in classrooms, in residence halls, on the bleachers at athletic events. It follows students as they study abroad, and it is the elephant in the room when students are learning to lead. The gender-laden experiences of our students have unanticipated consequences in their own lives and in society as a whole, yet those of us in higher education generally behave as if we live in a "postgender" world.

Women and men arrive at our campuses with different self-concepts. Their orientation toward academic work and leadership differs, and they participate differently in what we call engaged learning. Research suggests that college has little impact on these differences, or on helping students take them into account. That comes as no surprise to people who spend time with college students. What is surprising is that we pay little systematic attention to this issue.

That's too bad, because our goal, as educators, in exploring questions of gender should be to ferret out what works (and doesn't work), both pedagogically and socially, for men and women in college. Ideally we would explore ways to support positive outcomes and tendencies and to encourage development, awareness, and growth; yet most institutions fail even to study the issue.

I hope it is clear that I am not making assertions about individual women and individual men; any student may have a markedly different profile than the norm. However, consider the following, which reflect conclusions from national data and are supported by research at my own institution, the College of St. Benedict, and at Saint John's University, our partner institution:

- Women underestimate their abilities and express lower levels of self-confidence than their abilities suggest. Men overestimate their abilities and express higher levels of confidence than their abilities warrant. This difference arrives with them as first-year students and leaves with them as seniors. When I talk about this, or I hear researchers describe this finding, the audience always chuckles (boys will be boys, after all).

- Those conclusions lead some people to worry about women, and some to disparage men. But the issue is more complicated. Both of those profiles have some good attributes and some bad attributes, and there is an optimal level of self-confidence to ensure the best results. Underestimating one's abilities probably results in more time in academic preparation and a more team-oriented approach to problem solving. Higher levels of self-confidence probably support innovative practices and may help one nail a job interview.

- Men in college spend significantly more time in leisure activities (especially, for example, video-game play and athletic pursuits) than do women. College women are hyper-scheduled participants in co-curricular activities.

- Like my first example, this information yields chuckles. But if we look more deeply, important questions arise. Is there some happy medium that we could help our students achieve? Stressing greater attention to academic pursuits for men and more leisure time for women could better prepare students for work-life balance after college. Consider the consequences for the work force and for families if we are producing a generation of women who think they must work constantly at work and at home to achieve a baseline level of success—and a generation of men who think that they needn't work too hard to be successful.

- Women have higher GPA's than do men—when they enter and leave college—even when the sexes show equivalent aptitude on standardized tests. Is there absolutely something good about having the very highest GPA one can get? Women who work hard to achieve this should be applauded. But we need to understand better the reasons why men's GPA's are lower. Is it simply because they don't study as much on average, or is it in some cases because the learning takes precedence over the grade, something that we strive for as educators? Or could it be that men take more (good) academic risks?

Clearly, our conclusions about gender must be nuanced, and we would be wise to suspend assumptions about whether women or men are doing better or worse. But there are other areas where nuance isn't necessary to see that we could be more aggressive as educators in challenging gender-stereotyped choices.

For example, in a country with a scientific and technological brain drain, there continues to be a pipeline problem for women in mathematics and the physical sciences.

In a country where the health-care and education systems are deeply challenged, men continue to be underrepresented in the important fields of nursing and teaching. Yet one rarely hears of national efforts to engage more men in these fields.

In an ever-shrinking world, men show significantly less interest than women in studying abroad, interacting with other cultures, and learning a second language. Is this why women exhibit greater acceptance of diversity than do men?

In our current economic and political crisis, women remain in the minority in the field of economics, and they show markedly less interest in running for political office than do men. They do more of the background work of leadership and hold fewer titular leadership positions than men. This is true in college, and after college, including in the field of higher education. We need all forms of leadership, but we don't necessarily want approaches to leadership to remain highly correlated with gender.

As I reflect on these issues, I think about what has changed in my lifetime, and whether we are doing any better with gender. In the United States today, women have access to just about every educational opportunity and every career. But access doesn't guarantee outcomes. A gendered culture, mostly in unconscious ways, limits women's expectations for themselves and our expectations for them.

And while we were focusing on gaining access for girls and women, we neglected the needs of boys and men. We didn't plan well for the consequences of a society that taught one sex that it had to work harder to gain access, and the other sex that access was guaranteed. We find ourselves surprised each time we learn that the educational system is not serving boys and men as well as it might. We've barely begun to explore higher education's role in finding a balance that is good for all of our students and good for our country, and it is time we got started.

Women Face a Testing Time to Secure an MBA Place

By Emma Boyde
Financial Times, January 5, 2014

Business schools are eager to be seen as working towards gender equity. Harvard Business School, for example, has been experimenting with techniques to support female students. Other schools have professors who lecture on females in the workplace. Babson College runs the Center For Women's Entrepreneurial Leadership, which is targeted at female students who wish to run their own businesses.

Everyone, it seems, is keen to promote advantages for women.

Yet although women are making strides in education generally, accounting for a majority of university students overall in most developed countries, they remain in a minority in business schools.

Data from the Graduate Management Admission Council, which runs the Graduate Management Admission Test, might help explain why this is the case. The problem is that women appear to underperform men by about 20 points in the GMAT. In the 2011–12 testing year the mean total score for men was 557, while the mean total figure for women was 536. The top score in the GMAT is 800.

Lee Weiss, executive director of graduate programs at Kaplan Test Prep, says that a 20-point difference could make all the difference.

"When you're applying to top business schools, breaking the 700 barrier is very important and our latest annual survey of business schools shows a low GMAT score is the biggest application killer," he says.

"If the highest score for women was 690 and men got 710 that would put women at a disadvantage."

A similar gender disparity emerges in the Graduate Record Examinations (GRE) tests. The GRE scores are expressed as three separate numbers, one for verbal reasoning, one for quantitative reasoning and the last for analytical writing. The most recent test scores, for June 2012–June 2013, reveal that men and women perform equally well on verbal reasoning, scoring a mean of 150.5 each. Women outperform men on the analytical writing section with a mean score of 3.6 compared with 3.4 for men. On quantitative reasoning, however, men score 154.9 against women's 150.2.

The quant[itative] score might be what is holding women back, but altering the test to benefit those who find mathematics hard does not seem to be the answer.

There is no getting around the fact that you need to be highly numerate to do well in business school.

"First year at business school is going to be quantitatively demanding, so you need to be sure that they can handle it," says Laura Tyson, professor of management and director of the Institute for Business and Social Impact at University of California's Berkeley-Haas School of Business.

However, she does not believe women are less capable. She says that there is growing evidence from many parts of the world that the perceived difference between men and women on quantitative skills either does not exist or is getting smaller over time.

GMAT data from China, where women slightly outperform men on the test, would seem to support Prof. Tyson's theory.

It is unclear what weighting top schools give to women's GMAT or GRE scores during the admissions process. HBS says that it had a relatively high proportion of women students—they accounted for 39 percent of its MBA cohort in 2013—but added that it would like to "pass" on commenting on its admissions policy.

The Wharton School at the University of Pennsylvania, whose MBA class of 2013 was 45 percent women—making it a school with one of the highest proportions of women—was also reluctant to make any comment, as were deans from several of the top schools.

Both GMAC and Educational Testing Services, which administer GRE tests, say that they advise schools that it would be unwise to look at just one metric.

Clearly, however, a better score would put women in a better position. Elissa Ellis Sangster, executive director of the Forté Foundation, a non-profit consortium which aims to promote women in business and business education, says the problem could be due to lack of preparation. She says that Forté tries to encourage women to think about the three Ps: planning, preparation and persistence.

"Anecdotal information is that women often go in three to four years after graduation. They have lots of things going on in life. They take the test and are disappointed," Ms Sangster says, adding that the disappointment often leads to women giving up.

She says it is all about confidence and preparedness. "Preparing and persisting through that process is so important."

Simone Pollard, director of business school relations at ETS, would agree that preparation is the key to doing well at either GRE or GMAT. "They are all learned skills. These tests are testing what you know at this particular time. People are arriving at different milestones at different levels of preparation."

If consistency in GMAT scores is to be believed, and Tracey Briggs, director of media relations at GMAC says that it is one of the organization's chief concerns, then women are to be applauded for gradually closing the gap over time. The latest publicly available figures show the gender performance gap has narrowed from about 40 points in the 2002–03 testing year to the 20-point gap reported in 2011–12.

If women can also manage to close the gap in the other parts of their application, then gender equity in business schools could soon be a real proposition in the not-so-distant future.

But there are other factors at work. Prof Tyson says that one should ask why women do not apply, not why they are not doing so well. She points out that women are in the minority of GMAT test takers.

"Maybe they have already decided business school is not for them," she says.

"I think it's [business school] a terrific education because it gives you skills which are applicable to a variety of different sectors and activities."

The Role of Gender in Scholarly Authorship

Jevin D. West, Jennifer Jacquet, Molly M. King,
Shelley J. Correll, Carl T. Bergstrom
PLoS ONE, July 22, 2013

Introduction

Gender inequities and gender biases persist in higher education. After decades of high female enrollment in most PhD fields, women represent one-quarter of full professors and earn on average 80% of the salary of men in comparable positions.[1] A recent report[2] surveyed 1800 faculty across six science and engineering disciplines and found men publish significantly more in chemistry and mathematics, while women publish more in electrical engineering (there were no significant differences found in biology, civil engineering, and physics). A recent experiment tested the role of gender in hiring by asking 127 science faculty to evaluate potential lab manager applications and found faculty gave identical applications higher scores if the applicant had a male name.[3] Another recent analysis of commissioned articles in two prestigious journals published in 2010 and 2011 showed that women scientists are underrepresented; for instance, women wrote just 3.8% of earth and environmental sciences articles for *Nature* News & Views, although they represent 20% of the scientists in this discipline.[4] With the use of alphabetical authorship listings declining over time,[5] and given the complexity of evaluating intellectual contributions[6] in increasingly collaborative efforts, understanding patterns of authorship order becomes increasingly important.

Here we use the JSTOR corpus—a body of academic papers from a range of scholarly disciplines spanning five centuries—to examine trends in the gender composition of academic authorship through time. We pay particular attention to authorship order, given that first and sometimes last author publications are at least as important as raw publication counts for hiring, promotion, and tenure, particularly in scientific fields.[7] Studies of authorship in the medical literature reveal, for instance, that women have been historically underrepresented in the prestige positions of first and last author, and that while discrepancies have recently declined in the first author position, women remain underrepresented as last authors.[8, 9, 10, 11] To view authorship patterns in their disciplinarily context, we use a network-based community detection approach to categorize hierarchically each paper in our study corpus. This yields a hierarchical classification of all papers in our study and allows us to study and compare patterns of gender representation in individual fields of any size and scale.

Methods

The JSTOR Corpus

The JSTOR corpus is a digital archive of published scholarly research that spans the sciences and humanities from 1545 to the present day. At the time of this analysis, the JSTOR corpus comprised 8.3 million documents ranging from 1545 until early 2011, including 4.2 million research articles. Approximately 1.8 million of these documents (97% of which are research articles) cite or are cited by other documents in the JSTOR corpus and thus are amenable to network analysis. We call this group the "JSTOR network dataset". Moreover 94% of these 1.8 million articles are part of a single giant component of the citation network, such that any of these articles can be reached from any other by following citation trails forwards and backwards. We restrict our analysis to the JSTOR network dataset because this is the portion of the JSTOR corpus that we can hierarchically categorize using citation information. For a list of the main fields available in JSTOR dataset, see Table 1. The gender composition of the identified authors in the network dataset (21.9% female) is close to that of the identified authors in the entire corpus (20.8% percent).

Field	% female	authorships
Mathematics	10.64	6134
Philosophy	12.04	12190
Economics	13.68	69142
Probability and Statistics	18.11	28324
Political science - international	19.07	14908
Political science-US domestic	19.09	15705
Ecology and evolution	22.76	279012
Law	24.21	18503
Organizational and marketing	25.44	32119
Physical anthropology	27.05	16296
Radiation damage	27.69	7825
Classical studies	28.88	6372
Molecular & Cell biology	29.25	277032
History	30.47	15585
Veterinary medicine	31.81	10960
Cognitive science	32.12	12786
Anthropology	36.46	19900
Pollution and occupational health	37.57	32108
Sociology	41.41	44895
Demography	41.90	7600
Education	46.35	28635

doi:10.1371/journal.pone.0066212.t001

Mapping the Hierarchical Structure of Scholarly Research

The scientific literature can be viewed as a large network in which papers are linked by citation relationships.[12] The topology of scientific networks can be used to map the structure of science, and the map equation[13, 14] has proven to be a particularly effective method.[15] However, such maps of science have typically shown only a single layer of structure. To map the structure of scholarly disciplines, fields and subfields, we turn to the hierarchical map equation,[16] which reveals multiple levels of substructure within a network. Using the hierarchical map equation on the network of citations, we create a multi-scale map of the JSTOR network dataset in the form of a hierarchical classification that assigns each paper to a major domain, field, subfield, specialty within subfield, and so forth. For example, Bill Hamillton's classic 1980 paper "Sex versus asex versus parasite" is classified as residing in ecology and evolution : population genetics : Sexual and asexual reproduction : Sex and virulence. We used the May 13th, 2012 version of the hierarchical map equation code; improvements to that search algorithm made subsequent to our analysis may find somewhat flatter hierarchies than that reported here. While the algorithm made the decisions about how many fields exist and which papers are assigned to which fields, we manually assigned descriptive names to each field or subfield to facilitate navigation. The names are intended as a general indication of subject matter rather than as a definitive classification.

Determining Gender of Authors

We use US Social Security Administration records to determine gender from first names. The US Social Security Administration website makes available the top 1000 names annually for each of the 153 million boys and 143 million girls born from 1880–2010. (These data acknowledge only two genders.) We assume we can identify an author's gender if the author's first name is associated with a single gender in social security records at least 95% of the time, as with 'Mary', or 'John'. Otherwise, as with 'Leslie' or 'Sidney', we are unable to identify the gender and do not include that author in our analysis. Since in any given era, androgynous names are more likely to be females, this may slightly downwardly bias our estimates of women.[17] Similarly, we are unable to classify names that never appear in the top 1000 for either gender in the US records. As a result, authors of some nationalities may be underrepresented in our data set. In a few rare cases national differences may cause misleading assignments for non-US authors (e.g. 'Andrea' is typically a female name in the US but a male name in Italy). By this method we are able to assign genders to 6879 unique first names: 3809 female and 3070 male.

We extracted the first names of all authors in the JSTOR network dataset, discarding those authors who list only initials. An *instance of authorship* consists of a person and a paper for which the person is designated as a co-author. There are 3.6 million authorships in the JSTOR network dataset; of these we are able to extract a full first name for 2.8 million authorships (77%) associated with 1.5 million papers. (The exclusion of authors with only first initials may exclude women authors disproportionately, particularly in early eras when women may have been more likely than men to publish with initials to avoid potential discrimination.) Of these 2.8 million authorships with full first names, we are able to confidently assign gender to 73.3%. The remaining authorships involve names not in the US social security top 1000 lists (24.3%), or names associated with both genders (2.4%). The final data analyzed include all papers where we know the gender of one or more authors.

Gender and Authorship Order

We look at the gender composition of all papers with any number of authors in the JSTOR network dataset. For every field, subfield, and so forth, we calculate both the overall gender composition and the gender composition of each authorship position—first, second, third, etc. In some fields, such as molecular biology, the last author position of a paper conveys a special meaning: the last author is typically the principal investigator or group leader of multi-author effort. This is especially the case for papers with at least three authors. Therefore we also report the gender frequency in the last-author position for all papers with three or more co-authors. We then compare the gender frequencies at each author position with the overall gender frequency in the same field. If authorship order were gender-unbiased, we would expect to see the field-wide gender composition reflected at each author position.

Results

In an interactive online visualization at www.eigenfactor.org/gender, we report the gender composition by authorship position and overall, for each field, subfield, etc., of the JSTOR network dataset. Women represent 21.9% of the gender-identified authorships in the entire JSTOR network dataset, but these authorships are not distributed evenly in time across fields, or across authorship positions. For instance, women represent 17% of total single-authored papers in the JSTOR network dataset, but represented only 12% prior to 1990, while they account for 26% of single-authored papers after 1990. Figure 1 shows that the fraction of female authorships in general has increased substantially since the 1960s. However, some of this increase may result from increased ease of identifying woman authors as individuals because they have become more likely to use first name instead of merely initials.

FIGURE 1

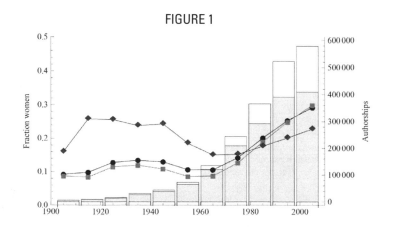

Studies of the economics literature have noted considerable differences in gender representation in subfields,[18, 19] and our analysis reveals a comparable pattern across the subfields within the JSTOR network dataset. Even within a field such as sociology that has a relatively even gender balance, different subfields can vary dramatically in gender composition.

Women are not evenly represented across author positions. Prior to 1990, women were significantly underrepresented in the first author position; subsequent to 1990 much of this gap has been closed. However, a new gender gap has emerged in the last author position—a position of prestige in the biosciences which represent more than half of the authorships in the JSTOR network dataset. Authorship order patterns vary among fields as well. And because conventions of author order vary across disciplines,[20, 5] underrepresentation of women in the last author position does not hold up in all fields. In mathematics, for instance, author order tends to be alphabetical irrespective of contribution, and in this field women are evenly represented—albeit at low frequency—across authorship positions.

As expected,[21] the proportion of multi-authored papers has increased over time. Some of the pattern in authorship order may be an artifact of this trend in parallel with an increase in the fraction of women over time.

Discussion

Only a century ago, women were forbidden from seeking degrees in most universities in Europe.[22] Women seeking a role in academia faced—and continue to face—difficulties at every stage, from admission (Magdalene College at the University of Cambridge was the last all-male college to become mixed, which occurred in 1988), to post-doctoral fellowships,[23] to hiring,[3] to tenure.[24] As both women and the belief that they belong in universities have infiltrated the academic system, the situation has greatly improved. Women have earned a higher proportion of bachelor's degrees than men since the mid 1980s.[25] In 2004, 48% of PhD recipients were women, up from 16% in 1972.[1] Despite this increasing equity early in the pipeline, women are still significantly underrepresented in tenure-track and research university faculty positions. Women occupy only 39% of full-time faculty positions and make up an even lower percentage of full professors.[1]

Since academic publishing is very important to being hired as a faculty member and being promoted, the underrepresentation of women as authors in academic publications and in more prestigious authorship positions potentially affects the representation of women faculty in academia. Our research shows that women are increasingly represented in JSTOR network dataset authorships: 27.2% of authorships from 1990–2012 are women compared to just 15.1% from 1665–1989. However, our results also show that the academic publishing environment remains inequitable. For instance, since 1990, women represent only 26% of single-authored papers in the JSTOR dataset.

In many fields, it is not just sheer number of publications, but author order that matters in promotion and tenure decisions. Here we show that women historically have been underrepresented in the first author position, though this is changing, and that women are currently underrepresented in the last author position. (Given these findings, we note the irony of our own authorship order on the present paper.) We should expect some lag between disparity in the first and last author positions, as it takes time for younger scholars to become leaders of research groups. But the difference between total female authorships and first authorships has been less than 2% since the 1960s, while the discrepancy between total and last authorships remains above 5%. This may reflect a "leaky pipeline" in which women disproportionately leave academia after graduate or postdoctoral training.

While our analysis can clearly delineate gendered patterns in authorship, the data do not allow us to uncover mechanisms that produce the gender disparities we find. Any number of mechanisms could be responsible. One possibility is that women submit fewer papers than men or that their contributions to papers are less significant than their male coauthors, thereby landing them in lower prestige positions on papers. While there is no evidence to support the claim of women's lesser contributions, women are less likely to be involved with collaborative research projects in many scientific fields.[26] A second possibility is that in informal negotiation among a team of authors about author position order, men negotiate more successfully for the more prestigious positions. While we know of no studies that specifically examine authorship negotiations, men, in general, do negotiate more than women[27] and are more likely to self-promote their accomplishments.[28] A third possibility is that there is a bias against women in the review process, such that when they are in the more prestigious author positions, papers of equal quality are less likely to be accepted than when men occupy the prestigious positions. This would produce an underrepresentation of women in journals that do not rely on gender blind reviews. While some have claimed, using correlational data, that gender bias is no longer a factor in producing gender disparities in academia,[29] controlled laboratory experiments and field experiments continue to find that biases negatively affect judgments of women.[30, 31] For example, a female applicant for science lab manager positions was less likely to be hired than an otherwise identical male applicant, based on judgments of competence by prospective hiring faculty.[32] Furthermore, the report "Beyond Bias and Barriers" reviewed the large literature on gender, bias and academic careers and concluded that subtle biases continue to affect women's careers in academia.[33]

Our analysis reveals several important patterns: while there have been important gains in parity in the first author position, with the proportion of women in first author positions now even slightly exceeding the overall proportion of female authorships, the proportion of women in the last author position and the proportion authoring overall remain disproportionately low. One strength of this study is that the large dataset represents a significant number of all academics, women and men, across many fields of study and over a large timespan. Though significant progress has been made toward gender equality, important differences in positions of intellectual authorship draw our attention to the subtle ways gender disparities continue to exist. The finding underscores that we cannot yet disregard gender disparity as a notable characteristic of academia.

Notes

1. West MS, Curtis JW (2006) AAUP faculty gender equity indicators 2006. Technical report, American Association of University Professors.
2. National Research Council (2010) Gender Differences at Critical Transitions in the Careers of Science, Engineering, and Mathematics Faculty. National Academies Press.
3. Moss-Racusin C, Dovidio J, Brescoll V, Graham M, Handelsman J (2012) Science faculty's subtle gender biases favor male students. Proceedings of the National Academy of Sciences, USA 109: 16474–16479. doi: 10.1073/pnas.1211286109
4. Conley D, Stadmark J (2012) Gender matters: A call to commission more women writers. Nature 488: 590. doi: 10.1038/488590a
5. Waltman L (2012) An empirical analysis of the use of alphabetical authorship publishing. Journal of Informetrics 6: 700–711. doi: 10.1016/j.joi.2012.07.008
6. Zuckerman H (1968) Patterns of name ordering among authors of scientific papers: A study of social symbolism and its ambiguity. American Journal of Sociology 276–291. doi: 10.1016/j.joi.2012.07.008
7. Wren JD, Kozak KZ, Johnson KR, Deakyne SJ, Schilling LM, et al. (2007) The write position. EMBO reports 8: 988–991. doi: 10.1038/sj.embor.7401095
8. Jagsi R, Guancial EA, Worobey CC, Henault LE, Chang Y, et al. (2006) The "gender gap" in authorship of academic medical literature–a 35-year perspective. N Engl J Med 355: 281–7. doi: 10.1056/NEJMsa053910
9. Feramisco JD, Leitenberger JJ, Redfern SI, Bian A, Xie XJ, et al. (2009) A gender gap in the dermatology literature? Cross-sectional analysis of manuscript authorship trends in dermatology journals during 3 decades. J Am Acad Dermatol 60: 63–9. doi: 10.1016/j.jaad.2008.06.044
10. Sidhu R, Rajashekhar P, Lavin VL, Parry J, Attwood J, et al. (2009) The gender imbalance in academic medicine: A study of female authorship in the United Kingdom. J R Soc Med 102: 337–42. doi: 10.1258/jrsm.2009.080378
11. Dotson B (2011) Women as authors in the pharmacy literature: 1989–2009. American Journal of Health-System Pharmacists 68: 1736–1739. doi: 10.2146/ajhp100597
12. de Solla Price DJ (1965) Networks of scientific papers. Science 149: 510–515. doi: 10.1126/science.149.3683.510
13. Rosvall M, Bergstrom CT (2008) Maps of random walks on complex networks reveal community structure. Proceedings of the National Academy of Sciences, USA 105: 1118–1123. doi: 10.2146/ajhp100597
14. Rosvall M, Axelsson D, Bergstrom CT (2010) The map equation. European Journal of Physics 178: 13–23. doi: 10.2146/ajhp100597
15. Lancichinetti A, Fortunato S (2009) Community detection algorithms: A comparative analysis. Physical Review E 80 056117: 1–11. doi: 10.1103/physreve.80.056117
16. Rosvall M, Bergstrom CT (2011) Multilevel compression of random walks on networks reveals hierarchical organization in large integrated systems. PLoS One 6: e18209. doi: 10.1371/journal.pone.0018209

17. Lieberson S, Dumais S, Baumann S (2000) The Instability of Androgynous Names: The Symbolic Maintenance of Gender Boundaries. American Journal of Sociology 105: 1249–1287. doi: 10.1103/physreve.80.056117

18. Boschini A, Sjögren A (2007) Is team formation gender neutral? Evidence from coauthorship patterns. Journal of Labor Economics 25: 325–365. doi: 10.1103/physreve.80.056117

19. Dolado JJ, Felgueroso F, Almunia M (2005) Do men and women economists choose the same research fields? Evidence from top 50 departments. Technical report, Centre for Economic Policy Research, London.

20. Endersby JW (1996) Collaborative research in the social sciences: Multiple authorship and publication credit. Social Science Quarterly 77: 375–392.

21. Wuchty S, Jones BF, Uzzi B (2007) The increasing dominance of teams in production of knowledge. Science 316: 1036–1039. doi: 10.1126/science.1136099

22. Etzkowitz H, Kemelgor C, Uzzi B (2000) Athena unbound: The advancement of women in science and technology. Cambridge University Press.

23. Wenneras C, Wold A (1997) Nepotism and sexism in peer review. Nature 387: 341–343. doi: 10.1038/387341a0

24. Spelke ES, Grace AD (2006) Sex, math, and science. In: Ceci S, Williams W, editors, Why Aren't MoreWomen In Science?: Top Gender Researchers Debate the Evidence., APA Publications.

25. England P, Li S (2006) Desegregation Stalled: The Changing Gender Composition of College Majors, 1971–2002. Gender & Society 20: 657–677. doi: 10.1177/0891243206290753

26. Fox MF (2001) Women, Science, and Academia: Graduate Education and Careers. Gender & Society 1: 654–666. doi: 10.1177/0891243206290753

27. Babcock L, Laschever S (2007) Women Don't Ask: The High Cost of Avoiding Negotiation-and Positive Strategies for Change. New York, NY: Bantam Dell.

28. Rudman LA (1998) Self-Promotion as a Risk Factor for Women: The Costs andBenefits of Counterstereotypical Impression Management. Journal of Personality and Social Psychology 74: 629–45. doi: 10.1037/0022-3514.74.3.629

29. Ceci SJ, Williams WM (2011) Understanding current causes of women's underrepresentation in science. Proceedings of the National Academy of Sciences USA 108: 3157–3162. doi: 10.1177/0891243206290753

30. Goldin C, Rouse C (2000) Orchestrating Impartiality: The Impact of "Blind" Auditions on Female Musicians. American Economic Review 90: 715–741. doi: 10.1257/aer.90.4.715

31. Correll SJ, Benard S, Paik I (2007) Getting a Job: Is There a Motherhood Penalty? American Journal of Sociology 112: 1297–1339. doi: 10.1257/aer.90.4.715

32. National Academy of Sciences (2007) Beyond Bias and Barriers: Fulfilling the Potential of Women in Academic Science and Engineering. Washington, DC: National Academies Press.

33. Burrelli J (2008) Thirty-three years of women in S&E faculty positions. Infobrief, Science Resources Statistics NSF 08-308, National Science Foundation.

Breaking the Code

Gender Stereotypes Hinder Women in Tech Fields

By Caitlin Byrd
Mountain Xpress, November 6, 2013

Once a week, the computer scientist dons ballet shoes and dances her heart out. The dancing began in third grade; computer science didn't start until college, and mathematics has been a constant. But as the only female member of UNC Asheville's student programming team, Hannah Sexton says she's used to being the only woman in the room.

"In general, it tends to be more of a male-dominated field," she notes. "It was interesting for me, because in middle school some of the best kids in math were females, but it seems as they get older it's more males."

Nonetheless, Sexton stuck with it. At Buncombe County Early College, she took Calculus I and II. "It was what challenged me, but in a way, I enjoyed it," the UNCA senior recalls.

So when she got to UNCA, Sexton expected to major in applied mathematics. But a required computer programming course prompted a course correction: She switched to a double major, adding computer science to the mix. And this year, Sexton joined the six-person programming team, which competes in the annual ACM International Collegiate Programming Contest. The high-profile event poses problems requiring both an understanding of complex mathematical concepts and top-notch coding skills.

The team's gender breakdown, however, reflects that of the tech industry as a whole. In 2011, women held 57 percent of all professional positions in the country but only 25 percent of technology jobs, according to U.S. Department of Labor statistics.

Meanwhile, the local tech industry is growing—about 3.5 percent in the last five years, says Ben Teague, economic development director for the Asheville Area Chamber of Commerce. That's good news for information technology professionals, computer programmers and software developers. But details about Asheville's tech sector remain sketchy: Most of the data is more anecdotal than empirical, and both men and women in the field here maintain that how the industry grows locally could be just as important as how quickly it develops.

Hacking It

Forty-two people gathered in a classroom June 1 at A-B Tech for Hack for Food, a 12-hour "hackathon" sponsored by Code for Asheville, a local nonprofit that's an arm of Code for America. Code groups aim to use technology and community resources to improve access to data and help modernize government.

Hack for Food participants were charged with creating a phone app that would promote access to healthy local food while addressing issues of food insecurity. Each person had a role. Some were city staffers or members of the Asheville Buncombe Food Policy Council; others were computer programmers writing lines of code or building data structures; some were Code for Asheville "brigade" members.

But looking back at the event, Code For Asheville co-captains Dave Michelson and Scott Barnwell noticed a missing link. Not one of the 13 participating women came from the tech industry.

Michelson and Barnwell can't account for the discrepancy, but it's much on their minds. "We're trying to be really proactive on it," notes Barnwell. "The awareness is there: It's just trying to figure out how we best address it. We've been talking about reaching out to the females that participate [in Code for Asheville meet-ups and the online group] and asking them what about this appeals to you, and what do you think would help in terms of recruitment."

Differing Perspectives

Rebecca Bruce believes there's a pressing need to address these issues—in the field, in the classroom and in society at large.

"Technological advancements, which are made by people in computer science and engineering, are shaping our culture. We need to have all sorts of understandings and input into that process of creating technology," says Bruce, a UNCA computer science professor. "The people who do this don't need to all be just one type of person—usually your white American male. So much is lost through having only that one perspective."

That lack of gender balance, she explains, can unintentionally affect the whole dynamic of what's considered acceptable.

"It can feel awkward to go into a room where you're the only female. On a deeper level, however, there is more to being outnumbered. Sometimes there are conversations and comments and things that fly around that aren't intended at all to be sexist but in fact are," she continues. "You do feel the need to prove yourself, or you feel threatened by the fact that maybe you really don't belong."

When she worked on the space shuttle program in New Mexico, Bruce recalls, there was no women's restroom at one of the testing sites. She had to use the men's room and post a sign when she went in there.

Lynn Banks knows that feeling all too well. After attending networking events hosted by Tech After Five and Meet the Geeks, Banks wanted to create a place where she felt she belonged, rather than situations where maybe 85 percent of the participants are male. So last year she teamed up with Constance Markley, Dalene

Powell and Pam Silvers to found Asheville Women in Technology. The group's goal, Banks explains, is simple: give women in the field a support system and mentoring opportunities.

It seems to be working. The group has about 70 active members, she reports, and on average, about 20 attend the monthly meetings.

"We always joke around and say there's no crying in technology: You've just got to pull your big-girl panties on and go with it," notes Banks, an engineer for TSAChoice. "But I don't think men understand the adversity women face in the workplace. They certainly have their own challenges that they meet each day, but we're quite different from them."

Female Pioneers

For women hoping to pursue a career in a STEM field (science, technology, engineering and mathematics), those challenges usually start early. Marietta Cameron, an associate professor of computer science at UNCA, still remembers when her sixth-grade teacher told her male classmates, "'I would be ashamed of myself if the girls in my class would beat up on me in math the way these two girls are beating up on you guys.' Later I realized it wasn't a compliment: This guy was saying women weren't supposed to be better than men in mathematics."

UNCA, notes Cameron, has no specific program encouraging young women to enroll in STEM fields. But A-B Tech received a nearly $200,000 National Science Foundation grant last year to recruit and retain women in its STEM programs, which include information-systems security, computer engineering, computer information, electronics engineering, mechanical engineering, networking and sustainability. Silvers, who chairs the school's Business Computer Technologies Department, believes the needed change can begin in the classroom. During the 2010–11 school year, she reports, women accounted for about 57 percent of the school's total enrollment but only 12 percent of students in its technology programs. Unofficial numbers, says Silvers, suggest that the percentage of women in those programs has now grown to 18 percent.

A large part of the recruitment effort, she believes, involves changing ideas about who works in STEM fields and what those jobs are actually like.

"A lot of times, the people we see pictured in stories or ads or anything about technology and engineering tend to be a male working by himself at a desk, as opposed to someone working on a team," she points out. "Part of the campaign we're doing is 'Picture yourself in technology.' It's providing the female role model, showing that other women have been successful in these careers."

Amy Daugherty, an environmental science major at A-B Tech, is already filling that encouraging role even though she's still a student herself, helping her peers stay the course. When a classmate grew dismayed about an exam grade and seriously considered leaving a STEM program, for example, Daugherty encouraged her to seek tutoring instead, gently reminding her that one grade is not the end. Having someone who understands the unique challenges women face in these fields, she maintains, can make all the difference.

"When it comes to men, they've had so many people help them: They have a very paved path. We've had a path that's been blazed by the wonderful women ahead of us, but it gets overgrown, because there's not enough of us to keep it cleared," Daugherty observes. "But I truly believe that the more I go through, the easier it's going to be for other women to come after me."

Cultural Programming

Banks, however, believes that while changes in the classroom are important, we also need a shift in cultural norms. "I think it has to start with parents and teachers— not automatically classifying females with Barbie dolls and princesses, and realizing that they'd enjoy dropping Mentos in a Coke bottle and watching it explode just as much as a little boy."

Sexton agrees. While she'd love to see more females in the field, she thinks, "It would have to come to a time when the population in general would not view certain jobs as being for women and certain jobs for men."

In a small way, that change may already have begun. Judging by his own experience, Michelson of Code for Asheville believes that a series of small steps and jettisoned assumptions can eventually add up to major change in the industry's makeup. "I've asked my son if he wanted to learn how to code," he reveals. "Now I wonder why I haven't asked my daughter, too."

Paul Graham's Right

Incubators Can't Fix Tech's Female Problem

By Cromwell Schubarth
Silicon Valley Business Journal, December 31, 2013

Y Combinator co-founder Paul Graham landed in hot water (again) over the weekend over remarks attributed to him about a lack of women tech founders in his accelerator program.

The comments appeared in a long Q&A in The Information, a recently launched tech news site, and were labeled sexist in a blog on Valleywag a few days later that sparked a weekend war of words on Twitter and elsewhere.

Graham on Monday posted a long blog saying his words were taken out of context. He explained his position on why Y Combinator isn't the right place to try to fix the lack of female founders in Silicon Valley and the greater tech world.

The Information subsequently defended its story and explained how it got published.

It hasn't been a banner year for Graham, who was labeled racist earlier this year for saying that hard-to-understand foreign accents would keep applicants from being successful at Y Combinator.

Let me start by joining those who say they have no reason to believe Graham is either sexist or racist.

I believe that Graham has strong beliefs about who will benefit most from a few months of schooling at Y Combinator—young people with strong coding backgrounds—and he concentrates his efforts on those founders. That's in part because Y Combinator is a three-month crash course for tech entrepreneurs who want to polish a pitch and refine their business model.

YC has helped propel many in its target group to pre-eminence in the world of tech incubators and accelerators.

The big question in the weekend debate was whether Graham and Y Combinator should do more to actively help young women succeed as founders who don't come to him with extensive coding experience.

To argue that YC is the place that should build up female participants' coding skills, I think, is attacking tech's lack of women at the wrong end of the funnel. Graham laid the blame on the fact that only a small number of girls are taking up coding in their early teen years.

His comments reminded me of a conversation I had this year with Ann Winblad, the successful software company founder and venture capitalist, when she was given the annual Innovation Catalyst Award from the VC Taskforce.

When I asked her why there aren't more women in venture firms and leading tech companies, Winblad told me:

"The setback is what's happening at the education level. It's disappointing how few women there are in computer science classes and math majors and other science classes at graduation. I was fortunate when I went to school that I was a double major in math and business. We didn't have a computer science major, but we started having classes. I took every single one of them.

"I recently spoke to about 30 13-year-old girls from various schools in the South Bay and about 25 of them said their favorite subject was math. So I made them pledge to me that when they went to college, they would grind their way through the math major. I made them pledge twice. I said, 'Look, I'm going to come and find you all in five years and make sure you held up to your pledges. I am proof of what you can do with a math major.'

"We are still doing a bad job as women and role models of how you need to educate yourself to actually be prepared to take the jobs to be leaders in the technology industry."

Some have suggested that tech leaders like Graham should do more to advocate and support programs that promote technology careers to young girls.

Fair enough. The money and support from Silicon Valley tech leaders going toward bolstering young women's technical skills should be increased until education disparities are erased.

But in pillorying Graham, his critics put the focus on an easy target with a history of unguarded comments rather than where it should be. The real solution is to get educators and parents to support young girls who show promise and interest in tech.

2

Cracks in the Glass Ceiling: Women Leaders

Erin McCarty, a software engineer at social gaming company Kabam, stands for a portrait at the company's headquarters. McCarty is the only female engineer in a seven-member team crafting the multiplayer-shooter game "Realm of the Mad God."

Working Women

Challenges and Advances in the Twenty-First Century

At the turn of the twentieth century, relatively few women in the United States worked full-time outside the home. But as young men left to fight in World Wars I and II, many women took up traditionally male jobs such as factory work to provide resources for the war and keep the country's industries running. After World War II ended and the United States entered a new period of prosperity, some women found they enjoyed their new careers, as well as their new roles in the public sphere that came with greater visibility outside the home. From the late twentieth to the early twenty-first centuries, the proportion of women in the workforce—particularly those with children—increased significantly, from about 46 percent in 1975 to nearly 60 percent by 2008.

However, women in the workforce have encountered a new obstacle, sometimes referred to as the "glass ceiling." Despite their growing numbers, female employees have been promoted less frequently than their male colleagues—especially into upper-level management—and paid less for the same work, regardless of their qualifications or performance level. Assumptions about child-rearing responsibilities have made managers question female employees' dedication to their jobs, regardless of whether those employees actually had children. And women have frequently faced workplace harassment, ranging from general assumptions of incompetence to outright sexual assault. Taken together, these conditions made some workplaces feel particularly hostile to women, especially in traditionally male-dominated fields such as science and engineering.

Despite these challenges, women have pursued careers in increasing numbers and are finally making some cracks in the proverbial glass ceiling. As of 2012, female executives held the chief executive officer position at twenty-three companies on the Forbes 500 list. The number of women entering STEM (science, technology, engineering, and math) fields continues to grow, as do the number of women pursuing advanced degrees and tenure-track professor positions in these fields.

Many powerful female executives strive to make lasting changes outside the business realm as well. As more women rise to powerful and visible positions within large international organizations, they give younger women the confidence to pursue a similar path. Many also make their mark on the world by using their financial resources and business acumen to lead philanthropic organizations that create lasting change for the less fortunate.

Equal Pay for Equal Work

The pay gap between men and women is a long-standing debate in the United States. President Barack Obama raised this issue in his 2014 State of the Union address, citing the common statistic that, on average, women make 77 cents for every dollar made by their male colleagues. This leads to questions about why such a discrepancy exists: Do women choose lower-paying careers (such as teaching and counseling) more often than men? Are women more likely than men to choose careers based on personal fulfillment rather than earning potential? Do gender-based harassment and unequal opportunities in the workplace unfairly keep women out of higher-paying careers or positions within their companies? Or are women simply paid less to do work that is identical to their male colleagues? Even the statistic itself sparks a debate about the data used to reach this conclusion. For example, if the data includes the large number of women who work only part time outside the home, this may disproportionately drive down the annual average salary for all women.

Answering these questions proves complicated at best, and attempts to legislate equal pay for equal work have fallen flat: the Paycheck Fairness Act, designed as a companion to the Lilly Ledbetter Fair Pay Act (2009), passed in the Democratic-controlled House in 2009 but stalled in the Senate before becoming law. It was reintroduced in 2012, but stalled yet again, with votes for and against split along party lines. Reform may be slow in this area until analysts can determine the true cause for the apparent gender pay gap, but this is easier said than done.

Women in Science and Engineering

One potentially contributing factor to the apparent pay gap may be the underrepresentation of women in STEM fields. These fields are traditionally male-dominated and also tend to be higher-paying than many traditionally female-dominated fields such as teaching and counseling. Increasingly, women are pursuing careers in these areas; however, there continues to be a lack of women among those who receive top honors in science fields, including the coveted Nobel Prize. The last time any women received a Nobel Prize in one of the three science categories was in 2009, when Elizabeth H. Blackburn and Carol W. Greider shared the Nobel Prize in Physiology or Medicine with fellow researcher Jack W. Szostak, for discovering how chromosomes are copied during cell division. In the last one hundred years, only fifteen women have received a Nobel Prize in a science category.

To better understand the reasons behind this lack, in 2012, the American Institute of Physics (AIP) conducted extensive global surveys of women in different subfields of physics. Some of their results determined that women make different career and lifestyle choices—such as raising families or making space for their husbands' career path—that put them in weaker positions for conducting prize-winning research. Still others suggest that female researchers tend to share the credit for their discoveries more than their male colleagues and thus might not receive the same personal accolades for their work.

The survey also revealed that women leave the physics field at some point between high school and graduate school at a much higher rate than men and thus never conduct the type of research that would warrant a significant prize. Further reports suggest that other science fields follow this trend as well. The *Guardian*, a British newspaper, conducted a study of British PhD students in chemistry: At the beginning of their program, 72 percent of women pursuing chemistry doctorates planned to become researchers, but that dropped to 37 percent by degree completion time. By contrast, 61 percent of men set out to become researchers, and only 2 percent changed their minds by the end. So even while a growing number of women pursue STEM fields, they also seem to be fleeing these fields at high levels—sometimes even after completing advanced degrees. However, it is not entirely clear why, or what can be done to keep them there.

Women in Business and Media

Much like science and technology fields, women in business and media are experiencing similar growing pains along with signs of progress. There are a growing number of female CEOs in *Fortune* magazine's well-known ranking of the top 500 US companies by revenue, including Mary Barra of General Motors, Marillyn Hewson of Lockheed Martin, Ellen J. Kullman of DuPont, Indra K. Nooyi of PepsiCo, Virginia Rometty of IBM, and Meg Whitman of Hewlett-Packard. As of 2014, women hold 4.6 percent of Fortune five hundred CEO positions, for a total of twenty-three women. Nearly half of them only started in these positions around 2011; but, however small, this tiny spike points to an important trend of women finally rising to the top ranks of large, multibillion-dollar global corporations.

Women are also increasingly rising to the top of major companies as C-level executives other than CEOs, such as Sheryl Sandberg, who left Google to become the chief operating officer of Facebook in 2008. In 2013, Sandberg wrote the book *Lean In: Women, Work, and the Will to Lead*, which addresses gender imbalances in high-ranking business management teams and strives to empower women to be more self-confident in pursuing leadership roles, especially in high-technology industries. At the heart of her argument is the idea that everyone—men and women—should be free to choose whether they wish to pursue a high-powered career, stay at home to raise their family, or something in between, regardless of traditional gender roles or stereotypes.

Additionally, women such as Oprah Winfrey and Martha Stewart are becoming media "moguls"—they started from simple television shows, then grew to broader representation through magazines and books, and finally took control of the media outlets themselves. The growth of women-controlled media outlets is significant because it allows women control over how they are represented in the media.

However, women in powerful business positions may be subject to personal and professional scrutiny in ways that their similarly-positioned male colleagues are not. In *Lean In*, Sandberg cited a study conducted by Columbia Business School and New York University professors that found that students viewed women who actively pursue business success as "bossy" and "aggressive," while they viewed men who exhibited exactly the same behaviors more positively. This discrepancy is often raised in debates about the lack of women in high-ranking business positions: some argue that negative perceptions of business-minded women prevent them from being "likeable" enough to rise to the top, while others suggest that women choose not to pursue business success as aggressively as men because they do not want to be perceived negatively. Businesswomen such as Martha Stewart have experienced this double-standard first hand: while Stewart did indeed spend time in prison and is the subject of several anecdotes about her "unlikeable" behavior, some question whether public perception of her rise to success and subsequent prosecution for insider trading would have been as overwhelmingly negative had she been male.

Women in Philanthropy

Despite their struggles, many female executives strive to make lasting changes outside the business world as well. Many participate extensively in philanthropic activities, using both their financial resources and business acumen to create sustainable programs to help others. For example, in 2006, Martha Stewart donated $5 million to found the Martha Stewart Center for Living at Mount Sinai Hospital in New York. In interviews, Stewart noted that the center, which is devoted to geriatric care, made an enormous impact in the lives of its elderly residents, many of whom had nowhere else to turn. She expressed the urgency of the need for changes in the elder care system in the United States, especially as the average age of the US population increases. She also observed that philanthropy is particularly important in situations where such urgent needs are not necessarily matched with public focus, and that successful philanthropy requires careful management, not just handing over cash or lending one's name to a cause.

Oprah Winfrey is another example of a successful businesswoman with a significant portfolio of philanthropic activities. Winfrey started as a talk show host and rose to control an enormous media empire that includes a magazine, a television station, books, product endorsements, and more. But in addition to her myriad business pursuits, Winfrey's extensive philanthropic efforts range from giveaways on her talk show to establishing larger, lasting programs such as the Angel Network and the Oprah Winfrey Leadership Academy for Girls in South Africa.

In interviews, Winfrey discusses the key elements to sustainable philanthropic activity, including the importance of building strong business infrastructure and finding other leaders who share your vision. And while not all of these efforts have been perfect—for instance, a dorm parent at her school in South Africa faced allegations of sexual abuse—her efforts contributed significantly to lasting changes in the lives of others. Like Stewart, Winfrey used her knowledge and understanding of business operations to find an effective and efficient way to share her wealth with those who could benefit.

Conclusion

The number of women in the workforce has grown significantly over the past century, but many challenges remain. Women continue to be underrepresented in technology and science fields, as well as in executive positions at large corporations.

However, as more women take on these roles, they inspire the next generation of girls to rise to the challenge of creating lasting changes both inside and outside the boardroom.

—Tracey M. DiLascio

Bibliography

Forbes, Moira. "Martha Stewart Opens Up on Philanthropy, Her 'Grave Setback' and What She Learned." *Forbes*. Forbes.com, 18 Sept. 2012. Web. 12 Feb. 2014.

Forbes, Moira. "Oprah Winfrey Talks Philanthropy, Failure and What Every Guest—Including Beyoncé—Asks Her." *Forbes*. Forbes.com, 18 Sept. 2012. Web. 12 Feb. 2014.

Friedman, Ann. "Martha Stewart's Best Lesson: Don't Give a Damn." *New York Magazine*. New York Media, 14 Mar. 2013. Web. 12 Feb. 2014.

Henderson, Nia-Malika. "Obama, Democrats Put Spotlight on Gender Pay Gap. Will It Matter?" *Washington Post*. Washington Post, 29 Jan. 2014. Web. 12 Feb. 2014.

Howard, Caroline. "The New Class of Female CEOs." *Forbes*. Forbes.com, 22 Aug. 2012. Web. 12 Feb 2014.

Ivie, Rachel, and Casey Langer Tesfaye. "Women in Physics: A Tale of Limits." *Physics Today*. American Inst. of Physics, Feb. 2012. Web. 12 Feb. 2014.

Leahy, Anna, and Douglas Dechow. "The Nobel Prize: Where Are the Women?" *Huffington Post*. TheHuffingtonPost.com, 24 July 2013. Web. 12 Feb. 2014.

Quast, Lisa. "Causes and Consequences of the Increasing Numbers of Women in the Workforce." *Forbes*. Forbes.com, 14 Feb. 2011. Web. 12 Feb. 2014.

Sandberg, Sheryl. *Lean In: Women, Work, and the Will to Lead*. New York: Random, 2013. Print.

United States Department of Labor. "Labor Force Participation of Women and Mothers, 2008." *Bureau of Labor Statistics*. BLS, 9 Oct. 2009. Web. 12 Feb 2014.

"Women CEOs of the Fortune 1000." Catalyst. Catalyst, 15 Jan. 2014. Web. 12 Feb. 2014.

The Shaping of Culturally Proficient Leaders

By Carmella S. Franco, Maria G. Ott, Darline P. Robles
Leadership, November 1, 2011

Three Latina superintendents share the stories of their childhoods, careers and challenges, and their vision to transform schools into places of equity and excellence.

Our careers crossed and converged throughout the years we served as superintendents. When together, we often shared our past histories and discovered how much we all held in common. We were together on many panels to discuss the role of the superintendent and the paths we followed to achieve this goal.

When we finally decided to write our stories with a commitment to help others achieve their leadership potential, we discovered through reflection that our personal and professional lives reflected our approaches to leadership. We met and pledged that we would begin the process of developing our book about leadership, published by Corwin Press in September 2011, titled *Leadership for Equity: A Culturally Proficient Society Begins in School.*

Our personal leadership stories emerged during conversations with Randall B. Lindsey and Stephanie M. Graham, who are renowned for their work on cultural proficiency. During our conversations, we discovered that our early life experiences shaped the leaders we became.

In her foreword to our book, Thelma Meléndez de Santa Ana writes: "These trailblazing women chronicle their childhoods, careers, and challenges and share their vision to transform schools into places of equity and excellence. Through the lens of cultural proficiency, their stories enhance readers' understanding of barriers to educational opportunity and equity, conditions that help promote success for underserved students, ways to leverage culture as an asset, and links between high-quality education for some and excellence for all learners."

Her words were humbling and reinforced the importance of sharing our personal stories in the hopes of inspiring colleagues to join us in this work.

Our Personal Journeys

We are all baby boomers who lived through major societal changes, including integration, demographic shifts in the nation's population, and the focus on accountability to address achievement gaps. It was clear that as we answered questions about our early years, our years as teachers, our early years as administrators, and ultimately our leadership roles as superintendents, we became bonded in our shared passion and commitment to provide equitable learning opportunities for all children.

Carmella Franco's journey began in Pueblo, Colorado, where she was raised in a large extended family that lived within a three-block area where English, Spanish and Italian were the daily languages. When economic necessity caused the family to move to Los Angeles to join her paternal grandparents, she found herself adapting to a new environment. Throughout her childhood, education was emphasized, and the arts were an important component of the experiences her family provided. Franco remembers her early years as having a magical quality.

Maria Ott's journey started in Germany, where she was born Maria Miranda Gutierrez. She was born to a father serving in the US military whose family had immigrated to California from Mexico and a German mother from a farm in a small town in Bavaria. At five years of age, she traveled from Germany to join her father's large extended family in East Los Angeles. Because English was not Ott's first language, she experienced the English learner journey as a child and became a life-long advocate for providing equitable opportunities for children learning English as a second language.

Being Raised in Diverse Environments

Darline Robles started kindergarten as a 4-year-old who experienced several moves during her early school experiences. The moves taught Robles how to adapt and be flexible in new environments. She was raised in diverse settings in which she learned about and came to appreciate many cultures, but also where she experienced and observed cultural biases and insensitivities. For most of her childhood, Robles lived in a single-parent home with a working mother. This situation produced a high level of independence, supported by a loving family that insisted on education as a top priority.

As co-authors, we developed a deep understanding and appreciation of our shared experiences and those unique to each one of us. We found that many painful situations that reflected our culture, language or female identity were hidden under the exterior of our professional successes. The conversations with Randy Lindsey and Stephanie Graham helped bring the memories to the surface, shaping an important new tool for educational leaders.

A Bridge for Personal Reflection and Growth

The Cultural Proficiency Leadership Rubric in our book adds to prior work by Lindsey and Graham and provides a concrete way for educators to reflect on personal beliefs and practices that place an individual or organization along the six-point continuum of cultural proficiency.

Beginning with descriptions of beliefs or practices that might be labeled culturally destructive, the continuum proceeds to describe behaviors that might be considered as cultural incapacity, cultural blindness, cultural pre-competence, cultural competence, and finally, cultural proficiency, where transformation for equity occurs.

The new Cultural Proficiency Leadership Rubric, like rubrics published in other books in the Cultural Proficiency series, is organized around five essential elements: assessing culture, valuing diversity, managing the dynamics of difference, adapting to diversity, and institutionalizing cultural knowledge.

Each element is defined along the continuum, and the rubric serves as a bridge for personal reflection and growth for educators seeking to transform classrooms, schools and school districts to ensure equity for all students. The connection between transforming schools for equity and transforming society for equity is a theme that is reflected both in the rubric and the book.

The Cultural Proficiency Leadership Rubric is a central element of the book, challenging the reader to put on the lens of cultural proficiency to view his/her own leadership behaviors. The rubric is important to leaders looking at the policies and practices of organizations by providing language to describe unhealthy and healthy conditions.

Each element of the rubric is described across the continuum and serves as an excellent tool for personal growth for the individual leader, as well as a professional development tool for leaders committed to transforming their organizations. Transformation for equity requires a commitment to a dramatic shift from tolerating diversity to institutionalizing equity as the worldview for the organization.

Stephanie Graham asked us to describe some of the challenges that we experienced as women of color administrators. Carmella Franco describes having to work twice as hard and being in constant pursuit of excellence. She also discusses her experience with professional jealousy and with unsupportive supervisors. Franco writes that she "observed that the increase in the number of women in administration has been threatening in and of itself; adding color to it is an additional complexity."

Viewed as a Leader Who Succeeds on Merit

Maria Ott responds to the question by describing how others wanted to define her as a Latina rather than a qualified administrator. She writes, "I was proud to be Latina, but I wanted to be viewed as a leader who had succeeded based on merit. . . . It has always surprised me when comments are made about increased numbers of people of color at the leadership level. There were few complaints when district leaders were predominately represented by white individuals; however, when too many people of color advance to that level, questions surface regarding the shift in leadership."

Darline Robles says, "Some people have underestimated me, and had low expectations about my work. That more than anything has annoyed me. When I have accomplished something, some seem to be surprised, as if I, a woman, a Latina, could not do it."

Randy Lindsey asks the three authors to answer a complex question, "How do women become identified with being in charge, without being identified with negative or unfeminine ways?" Ott answers: "Women must not hesitate to show their strength in leadership roles. Women should know their personal compass well so that they are consistent in their focus and clearly articulate their passion for creating successful educational environments for all children. Others look for consistency in the behavior of their leaders, and not being clear about what you stand for is one of the reasons that others will not follow. It is better to have disagreement with your priorities than to be someone who wavers in his/her beliefs."

Robles answers the question directly, "You just lead. I don't think you can worry about how you will be identified or else you will be stuck and not move forward. People will always have an opinion about you—correct or not. As a leader, you must be who you are, be authentic. It is interesting how language will be used differently to describe a woman's commitment to her work. Often I would hear others describe it as being emotional rather than passionate about making sure students who have been underserved for too long are provided with strong teachers to ensure they have access to quality education. I always welcomed the opportunity to provide alternative language."

Franco said, "Obviously, women need to learn to play with the 'big boys,' but I don't interpret this as 'acting' like them. That being said, I believe that there are distinctive ways that both men and women in leadership roles portray themselves: conducting business in a conservative and serious manner, being viewed as a business leader, in charge of a multi-million dollar operation, dressing appropriately for the position."

Franco continued, "The issue of negative perceptions of women being in charge will be there as long as there is a dearth of women in top CEO positions. This has been a hard wheel to turn, and it continues to move very slowly. The logical interpretation is that women are not viewed as being able to run a major business; consequently, men continue to be named to those positions."

Improving Student Achievement

The fact that we shared the experience of being women in leadership roles—Latinas that encountered stereotyping and biases regarding our professional potential—brought the three of us closer as friends and professional colleagues. We all have successfully improved student achievement and provided important leadership in both mid-sized and large districts.

Franco's career as superintendent of Whittier City Schools for 12 years, retiring in 2008 to immediately assume the role of interim superintendent for Woodland Joint Unified, prepared her to serve as the first state trustee, with full authority over the school board, assigned to a district for academic performance issues. She is starting her second year in the Alisal School District with the goal of leading the district back to independence from state oversight.

Ott served seven successful years as superintendent in the Little Lake City School District, leaving in 2000 to work beside Roy Romer in stabilizing and leading the Los Angeles Unified School District as the senior deputy superintendent. In 2005, she was appointed to lead the Rowland Unified School District. The district has initiated major transformational work around teaching and learning and continues to be recognized as a cutting-edge district.

Robles led the Montebello Unified School District before accepting the position of superintendent of the Salt Lake City School system, where she served for eight years. In 2002, she was appointed as the first Latina to lead the Los Angeles County Office of Education. Robles retired in August 2010 to develop a master's program in school administration at the University of Southern California. As a faculty member, Robles is positioned to influence the quality and content of preparation programs for educational leaders at USC and universities across the nation. She was recently appointed to the President's Advisory Commission on Educational Excellence for Hispanics.

The conversations modeled and encouraged in *[Leadership for Equity]* take courage and the ability to open one's thinking to a new awareness level related to cultural proficiency. We have the opportunity to have courageous conversations that will break down barriers to success for historically underserved students, closing gaps and providing educational access. But we must first be willing to identify priorities and create conditions in schools and districts that remove the inequities that are microcosms of inequities in society.

All Boats Rising

[Leadership for Equity] is designed to help you begin important conversations about educational equity. We invite you to use our stories and the questions we pose to lead for equity so that opportunities and achievements increase for all students, especially for students who are underserved by present and past policies and practices. As asserted by Thurgood Marshall, the improvement of opportunities for those least well served in our society results in "all boats rising."

Do Women Lead Differently?

By Sherry Ricchiardi
American Journalism Review, December 1, 2011

Jill Abramson, the first woman to serve as executive editor of the *New York Times*, says female journalists don't have "a different taste in stories or sensibility." A number of top newsroom managers and researchers beg to differ.

Like many female journalists, Jane Eisner rejoiced when the *New York Times* smashed the glass ceiling and named a woman executive editor of the world-renowned newspaper. Yet she found herself in "respectful disagreement" with the new boss, Jill Abramson, just days after the changing of the guard on September 6.

The point of contention surfaced when *Times* Public Editor Arthur S. Brisbane asked Abramson if readers would see a change because a woman is now in charge. The native Manhattanite was entering terrain that had been ruled by white males since the newspaper's founding in 1851.

In her response, one line jumped out: "The idea that women journalists bring a different taste in stories or sensibility isn't true," Abramson said in the column that ran in the *Times* on September 10. She went on to explain that everybody at the newspaper recognized and loved a good story, and it is rare that there are disagreements.

Eisner had no quarrel with that. It was Abramson's denial of the influence of gender that led the veteran journalist to argue on her blog that we all define a good story through personal prisms and experiences, and that a woman might see something a man might miss—and vice versa.

"I was surprised she said it. I wish I had an opportunity to ask her more about it," says Eisner, who spent 25 years at the *Philadelphia Inquirer* and in 2008 became the first female editor of the national Jewish news organization the Forward.

She wasn't the only one perplexed by Abramson's response. The comment quickly hit the blogosphere, rekindling an age-old debate over whether gender makes a difference when it comes to newsgathering and management style. Uttered by one of the most powerful women in American journalism, the words did not sit well with many females in the profession.

In October, *Gawker* raised the question: "Do Women Do Journalism Differently?" The response: "Jill Abramson says no."

Megan Kamerick, immediate past president of the Journalism and Women's Symposium, better known as JAWS, wants to ask Abramson two questions: "Did you really believe what you said, and can you explain what you meant by it?" Kamerick,

---

a reporter for the *New Mexico Business Weekly,* wonders if Abramson felt compelled to make the gender disclaimer because of her new position. "No man would be under the scrutiny she's under," she says. "Everything she says is going to get amplified, dissected and picked apart."

Abramson turned down AJR's request for an interview. But other top female media managers did speak out about the distinctness of female leadership and their own career experiences. It's a given that not all women have the same traits or management styles. But all of those interviewed believe that, in one way or another, femaleness is a factor.

"I think it's true we're all identical in loving a good story, but not all editors will define a good story identically," says Ann Marie Lipinski, who in 2001 became the first female editor of the *Chicago Tribune*, a position she held for seven and a half years. "Do I think gender plays a role in that case? I suspect at times it does. Being a woman gives you access to some experiences in life that men don't have, just as the reverse is true."

When she was editor of the *Tribune*, Lipinski, now curator of the Nieman Foundation for Journalism at Harvard University, didn't think of herself as a role model. Some women on her staff evidently did. One of her last conversations before leaving the paper was with a reporter who told her, "I haven't said it all these years, but I wanted you to know what a difference it made to me to know there was a woman in that office."

Abramson's own newspaper has explored the topic of female leadership. An August 2, 2009, *New York Times* article, "Do Women Make Better Bosses?," provided insight into the influence of gender on management styles.

Alice Eagly, a social psychologist at Northwestern University, has read hundreds of studies that compare women and men as managers. In the *Times* article, she concluded that females tend to be more collaborative and democratic than male managers. "Compared with men, women use a more positive approach by encouraging and urging others rather than a negative approach of scolding and reprimanding. . . . Women attend more to the individuals they work with, by mentoring them and taking their particular situations into account," Eagly told the *Times*.

Eagly cautioned that main differences were "on the average" and there were exceptions. There was no "one size fits all" modus operandi.

Her findings reverberated during interviews with women who run news operations today and others who used to do so.

Karen Magnuson makes no bones about it—she is a "people person" who likes to give hugs and connect with staffers in her newsroom at the *Democrat and Chronicle* in Rochester, New York. "I am demanding, but I also am warm and fuzzy," says the editor and vice president for news.

Could she imagine a male editor describing himself that way?

"Probably not, but I am proud to be both," says Magnuson, former president of Associated Press Media Editors.

On October 19, she hosted a "watchdog retreat" at her home. Staffers spent the afternoon brainstorming ways to expand and advance their investigative reporting on multiple platforms. At 5 p.m., she broke out wine, beer, cheese and crackers so people could wind down before they headed home. "Great way to relax with staff," Magnuson says.

When she was hired as managing editor 12 years ago, she was the lone woman in news budget meetings with white males. She credits former editor Tom Callinan for charging her with diversifying the staff. "To know I had the support of my editor and that this was a priority meant the world to me," says Magnuson, who took over the Number 1 spot when Callinan left the paper in 2001. She praises him for seeing gender balance and diversity as important to the newsroom.

She agrees with Abramson's point about gender "to a certain extent." It's more about personality and background, she says. "But I do believe that female editors can bring a different perspective to the job, especially if the position has been male-dominated."

It's not unusual for female news managers to credit male colleagues who helped pave the way. Charlotte H. Hall was in the field for 33 years before she had a female boss, but "I had wonderful male editors; I'm not complaining," says Hall, who retired as editor and senior vice president of the *Orlando Sentinel* in October 2010. "They were my mentors, and I wouldn't have gotten where I did in management without their help and sponsorship."

Diane McFarlin, president and publisher of the *Sarasota Herald-Tribune* since 1999, lists Seymour Topping among her mentors. She met Topping after the New York Times Co. bought the *Herald-Tribune* in 1982 and the veteran Timesman arrived to help with the reorganization. He took the 28-year-old assistant managing editor under his wing. "I was blessed to have men like that who were gender blind," McFarlin says.

The *Washington Post* reported that during comments to newsroom staffers on June 2, Abramson talked of standing on the shoulders of men who hired and promoted her, including Bill Keller, the executive editor she replaced, and former *Times* Executive Editor Joseph Lelyveld. She also credited women at the *Times*, "who had to fight battles just to get in the door."

Some women have wrestled with themselves about whether news judgment and leadership skills were gender blind. When she became executive editor of Hampton Roads' *Virginian-Pilot* and *Ledger-Star* in 1984, Sandra Mims Rowe remembers saying, "Oh, no, there is no gender aspect, no chromosomal impact to news judgment. It's all the same." She was 31 years old at the time. Today, she views things differently.

"I said that at the beginning almost defensively," says Rowe, who became executive editor of Portland's *Oregonian* in 1993. "I will be interested to see what [Abramson] thinks three years from now. I am not saying that smugly. I am talking from experience. My own view evolved over time."

Under Rowe's watch, the *Oregonian* garnered five Pulitzer Prizes before she retired in 2010. She believes that 90 percent of the time, a page one story is so obvious "you could spot it blindfolded at 20 paces back."

Then there's the other 10 percent.

"Of course there is a gender component. We are a combination of our life experiences, and that is a factor in news judgment," says Rowe, who earlier this year became chair of the Committee to Protect Journalists.

She cited the following example: Rowe was editing the *Virginian-Pilot* in October 1991 when Anita Hill testified at Clarence Thomas' Supreme Court confirmation hearing. Hill spoke about offensive statements she said Thomas had made to her at work. She described how he talked of viewing pornographic films showing women having sex with animals and rape scenes. She testified that he bragged about his sexual prowess and wondered aloud one day, "Who has put pubic hair on my Coke?"

As the story unfolded, Rowe presided over news meetings attended primarily by men. Here's how she recalls the discussion. "The first day, the guys were all going, 'Oh, phew, what do we do with this?' Everybody was churning over the graphic nature of it. I remember saying, 'There is not a woman in the workplace who does not understand this or have some familiarity, whether or not it has happened to her.'

"That was absolutely influenced by my gender. I was seeing the larger picture that I knew existed. This was about sexual harassment in the workplace."

Pulitzer Prize–winning author Anna Quindlen faced a similar scenario while she covered the hearings as a columnist for the *New York Times*. "Some of my colleagues were either skeptical or bemused by the workplace harassment [Hill] described," Quindlen wrote in an e-mail interview. "The women I knew were neither. We were just weary. We'd heard so much dumb, sexist, even abusive stuff during our lifetimes that little shocked us. The columns I wrote about those hearings therefore deeply reflected my experience as a woman. No question."

Wanda S. Lloyd, executive editor of the *Montgomery Advertiser* in Alabama, has no doubt female sensibilities play a role in how she runs the newsroom. When a local woman was murdered three months after getting married, the paper ran a routine crime story, which Lloyd describes as "very well done." But she wanted more.

She met with the reporter and sent him to family members in pursuit of details. "It wasn't just about the crime; it was about the woman. We had a story the next day quoting the daughter saying he abused her from the minute she said, 'I do,'"Lloyd recalls.

On the heels of the coverage, Montgomery's Family Sunshine Center, a shelter for victims, asked the *Advertiser* to host a roundtable on domestic violence for community leaders. The paper also ran a weeklong series titled "Domestic Silence."

Would a male editor have been as sensitive to the issue? "I would hope so," says Lloyd, one of four editors of the book *The Edge of Change: Women in the 21st Century Press*. Lloyd cites diversity as a linchpin for more balanced news decisions.

Case in point: Megan Kamerick tells of a JAWS board member who worked at a newspaper where the sports editor failed to cover a local women's basketball team that advanced to the tournament finals. But he did publish a story about a mediocre men's team. When outraged readers asked why, the sports editor said he forgot. Kamerick wonders, "Would he have forgotten if there had been a woman on the sports desk?"

Ten years ago, the *Sarasota Herald-Tribune* was a prototype for how women manage a newspaper. I visited the newsroom for a story in *AJR*'s January/February 2001 issue, "Where Women Rule." At the time, the paper had an all-female leadership team. Diane McFarlin had been in the publisher's chair since 1999, Janet Weaver was executive editor and Rosemary Armao was managing editor.

The women provided a blueprint for changing macho newsroom culture. During interviews, staffers praised the flexible scheduling system, especially for those juggling childcare. A city editor related how his schedule allowed him to spend time with his son after preschool classes some afternoons before returning to work.

Reporters talked about accessibility of supervisors and the lemon meringue pies and brownies that magically appeared during stressful times. They praised the more benevolent atmosphere.

The three women didn't define the differences as just being gender-based; they believed they reflected changes in the industry as a whole. Weaver and Armao have since left the *Herald-Tribune*, but McFarlin talks about a "transitional phase" in which a younger generation of journalists, female and male, seeks more balance between work and family life. McFarlin speculates that could be one reason some young women are not aiming for the top.

She sees a marked difference in her generation of female newsroom leaders. For them, the job tended to be all-consuming. Back in 2001, she said in an interview that "nothing was as stimulating as the newsroom. Nothing as interesting or enjoyable."

Looking back, "I thought, 'Yikes, that sounded horrible,' but for my generation of women, all of a sudden doors were opening and we thought, 'My God, we have to go through them.' We can't just say, 'never mind.' We felt compelled to go through the doors women before us had opened. Today there is more opportunity; women feel they have more choices. And that is OK."

Whatever the reason, the number of female journalists in supervisory positions and in the newsroom overall has stalled. According to the American Society of News Editors' newsroom census, the figures have remained basically the same over the past 10 years. In 2001, women accounted for 34.4 percent of newsroom supervisors; today it's 34.6 percent. The percentage of women in the newsroom has decreased slightly to 36.9 percent from a high for the decade of 37.7 in 2006.

Nobody knows the numbers better than Charlotte Hall. Over the years, Hall has kept an eye on the number of women running America's largest circulation newspapers. "Sadly, at times it was zero," she says.

When she looked at the nation's 10 largest newspapers in October, she found only one female editor: Jill Abramson. By Hall's calculation, of the 30 papers with the highest circulation, six, counting the *New York Times*, have newsrooms run by women—the others are *Newsday,* Minneapolis' *Star Tribune*, the *Baltimore Sun*, Cleveland's *Plain Dealer* and the *Sacramento Bee*. "It's never been more than a handful," Hall says.

When she was named editor of the *Orlando Sentinel* in March 2004, Hall didn't dwell on bringing a woman's viewpoint to the job. When budgets were slashed, she had to cut everywhere, but she favored keeping hard news and watchdog journalism over preserving the full range of feature beats. That flew in the face of popular stereotypes about women's taste in news.

But she was conscious of female representation in stories. "Do women editors go out of their way to seek out female voices? That may be," says Hall, a past president of ASNE. "We may sense a lack of balance in stories more readily than a man."

When Hall was named editor of the *Sentinel,* she moved a sentence about being the first woman in the job out of the lead of the paper's press release on the development. "I felt somehow that categorized me," she says. "I even felt that when Jill was named. Too much was made of the fact that she was the first."

On October 24, *Forbes* ran a story on "The 10 most hated and pervasive stereotypes about powerful women." The third on the list was "tough," and Abramson was used as an example. "Despite her complexities, she must contend with being called 'tough' and 'brusque,' making the 'she's-tough stereotype' her least favorite," the article said. Then this quote from Abramson: "As an investigative reporter, I had tough standards and a formidable way of framing and reporting stories, but I don't think of myself as a tough person."

Yet that was a common theme in the stories about her appointment.

On June 2, a Politico story quoted Al Hunt, executive Washington editor of *Bloomberg News,* saying Abramson's "got more balls than the New York Yankees." Hunt hired Abramson in 1988 when he was the *Wall Street Journal's* Washington bureau chief. The same Politico story cited an anonymous quote about Abramson in a 1999 *Village Voice* story: "Balls like cast-iron cantaloupes."

On June 7, the *New York Observer* quoted *New Yorker* writer Jane Mayer, a longtime Abramson friend, as saying, "She can both kick ass more than anyone as a news person and make a great salad dressing. That's the ultimate liberation." While the two were at the *Wall Street Journal,* they coauthored a book, *Strange Justice,* about the Clarence Thomas confirmation hearings. "She is tough as nails," Mayer told the *Observer.*

The headline for a June 2 Slate story: "Jill Abramson: Built Truck Tough." That was a reference to a May 2007 incident in which Abramson was hit by a truck when she was on her way to work out at the Harvard Club in New York City. The reporter wrote, "She broke her femur and fractured her hip and spent three weeks in Bellevue Hospital. But you shoulda seen the damage to the truck."

In an article on Abramson in the October 24 *New Yorker,* media writer Ken Auletta described how as managing editor "many in the newsroom considered her to be intimidating and brusque; she was too remote they thought." Toward the end of the story, Auletta portrays the new executive editor roaming around the three newsroom floors bestowing compliments.

"At the 10 a.m. page-one meeting, she went out of her way to praise editors for their work," Auletta wrote. " 'She really is trying,' "one editor says. " 'How long it will last, I don't know.' "

Pink brain, blue brain. Does sex really make a difference when it comes to management?

Women in high-level positions seem to exhibit the same leadership behavior as their male counterparts, according to a March 2010 article in *Psychology Today*. "It could be the case that only women who exhibit the same sorts of leadership styles and behaviors as male leaders make it through," psychologist Ronald E. Riggio wrote.

Women and men attack problems with similar goals but different approaches, according to Michael G. Conner, a researcher and clinical psychologist from Portland, Oregon. For women, sharing and discussing provide opportunities to strengthen relationships. Men tend to dominate and assert their authority. "There are no absolutes, only tendencies," Conner says.

In her landmark 1982 book, *In a Different Voice*, psychologist Carol Gilligan explored psychological theory and women's development. Through her research, Gilligan concluded that women are more likely to consider moral problems in terms of "care and responsibility in relationships" rather than with the more typically masculine examination of "rights and rules." She believed that morality based on rules alone was incomplete and could become harsh and domineering.

How does that play out in a newsroom?

"Jill Abramson is very much in the culture of the *Times*, which is largely a male culture, so she had to prove she could be like one of the boys to get in the position she is in," says Gilligan, a professor at New York University. "But does she really think she won't bring something new, something original? It just depends; she may or may not."

Gilligan poses a question: "Is it possible to have no women in leadership positions and lose nothing of value in human experience? I am not saying all women are different, but this is an incredible opportunity for [Abramson]. I hope she takes it."

For the first time, a woman and an African American hold the two highest newsroom positions at the *New York Times*. Former *Los Angeles Times* Editor Dean Baquet moved from *New York Times* Washington bureau chief to the managing editor's office. For many, it is an emotional moment.

"Frankly, I wept," Anna Quindlen says. Quindlen joined the *Times* in 1977, three years after a class action lawsuit was filed against the newspaper over sex discrimination in hiring, pay and promotion. Seven women at the paper brought the suit on behalf of 550 female *Times* employees. The suit was settled in 1978 with the paper committing to an affirmative action program.

During the announcement of her promotion, Abramson publicly recognized Quindlen and others who preceded and supported her. She singled out the late *Times* reporter Nan Robertson, author of the best-selling book *Girls in the Balcony*, which is about discrimination at the paper.

Paul Delaney, who spent 23 years at the *Times* as a reporter and editor, applauds the choices of Abramson and Baquet. "Both are great journalists, and I do expect great things," says Delaney, who for eight years was an editor on the *Times'* national desk. When he heard the news, his mind drifted back to a bleaker time at the newspaper.

He recalls a lawsuit filed in 1972 by minority group members charging that newsroom managers favored white men in hiring, promotion, beat assignments and wages. According to Delaney, at the time not one black had risen above the position of reporter, and the highest-ranking woman was an editor in "women's news." Women and minorities joined together in spirit during the long struggle, says Delaney, who was one of the founders of the National Association of Black Journalists in 1975.

Abramson's comment on gender neutrality surprised him. "Maybe she was being coy; maybe she didn't want to upset the white guys on the staff. I can't believe she meant it deep down," says Delaney, who recently completed a memoir about his career at the *Times*.

For all the hoopla over Abramson's ascent to the pinnacle, what could it mean for women in journalism?

In a June 2 column, the Poynter Institute's Jill Geisler called Abramson's appointment "a big victory in the face of a big void." Both real and symbolic, it could serve as an inspiration, she said. Here are the ways she believes it could make a difference:

- "It can tap old-school publishers on the shoulder and remind them to look beyond their comfort zones when it's time to promote. Old habits die hard. New success stories help kill old habits.

- "It can encourage women in today's newsroom to stick around longer. A 2002 study by the American Press Institute found significantly more women than men in newsroom management were considering leaving the industry. They were less satisfied with their responsibilities and less optimistic about promotions than their male counterparts.

- "It can serve as an inspiration to today's journalism students, many of whom are women. It takes fortitude to pursue a career path in an industry under challenge. Seeing a woman lead a legacy institution into the digital future can be a powerful motivator."

It's premature to predict what impact Abramson's presence will have on the *New York Times* as it moves deeper into the digital world, or on the journalism profession itself. But if diversity is a hedge against unconscious biases and blind spots, as many have suggested, the *Times* appears to be headed in the right direction.

In Praise of Sheryl Sandberg

The Controversial Facebook Executive's Book Is Exactly the Right Kind of Self-Help

By Christine Rosen,
Commentary, May 13, 2013

In his 1943 paper, "A Theory of Human Motivation," the psychologist Abraham Maslow outlined what he called our "hierarchy of needs." Using the image of a pyramid, Maslow described its base as human beings' physiological needs (such as food and shelter), on top of which came our needs for security, for healthy social relationships, for esteem from others, and finally, at the apex, the need for self-actualization, which included such things as creativity, problem-solving, and morality. The story of our lives is the story of our progression through this hierarchy, Maslow believed, and we were not all destined to reach the top. "The story of the human race is the story of men and women selling themselves short," he observed.

Maslow's particular brand of humanistic psychology is no longer in fashion, but it lives on in diluted form in the advice and self-help industry, whose latest purveyor is Sheryl Sandberg, chief operating officer of Facebook and author of *Lean In: Women, Work, and the Will to Lead* (Knopf, 240 pages). Like Maslow, Sandberg is concerned with people reaching their full potential. Like him, she draws on elite examples to make her case: Maslow was partial to Albert Einstein and Gandhi, while Sandberg prefers former economic official and Harvard president Lawrence Summers and Facebook founder Mark Zuckerberg. Unlike Maslow, Sandberg's message is targeted specifically to women.

The message is both bracing and long overdue. While she acknowledges that barriers to women's success still exist in the workplace, Sandberg focuses on something else: the fact that women aren't exhibiting as much ambition as their male counterparts. And Sandberg thinks she knows the reason why: "We hold ourselves back in ways both big and small, by lacking self-confidence, by not raising our hands, and by pulling back when we should be leaning in," she writes. "Getting rid of these internal barriers is critical to gaining power." In other words, ladies, stop curling up at the end of your workday with your Tension Tamer herbal tea and your perceived slights and your fantasies of a mentor who will sweep you off your feet and into the executive suite. Work harder. Put yourself forward. Stop using the future possibility of children as an excuse to check out of your career when it's just getting started. Self-actualization is possible, Sandberg suggests, but you have to take responsibility for pursuing it. And you can't do that with advice gleaned from *Eat Pray Love*; instead, think Strive Work Achieve. As a friend of mine who owns her own business said with a sigh of relief after reading the book, "Bossiness is back!"

Of course, women who don the bossy boots are guaranteed criticism for doing so, and Sandberg has been getting it from all sides. Conservatives have chastised her (correctly) for uncritically endorsing outdated feminist assumptions like the notion that an ideal world is one that achieves perfect equality between men and women in all parts of life. And culturally conservative critics have faulted her for failing to consider the needs of the children of ambitious dual-income couples and for downplaying what they believe is the unique role that mothers play in society.

On the other end of the spectrum, feminists and socially liberal critics (many of whom are themselves members of the elite) have suddenly discovered their populist pitchforks and begun waving them at Sandberg's supposed hypocrisy in offering advice to working women when she herself has so much wealth and so many resources at her disposal. And economic leftists have condemned her uncritical acceptance of the increasingly harsh demands of capitalism on its elites.

It's easy to focus on Sandberg's privileged perch and, quite frankly, to envy her ability to summon armies of nannies and housekeepers, even though she acknowledges them upfront and with great appreciation. But it is harder to find fault with her assertion that all these choices have consequences, hers as much as everyone else's. She admits that because of her own ambitions and work schedule she has "missed a level of detail" about her children's lives, and she confesses that she "always wants to do more" for them. Sandberg is honest about her ambivalent feelings while also taking responsibility for the choices she has made (rather than casting about for others to alleviate the consequences of them). Her tone harks back to self-help manuals of previous eras, before everything was Oprah-fied and then politicized and authors hoped to cultivate some grit in their readers rather than leave them wallowing in victimhood. Reading her book, I felt as if the weight of a thousand scented candles and New Age bromides had suddenly been lifted. Sandberg is like the lovechild of Susan B. Anthony and Dale Carnegie, with a heavy dose of 21st-century business acumen thrown in.

Her sensibility makes her something of an outlier among her peer group. Sandberg's generation was raised on the messages of second-wave feminists, many of whom made it to the top of fields that were sparsely populated with other women at the time. Their hope and expectation was that the next generation—Sandberg's—would follow eagerly along the path they forged and thus break the patriarchy's grip on power. That didn't happen, and as Sandberg recalls, she and her peers had to endure many boulevard-of-broken-dreams speeches like the one she heard from Judith Rodin, president of the Rockefeller Foundation: "My generation fought so hard to give all of you choices. We believe in choices. But choosing to leave the workforce was not the choice we thought so many of you would make." Rodin's generation of feminists very much needed a villain to help them make sense of this story: Who or what had done this terrible thing to all of these promising young women?

How unpleasant it must be, then, to hear one of those women say: Maybe we're the problem. For them, Sandberg is committing the cardinal sin of blaming the victim. And although she gives an obligatory nod to the arguments about flex time, maternity and paternity leave, and the like, she is more interested in exploring the consequences of women's own choices. Achievement at the highest level requires trade-offs, whether you are male or female, and Sandberg's candor in describing her own only makes the force of her argument more challenging to the feminist notion that the problem can never be attributed to us (the women), but them (the men, the institutions they run, the government). The black-and-white, Manichean universe of female oppression and male domination in the workplace starts to look a lot grayer after reading Sandberg's book.

Even more appalling to feminist sensibilities, Sandberg suggests that women embrace some of the techniques that have proven so successful for men: Take credit for your work; sit at the table; stop apologizing for yourself and indulging your feelings of self-doubt; quit making excuses. "Taking initiative pays off," Sandberg writes. "It is hard to visualize someone as a leader if she is always waiting to be told what to do." But this supremely rational advice directly undermines a key part of the feminist message about women in leadership: the idea that it is the workplace (and men) who should conform to women's ways of doing things (which are, it is always assumed, superior to men's). Sandberg notes the contradictory messages women receive: Be aggressive, but not too aggressive; be nice, but not a doormat. But instead of blaming this situation on a patriarchal corporate conspiracy, she acknowledges the frustration of this unfair reality and then does the unthinkable: She offers advice. Yes, aggressive women are seen as unlikable even when men acting the same way are not (social-science research has shown this time and time again). So use *we* instead of *I* when negotiating that raise. Be nice but also be insistent. Smile.

Is this fair in an existential sense? Of course not. But who said life is fair? How many men in the workplace feign an interest in golf or pretend to appreciate their boss's sense of humor in order to get ahead? Sandberg suggests resisting "Tiara Syndrome," a phrase coined by the founders of a women's consulting group to describe how women "expect that if they keep doing their job well someone will notice them and place a tiara on their head." Instead, she advises, take some initiative, even if the system you are working in isn't ideal.

Tiara Syndrome isn't the only myth Sandberg properly pummels. She also takes on what might be called the "Mentor Myth." As Sandberg tells it, young women in the workplace view the perfect female mentor just as little girls envision glittery rainbow-colored unicorns: powerful creatures whom they have only to discover for their lives to change forever. Sandberg recounts the many times that young women who are complete strangers have come up to her after speeches or meetings asking her to be their mentor. "The question is a total mood killer," she says. She has the wit to admit that "we've brought this on ourselves" with incessant and boosterish encouragement of the idea that young women need female role models and advisers. You can't throw a brick in the feminist community without hitting a female leadership academy (Gloria Steinem and Naomi Wolf each founded one). But Sandberg is withering in her criticism of this notion, comparing these young women's attitudes with that of Sleeping Beauty: "Now young women are told that if they can just find the right mentor, they will be pushed up the ladder and whisked away to the corner office to live happily ever after. Once again, we are teaching women to be too dependent on others."

Sandberg is not criticizing mentorship; throughout the book she is generous and unstinting in her praise of the people whose advice and counsel helped her get ahead. What she resists is the notion, inculcated in a generation of young women raised on the drumbeat of Girl Power, that you deserve a mentor simply by showing up and having ovaries. And she notes the tendency among these young women to assume that the mentor's role is to devote herself to the care and nurturing of the mentee. After helping a bright woman rising through the ranks at Google (where Sandberg worked before moving to Facebook), she confessed to some surprise when the woman claimed never to have benefited from the guidance of a mentor. When Sandberg asked what her idea of a mentor was, the woman responded that it was someone she would talk to about her career for an hour a week. "I smiled," Sandberg writes, "thinking, *That's not a mentor—that's a therapist.*"

Many of Sandberg's mentors were men (such as Larry Summers, for whom she worked during the Clinton administration), and this, too, rankles her critics, several of whom have implied that her sponsorship by men (and continued success in the male-dominated tech industry) casts doubt on her credentials as a card-carrying member of the sisterhood. But it is her position as an outlier in her field that makes her insights persuasive. Sandberg paints an ambiguous yet more compelling portrait of female leadership, one that resonates because she has exercised leadership herself. As for uniquely female styles of leadership, however often they reign in specific instances, history and common sense suggest they are more fiction than reality in the aggregate. (I worked for an all-female organization for many years, and I can attest, *Lord of the Flies* had nothing on that office environment.)

Sandberg even wades into the roiling waters of women's complex feelings about other women—the "mean girl" problem, for lack of a better term. If you spend much time perusing feminist literature about women in power, you would assume that older women in the corner office are all waiting with open and nurturing arms to embrace the next bright young female thing rising through the ranks. But as Sandberg suggests, sisterhood isn't always powerful; all too often it's simply pettily vindictive. Case in point: Current Yahoo! CEO Marissa Mayer, who had the audacity not only to accept that high-powered position when she was pregnant, but also to be utterly transparent about her plans for working almost immediately after the birth of her child. A nurturing world of feminist leaders should have embraced such a decision, both for its honesty and its trailblazing. Instead, Sandberg writes: "The attacks on Marissa for her maternity-leave plans came almost entirely from other women. This has certainly been my experience too."

Perhaps the best piece of advice Sandberg offers is personal, and it reads like something out of a Jane Austen novel (not the prose, of course): "I truly believe that the single most important career decision that a woman makes is whether she will have a life partner and who that partner is." This is a far cry from Gloria Steinem's tossed-off observation that "a woman without a man is like a fish without a bicycle"; indeed, Sandberg makes it clear throughout the book how crucial her husband has been to her own success and her ability to juggle an ambitious career and a family. Even when Sandberg is encouraging men to "lean in to their families" by helping more with domestic tasks, she doesn't spare women criticism. She notes how often women engage in "maternal gatekeeping" behaviors, asking husbands to take on domestic tasks but then behaving in a critical or controlling way when they perform them (in the nonacademic literature, this is known by its more familiar term, "nagging").

Taken together, Sandberg's advice makes a compelling case for the argument that, contra decades of feminist propagandizing, female self-actualization is not and should not be the goal of businesses. Equal pay? Equal rights under the law? Benefits and flexibility that allow all parents to have more balanced lives? Absolutely. But a world that requires Abraham Maslow's hierarchy of needs on the corporate spreadsheet? No thanks. Sandberg's *Lean In* stands as a necessary corrective to a feminist movement that has migrated away from the pursuit of concrete political goals toward the pursuit of gauzier things like self-actualization. Women should abandon the notion that they can or should "have it all." As Sandberg correctly notes: "The greatest trap ever set for women was the coining of this phrase."

Sandberg reminds us that women can do a great deal to improve their own lives at the individual level, whether that is speaking up at a meeting or taking seriously the challenge of finding a good life partner. But she worries that "women will continue to sacrifice being liked for being successful." She insists that, to the contrary, "taking risks, choosing growth, challenging ourselves, and asking for promotions (with smiles on our faces, of course) are all important elements of managing a career." She is cruel to be kind, but in the right measure, as the seventies-era pop song goes. Fifty years after Betty Friedan told women what they suspected but couldn't articulate in *The Feminine Mystique*, Sheryl Sandberg, in her charmingly stoic way, is telling us what we know but won't admit. In this, her advice echoes that of a more traditional (and ancient) Stoic who was also a wise leader. In his *Meditations*, Marcus Aurelius advised: "Don't go on discussing what a good person should be. Just be one."

The Corporate Mystique

Sheryl Sandberg and the Folly of Davos-style Feminism

By Judith Shulevitz
New Republic, March 25, 2013

About two-thirds of the way through *Makers*, the PBS documentary charting the rise and fall of modern feminism, we learn the exact moment the American women's movement died. OK, maybe "died" is too strong a word. Let's say it had a really big stroke. On June 30, 1982, the Equal Rights Amendment passed its deadline for ratification and expired. And with that—narrator Meryl Streep tells us—the march-in-the-streets energy that had pulled women by the tens of thousands out of their kitchens and into the world just sort of dribbled away. Over the decades that followed, the work of reforming a sexist society would fall to individual "groundbreakers." These were women such as Meg Whitman, who headed off to her job at Procter & Gamble in the suit-and-bow-tie uniform of 1980s female executives, and Brenda Berkman, whose lawsuit toppled the gender barrier at New York City's fire department.

Women's opportunities have multiplied exponentially since 1982. Women now outnumber men at universities and in the middle management of many companies. But the conversation about feminism seems stuck more or less where it was 30 years ago. We're still talking about mentors, glass ceilings, and the impossibility or desirability of having it all. What we are not talking about in nearly enough detail, or agitating for with enough passion, are the government policies, such as mandatory paid maternity leave, that would truly equalize opportunity. We are still thinking individually, not collectively.

The new face of boardroom feminism, of course, is Facebook Chief Operating Officer Sheryl Sandberg. Now, it's nearly impossible to dislike Sandberg, or to be unimpressed by her wry candor and the indisputable truth of her message. Women do hold themselves back in the workplace, give away too much when they negotiate, and overcorrect for nasty stereotypes about pushiness. Sandberg's book, *Lean In*, is very personable. It's a disarmingly self-deprecating career-management advice manual that doubles as a feminist manifesto. And you have to admire her for using her considerable clout to help other women.

There is a lot of name-dropping in *Lean In*, and the names are largely men's: Mark Zuckerberg, Larry Summers, Eric Schmidt. (Sandberg works under Zuckerberg at Facebook; she worked for Schmidt at Google and for Summers at the U.S.

Treasury Department.) I drop these names myself not just to show that Sandberg knows what she's talking about when it comes to breaking into a man's world, but also to pinpoint that world on the social map. Sandberg isn't aiming for women to take over the corner office in which Don Draper used to drink whiskey. She wants them to commandeer the private jets of today's hardworking and largely sober super-elite–which is still as male-dominated as the "Mad Men" ad agencies were. "As the ninety-nine percent has become steadily pinker, the one percent has remained an all-boys club," observed Chrystia Freeland in her book *Plutocrats*.

Another term for Sandberg's reference group is "Davos Man," that by-now cartoonish figure named for the town in the Swiss Alps where CEOs and finance ministers meet every year to plot a better world. (As it happens, Sandberg was the confab's only female co-chair in 2012.) It's an item of faith for Davos Man—or Woman—that global leaders are more effective agents of social change than activists and bureaucrats. Sandberg's "lean-in" philosophy sure *sounds* like self-help for would-be C-level executives: Claim a place at the conference table; don't give your job less than your all when planning to start a family; if you're asking for a pay raise, smile and say "we," not "I." But I think Sandberg believes that women able to master this artful combination of submission to actual conditions and aggression ("I read the phrase 'lean in' as a weird version of 'man up,'" the sociologist Shamus Khan told me) will maneuver themselves into a position to mitigate the family-unfriendly culture of America's most competitive companies. And maybe they'll even get men to share the housework. "A truly equal world would be one where women ran half our countries and companies and men ran half our homes," Sandberg writes.

But how much, really, can individual women do? Sandberg cites research to back up her theory that women in management foster better work-life policies and help close the gender pay gap. I pulled up the most substantial paper in her footnote, however, and it concludes that the companies most likely to achieve a critical mass of female executives and therefore have more female-friendly workplaces are the ones that hold federal contracts—which means they've got to follow government affirmative action guidelines.

Marissa Mayer's story suggests that Sandberg's optimism is unwarranted. When Yahoo's new female CEO told her employees last month that they'd have to stop telecommuting and show up in the office, it became clear that she did not see her job as helping men and women live in Sandberg's "truly equal" world. Mayer's job is to run Yahoo. She wants to energize a dysfunctional company in which, insiders say, telecommuting has become an excuse for doing too little work under too little supervision. But Yahoo employees now understand that, when unregulated market forces go head-to-head with policies that facilitate gender equality, the policies stand down. It doesn't matter who runs the company.

I'm well aware that feminists have been discrediting other feminists by calling them elitist since the beginning of the women's movement. The most notable victim of this unsisterly populism—as *Makers* reminds us—was Betty Friedan. *The Feminine Mystique*, published 50 years ago this February, addressed a privileged sector of the *American* population: white, middle-class housewives. When the liberal women's movement morphed into the radical women's lib movement, Friedan was dismissed as irrelevant for not talking enough about the plight of black women, working women, and lesbians.

The charge was true, but missed the point. The reason *The Feminine Mystique* caught on so fast and to such revolutionary effect was that the American housewife saw herself in it. Sandberg and most of the other women discussed in *Lean In*, on the other hand, are anything but average. They camp in the dormitories of Harvard, occupy offices at McKinsey and Goldman Sachs, and wind up in Palo Alto and the Upper East Side. They inhabit a tiny transnational bubble floating out of reach of the middle class, which itself is slowly vanishing.

Competent female executives run better companies than incompetent male executives, but they're no more likely to make universal day care the law of the land. If Davos Woman had dominated feminist discourse when the Triangle Shirtwaist fire killed nearly 130 female sweatshop laborers in 1911, would she have pushed for the legislation that came out of that tragedy–the fire codes and occupancy limits that made workplaces safer for women, and men, for generations to come?

America's women's movements helped deliver a fairer world for everyone–upper-middle class, middle class, and working class—not because they produced more leaders, but because those leaders, and the rank-and-file who worked with them and even went to jail with them, changed the rules of society. They helped women get the vote, abortion access, domestic-abuse statutes, and the Family and Medical Leave Act, *de minimis* as that is. No corporate boss, even one as gallantly outspoken as Sandberg, can match that.

Oprah

Blazing the Trail to Her Destiny

By Miki Turner
JET, February 2, 2011

It's been a very long time since Oprah Winfrey was able to walk into a room unnoticed. The television icon who now runs her own network (OWN), an all-girls academy in South Africa and produces films—sometimes with her pal Tyler Perry—made an appearance at the Television Critics Association press tour in Pasadena, California, last month. When Winfrey came onstage, some folks didn't know whether to applaud or bow—or both.

Winfrey, whose show has been the top-rated daytime talk show for 25 years, is like the Queen of England, Martin Luther King Jr. and Harriet Tubman all rolled into one.

Grace. Power. Defiance.

Yet, even though she's been one of the most famous and influential people on the planet for nearly three decades, there once was a time when few people cared when or if she entered a room.

"That would be third grade, fifth grade, that would be seventh grade, eighth grade," she said with a laugh. "I started getting noticed in high school because I was the student council president by the time I was in 11th grade. So, not since 11th grade, but before that, yeah."

Winfrey, however, doesn't miss her brief dance with anonymity. Inspired by the words and works of Maya Angelou, Sojourner Truth, Langston Hughes, James Weldon Johnson and others, Winfrey has been blazing trails since she was old enough to channel "the energy and spirit" of her role models. They helped her overcome the adversity in her formative years—molestation and teen pregnancy—and they continue to guide her fortunes as one of the wealthiest women in the world.

"I accept that the attention and notoriety and fame is just a part of what I do," Winfrey said during a telephone interview with *JET* from her office at Harpo Studios in Chicago. "When you go out, it's like a parade when you're in the public eye. And if you don't want to be a part of the parade, then don't go out.

"I have always felt that I was a part of the seed of the free, and as part of the seed of the free you had a responsibility to all of those people who come before you."

Even with millions of adoring fans, Winfrey's validation still comes from the way she's been able to challenge the way people think, act and behave. Television is her vehicle, and she would prefer to use it to educate.

"All of us have different platforms," Winfrey said. "Mine just happens to be on television, where I get to speak to millions of people. What validates me is being able to do the work that I know I should be doing, to be on purpose with my work. It's not just about being on television, it's about using television for a purpose that is greater than myself—and that is to help lead people to the best of themselves."

She's been displaying her best self since beginning her television career at 19, becoming the youngest and first Black correspondent ever at WTVF in Nashville. From there she headed north to Baltimore and co-anchored the 6 p.m. news at WJZ in 1976 and became the co-host of *People Are Talking* two years later. In 1984, Winfrey hit the Windy City to host *A.M. Chicago*. One year later, the phenomenon now known as *The Oprah Winfrey Show* was launched. It's compelling and entertaining, and it's introduced us to Oprah's favorite things, classic books and new best-sellers, her boyfriend, Stedman Graham, and her best friend, Gayle King, among other things. She will end her show on May 25.

Sometimes Winfrey hit all the right notes—effecting change while earning through-the-roof ratings. But sometimes, by her own admission, her show did more harm than good—like the time she tried to cure a group of hostile skinheads and Ku Klux Klansmen. When one of them called her a "monkey," she realized she was only giving those hate-mongers a platform to spew their poison.

"That was a life-changing moment for me," Winfrey said wistfully. "I touched one of them and he said, 'Take your hands off me.' I thought, 'I've brought this terrible energy into my studio,' which is like my home, it's my space. That was when I decided I would never be in that position again. It forever changed the way I look at what this platform is."

Winfrey has become an Oscar-nominated actress for her supporting role in *The Color Purple*, a noted philanthropist and a multimillion-dollar brand. But like all trailblazers, she has her share of critics. When OWN launched on Jan. 1, some critics wrote that the network that Winfrey had promoted as enlightening and empowering was, in their view, redundant and boring. Others, like former BET owner Sheila Johnson, criticized Winfrey for not providing enough opportunities for Black folks.

"The 'haters' you don't pay any attention to," Winfrey said. "Criticism has its place. Criticism with thoughtfulness and analysis is something I can listen to. People who want to watch (OWN) and see the best of themselves, that's who I'm talking to. If that's not what you want to see, I'm not talking to you and that's OK. There are 500 other channels you can watch. I'm not trying to please everybody. I'm only trying to please people who want to hear it."

It appears that her supporters still heavily outweigh her critics and want to hear whatever Winfrey has to say on her show, her network or in the frigid ballroom of a five-star hotel in Pasadena. But when asked whether she'd like to be remembered as a television icon or a visionary philanthropist who let her little light shine bright enough to positively impact millions of people, Winfrey let someone else's words speak for her.

"I'm going to answer that question with a Maya Angelou quote for you," she said. "When I opened the school, I said to Maya that this was going to be my greatest legacy. And Maya said, 'You have no idea what your legacy is going to be. Your legacy is every woman who watched the show on battered women and decided I will no longer let a man hit me. Your legacy is everybody who watched the show on the 65-year-old who decided to go back to college and get her degree, and then someone else decided maybe I can do better and I'll go back to school or get a better job and improve myself. Your legacy is every child of divorce who ever watched a show that you did on children of divorce and because of that you see the healing from it.'

"So, the answer is, I don't know what my legacy is going to be. I believe your legacy is tied to every life that you are able to touch while you were privileged to be here on Earth. Every life that you were able to touch and what impact that had on that individual person."

Sustaining the Feminist Movement

Generations of Women Donors
Are Building Lasting Change

By Alison R. Bernstein
Ms. Magazine, Fall 2013

In the early 1900s, Katharine Dexter McCormick, a biology major from Chicago and one of just a handful of women at the Massachusetts Institute of Technology, decided to take on the university's administration. In those days, women were required to wear hats to class—even in science laboratories. McCormick, the daughter of wealthy, progressive parents, protested that the fabrics and feathers were a fire hazard in the lab. After some debate, M.I.T. backed down, abolishing the silly, dangerous rule.

This early incident foreshadowed McCormick's lifelong commitment to women's equality: She became a pioneering feminist philanthropist, singlehandedly funding the research and development of the birth-control pill. And she wasn't the only woman of her time opening her purse for women's rights. A century ago, women of means with a political or social-improvement agenda often put their money where their mouths were. Whether their wealth came through inheritance, business success or divorce settlements, women philanthropists played important roles in shaping America's reform movements in education, health, welfare and, especially, women's voting rights.

At the turn of the 19th century, for example, Alva Vanderbilt Belmont was the principal benefactor of the women's suffrage movement, while famed suffragist Susan B. Anthony put up funds from her life-insurance policy to guarantee that women could be admitted to the University of Rochester. Katharine Drexel provided education for girls of American Indian and African American backgrounds; Margaret Olivia Slocum Sage endowed the social science/social welfare reform foundation that still bears her late husband Russell Sage's name. And highly successful businessperson Madame C. J. Walker invested in black colleges—especially one in Florida that was established by civil rights advocate Mary McLeod Bethune.

With the advent of the Second Wave of the women's movement, mainstream philanthropy, too, paid attention to leveling the playing field for women. Major foundations such as Ford, Carnegie and Rockefeller—whose white male founders had not been prominent advocates for women's equality—were nonetheless in the vanguard of funding projects to advance the life chances of girls and women.

The Rockefeller family has provided significant support to the African American women's college Spelman; the Ford Foundation can take real credit for developing the field of women's studies both in the U.S. and overseas; and the Carnegie Corporation, in the 1970s and 1980s, focused on advancing women's leadership.

Even so, the 1980 report Far from Done, issued by the now-defunct organization Women and Foundations/Corporate Philanthropy, noted that only 6 percent of all foundation dollars were directed to projects aimed at specifically women and girls. While several major foundations were paying attention to "women's issues," the vast majority of the almost 90,000 private U.S. foundations were not.

So where are the philanthropic McCormicks, Sages and Walkers these days? After all, women now constitute 45 percent of millionaires in the U.S. And this percentage is likely to rise with increasing numbers of women making significant fortunes in high tech and other growth industries. In addition, since women are living longer than men, there will be more intergenerational transfers of wealth to wives, ex-wives, sisters and daughters.

You might not know many of their names (yet), but important feminist philanthropists are definitely out there, and they're trying to change not just women's lives but the whole notion of "women's philanthropy"—a concept that emerged in the 1980s.

The Ms. Foundation for Women, established in 1972 as an outgrowth of Ms. magazine (but not connected to the present-day magazine), was the first of its type to focus specifically on women and girls. By 2012, the U.S. was filled with 160 women's foundations and explicitly women's funds—part of a Women's Funding Network (WFN) launched in 1985. When it began, WFN served as an umbrella for just 20 organizations and $1.2 million in funds; today, the network makes $70 million in grants annually.

Another facet of women's philanthropy today involves networks of individual women donors who take collective action on behalf of progressive causes for women and girls. The Women Donors Network, begun in 1991, now has nearly 200 individual members nationally who leverage their giving around such issues as reproductive rights and reducing gender-based violence. Women Moving Millions, started in 2007, has more than 150 members who each pledge at least $1 million over her lifetime to advance opportunities for women and girls.

To understand the new modes of women's philanthropy, I recently interviewed several notable women donors, ranging in age from their late 30s to mid-80s and diverse in race, region and profession. With such diversity, I didn't expect all of them to have the same view of philanthropy—more specifically feminist philanthropy—and I wasn't wrong.

For example, while all felt comfortable claiming the label feminist, not all called themselves "feminist philanthropists." On the one hand, Celeste Watkins-Hayes, a distinguished younger African American scholar and donor to black women's causes and black women's studies (particularly Spelman College), says, "I am a feminist, if by that you mean someone who believes in gender equity and eliminating all forms of discrimination on the basis of gender."

But another younger philanthropist with whom I spoke, self-made multimillionaire Mellody Hobson, preferred to call herself a "humanist philanthropist." The president of Ariel, a Chicago financial services firm that is one of the largest minority-owned money management companies in the U.S., says that in her industry, "discrimination based on race is far more prevalent than gender-based discrimination." Education is her highest philanthropic priority, but not specifically for women and girls because, she noted, "minority men and boys were even more at risk of falling off the social mobility ladder which education had historically provided."

Veteran feminists Donna Hall, president and CEO of the Women Donors Network, and Peg Yorkin—the most significant single feminist funder over the last quarter century, having given more than $15 million to the Feminist Majority Foundation—both describe themselves as feminist philanthropists, but they note that you don't have to be a woman to be a feminist philanthropist. They agree that there is such a phenomenon as women's philanthropy, but didn't automatically assume it was feminist in terms of funding women-specific social movements and institutions. In fact, both seem concerned that women's philanthropy is not always as focused as it should be on funding women's movements over a sustained period of time.

Like Hall and Yorkin, Susan Berresford—the first woman to serve as president of the nation's second-largest philanthropy, the Ford Foundation—calls herself a feminist philanthropist, but argues that there is "much more complexity to the way in which feminist donors need to understand issues today." She looks for philanthropists to make a more intersectional analysis of feminist issues, including LGBT rights, the underrepresentation of minority men in higher education and the overrepresentation of minority men in prison.

Jacki Zehner, a former Goldman Sachs partner who now heads Women Moving Millions, isn't concerned about donors calling themselves feminists as long as they are advancing women's and girls' opportunities. "Feminism," she told me, "is a lens through which to engage in long-term progressive change regardless of the topic . . . it's not a category." As for men participating in feminist philanthropy, she says that "fewer men donors [than women] are prioritizing women and girls, but more are [than before]."

Jennifer Buffett, part of the younger generation of women philanthropists who, with her husband, Peter (son of business magnate/philanthropist Warren Buffett), 42, cofounded the NoVo Foundation to advance opportunities for women and girls, argues that many younger men are feminist in their support for women and girls. Nonetheless, she recognizes that there is a "great imbalance between the genders— men's impulses are more valued than women's." Thus she and her husband are committed to investing in women and girls so that the grantees might infuse values of collaboration and nurturing—which Jennifer Buffett associates with women—rather than the competition and violence she associates with men. "We need feminism," Buffett concludes, "to help heal the world."

Gretchen Wittenborn Johnson, wife of Johnson and Johnson heir Jim Johnson, is convinced that men and women donors have varied approaches to giving. "Different things motivate and drive us," says Johnson, 70. She is a strong supporter of promoting women leaders in all sectors, especially education and the environment, while her husband does not prioritize funding women's leadership (nor does he oppose it).

Yorkin, 86, is the most outspoken about the differences between men and women donors: "Women do it with their hearts; men with their minds." Moreover, she observed that she gives money to "strong feminist organizations," which she feels "isn't always true of a newer, younger generation of donors." What matters to Yorkin is whether women and men donors act "in a way that supports women's empowerment."

Feminist philanthropists appear to be doing something different in at least four ways. First, many prefer collective approaches—networks and collaborations. They like stretching their resources by leveraging other donors, and they like sharing insights and possibilities.

Second, they worry about advancing girls' and women's opportunities to a greater degree than does mainstream philanthropy—perhaps because they apply a "gender-sensitive" lens when looking at proposals or funding approaches. Third, they are likely to involve men as allies in their efforts to "level the playing field." This may be as simple as realizing that making more opportunities available for girls and women requires that men become engaged in feminist projects.

Finally, feminist philanthropists—if not all foundations and donors—are demanding more accountability from their grantees than in the past. They want to know what difference their funding is making, and they frequently rely on quantifiable metrics to learn what's working. This trend seems to be especially true of women philanthropists, according to the Center on Philanthropy at Indiana University. Surveys conducted by the center indicate that women donors are more engaged than men in the work of their grantees, and as a result want to have a prominent role in determining how their dollars are being spent.

This is both good news and bad. The good news is that feminist projects are likely to get more serious attention from women funders (and a "few good men") who support gender equity as a core value and are willing to take the long view. This could translate into sustained commitments and more impactful giving. It could also translate into movement building—not just funding single-issue or "siloed" projects, but organizations that tackle multiple aspects of women's empowerment.

The downside of these trends is that "engaged" donors are tempted to dictate the outcomes of their grant-making. In keeping with feminist principles, these donors should instead trust those closest to the problems of inequity and gender-based discrimination to decide themselves what needs to be done and how. In this way, feminist donors will chart a truly path-breaking course—funding long-term projects that will inevitably shape a more humane and equitable future for us all.

Glass Ceiling

Why Women Aren't Coaching Men's D-I Hoops

By Nicole Auerbach
USA Today, November 12, 2013

Confused, Bernadette Mattox peered down at the note on her desk.

It said Tubby Smith had called from Kentucky. She thought he'd simply gotten her number by mistake; earlier, she had called Kentucky's women's basketball office to confirm some scheduling details on behalf of the Georgia women's basketball program. Somehow, she figured, her message had gone to the wrong staff.

But when she called Smith back later to apologize and clear up the confusion, he surprised her with a question first. Would she be interested in joining Rick Pitino's staff and becoming the first female assistant in Division I men's college basketball?

Mattox went to interview in Lexington, where Pitino outlined her responsibilities. She wouldn't be on the road recruiting, but everything else would be identical to what he asked of his other assistants. "I was very appreciative of the fact that he respected me enough—or a female enough—that he thought I could come in there and do what the guys did," says Mattox.

"You first have to give credit to Rick Pitino for having that type of vision," Smith says. "At that time, no one dreamed of having a female coach on their staff, much less at Kentucky."

Pitino wanted to hire her. His athletic director, C. M. Newton, gave him the green light.

"Frankly," Newton says, "my only thought process was, 'If she's truly a coach and you're going to treat her as a coach, then you're free to hire whoever you want. If you are doing this as a token and she's not going to (have) coaching responsibilities, then don't do it.'"

"That was the only stipulation I put on it."

This was 1990.

Since then, only two other women have become full-time assistants on Division I men's college basketball staffs, according to *USA Today* Sports research: Stephanie Ready at Coppin State and Jennifer Johnston at Oakland University. Both times, like Mattox, the women were sought out for the jobs; they didn't apply. And both Ready and Johnston were out of the men's game by 2002.

Women work in the realm of men's college basketball in various ways—some in administrative roles, some as athletic trainers, for example—but so few as coaches. From 2003 to 2011, the Equity in Athletics Data Analysis database lists six full-time female assistants on Division I men's basketball staffs. But queries to the schools listed as their employers uncover the real number: 0.

There have been no female head coaches in Division I men's basketball, either.

"I remember Bernadette working for Rick, and the incredible fanfare," Big East commissioner Val Ackerman says. "That was thought to be the turning point. Many of us had a great sense of anticipation that it was going to create this new avenue, and it sort of ended. It's like it died on the vine."

It's particularly puzzling to those who coached with Mattox.

"There have been a lot of men who have crossed over into the women's game, but not a lot of women who crossed over into the men's game," says Florida coach Billy Donovan, who coached alongside Mattox at Kentucky. "I really thought when Coach Pitino did that it would really open up a lot of doors and opportunities."

* * *

So why hasn't it?

The most common answers may sound familiar.

Women don't actively seek coaching jobs in men's sports, so there is no pool of female applicants for men to hire from. Then, because there are no women coaching men's teams, there are no female role models encouraging others to cross gender lines. The cycle perpetuates itself.

Even Pitino, who received plenty of attention for hiring Mattox, says he's never received an application or call from a female coach.

"The pool is still relatively small," says Atlantic 10 commissioner Bernadette McGlade. "(Women) are not only not in the men's game, but their numbers are dwindling in the women's side of the game. . . . It's not like there's this great demand and they're just not getting hired."

When Title IX was passed in 1972, more than 90 percent of women's collegiate sports teams were coached by women, according to a study from Brooklyn College professors emerita R. Vivian Acosta and Linda Jean Carpenter. Acosta and Carpenter found that in 2012, only 42% of women's teams were coached by female coaches. Women's basketball fared a bit better; 62% of its head coaches were women last year.

Much of these statistics can be tied back to Title IX itself. In the decade following its implementation, many schools merged their men's and women's athletic programs. Most of the time, they made the man who ran the men's side the new athletic director overseeing the new athletic department. Women who had run the women's physical education or athletic departments were either demoted or moved out of administration altogether.

With fewer high-level female administrators, it became more difficult for women to get head-coaching jobs, a trend that has continued to this day. A 2012 survey by the Institute for Diversity and Ethics in Sports at Central Florida revealed only 8.2% of Division I athletic directors were female.

Patrick Nero, athletics director at George Washington and a former chairman for the NCAA Committee on Women's Athletics, attributed some of the decline in women coaching women—and the stagnant, low number of women coaching men (less than 3% of all sports, usually individual sports like track or swimming)—to increasing demands on time.

"The pressures of coaching any sport, male or female, has changed at the collegiate level over the last 30, 40 years," Nero says. "There were issues that were looked at in regards to work-life balance. In regards to moving. Moving families, moving spouses. It seemed to be more of a challenge on the women's side."

Ackerman outlined some of what she called "extraordinary demands."

"Coaching is 24/7," she says. "You're never off. If you're out of practice or traveling, you're on the phone with recruits. If you're a parent and have family obligations, men and women—though women tend to get harder hit—that's, as a result, created a fallout."

The flipside, however, is that male coaches seemingly have had no problem entering women's sports and finding success. The most prominent example is Geno Auriemma, who has won eight NCAA women's basketball championships at UConn.

Even male coaches without prior experience in the women's game have entered it in recent years. In 2005, Providence plucked Phil Seymore from his men's assistant role to become the women's basketball coach. In 2011, Virginia Tech hired Dennis Wolff, who had been the men's basketball director of operations and assistant to then–head coach Seth Greenberg, to run its women's program. During this influx of male coaches into the women's game, more female coaches have felt pressure to stay in the women's game.

"The men's ranks are primarily a male-dominated workplace, while the women's coaching ranks have been integrated for several decades now," says Ellen Staurowsky, a professor in Drexel's school of sport management who focuses on issues of gender equity. "We continue to have an entrenched sex-stereotypical way of viewing coaches in general that favors male coaches in general. I think there are so many assumptions around whether women have the capacity to coach men, whether women can lead men—all in contradiction of the 21st century worldview where we have women leaders in all manners of industry. In this particular sector, we've yet to make those kind of inroads."

* * *

In truth, there's no way to explain away this phenomenon without examining the stereotypes that lie beneath it.

Male players won't want to play for women. They won't respect them. They won't take orders from them. Women are too soft, too emotional, too fragile. Even if they played the sport, they can't possibly understand it as well as their male counterparts do. And, of course, women don't belong in the men's locker room.

Mattox, Ready and Johnston debunk all of those claims.

All three report having overwhelmingly positive experiences with players. They say their backgrounds helped (Mattox was Georgia's first All-American; Ready and

Johnston both played college ball, too), and they built relationships with players during off-season individual workouts. Still, it took time to earn respect.

Oakland coach Greg Kampe says Johnston "did a heck of a job" for him, and if he'd had to do it all over, he'd hire her again.

"I thought our players—after it took a little while to get used to it—I think they really appreciated that she was on the staff," Kampe says. "She brought a different perspective, especially with off-court situations. They would go to her with social issues, from girlfriends to everything."

At both Kentucky and Coppin State, players fell into line quickly.

"You've got to understand something about Coach Pitino—whatever he said, we believed," says John Pelphrey, who played at Kentucky for Pitino. "He could have told us the sky is pink today, and it'll be pink for the rest of time, and we're like, 'OK.'

"So, the way he delivered it to us was: 'Bringing (Mattox) on board, this was only going to make us better. She was a tremendous player. She not only can coach and game plan, but she's going to be tremendous for you guys off the floor. She had a completely different perspective than anybody else on our coaching staff.' That was it."

Coppin State coach Fang Mitchell simply walked into a team meeting, introduced the players to Ready and asked if they had any questions.

"They said no, and we went on from that point," Mitchell says. "It's still my program, and they're trying to get on the floor." He laughs.

Quickly, players discovered these women were quite knowledgeable about the game. They were sharp and could adjust to handle different personalities. They were tough. They were effective recruiters, hitting if off particularly well with parents of recruits.

Concerns about locker room access were overblown, Mattox says. "Why should I be in there?" she says. "A head coach of women's team who is male wouldn't be in there." Pitino himself wouldn't go in until it was time to speak to the team, she says.

Fellow coaches on staff soon admired their female colleagues both for their coaching competence and their temperament in difficult situations. Donovan remembers Mattox's grace when dealing with all the media attention. Kampe recalls a game against IUPUI where a man heckled Johnston, screaming sexually-charged commentary, to the point where Kampe felt he had to do something.

"I stopped the game, went to the referees and asked for the guy to be removed, and told them what he was saying," Kampe says. "I've never done anything like that in my life. It was really bad, and those are the things that are out there. It's different. It's hard.

"I don't want to compare it to Jackie Robinson, but the things that were said and yelled at him are going to be said and yelled at a female. They were. I experienced it."

* * *

"Did you play basketball?"
All these years later, Ready still bristles at the question and its underlying insult. She'd been milling around a Las Vegas gym, watching AAU teams and recruiting

players to Coppin State, where she was the first female assistant with off-campus recruiting responsibilities. It seemed everyone who was anyone was there; if you have any ties to men's college basketball, you go to Vegas in July.

Most of the coaches she met there accepted her as one of them. But not all.

"There were some people who were really rude and very obnoxious," Ready says. "I could tell you some stories, but they were the minority. Generally, those coaches that acted that way were the ones who were insecure about their own abilities. They felt threatened."

One male coach approached her and asked her if she had played the sport. After her initial shock wore off—she asked him to repeat the question—she said, "Of course I played." Still stinging, she turned the question back on him. Had he played? No. Had that been a problem for him in a male-dominated field like men's college basketball? No.

Ready's experience is typical of women who work in sports. Last month, Condoleeza Rice's selection to the College Football Playoff selection committee resulted in a wildly outdated backlash, highlighted by former Auburn football coach Pat Dye's comments: "To understand football, you've got to play with your hand in the dirt."

Time and time again, coaches who did not play their sport at the collegiate or professional level have found success coaching it. This past summer, Erik Spoelstra led the Miami Heat past the Gregg Popovich–coached San Antonio Spurs in the NBA finals. Neither coach played in the NBA—yet both coaches have combined for six NBA championships.

"What players respond to, more than anything else, are people who know their craft," says Arizona State coach Herb Sendek, who coached with Mattox at Kentucky. "In the NBA, I think sometimes a lot of thought is given to guys who played in the NBA, but I think ultimately, that is trumped by guys who really know their craft. For example, you have in the Finals, Pop and Spoelstra. Neither guy played in the NBA, but both guys command tremendous respect because they're prepared and they know their craft and they help guys get better.

"That's what players want. They want people who know their craft and who can help them get better. If it's Bernadette, great. If it's Gregg Popovich, who was never an NBA player, fantastic."

Women have served as men's head coaches at lower college divisions, as well as in high school and AAU. Some currently serve as directors of basketball operations at the Division I level, including on Kampe's staff. Others work in academic roles, assisting players with off-court responsibilities. That's not unique; former Georgetown coach John Thompson Jr. hired a woman, Mary Fenlon, as his academic advisor back in 1972, and she was around the Hoyas program until 1999.

There are obvious benefits to having a woman on a men's staff—for the players, their families and the school brand. Ready remembers coaches and spectators approaching her at AAU tournaments, asking what team she represented. Players, like Pelphrey, found value having a new voice and a different perspective on their coaching staff.

A number of coaches said it would be smart to hire women to work in men's college basketball, considering how many elite players come from single parent homes.

"There are a lot of single moms out there, grandmothers raising kids. That's just the truth of the matter," Ready says. "Of course they're going to be more comfortable talking to another woman. Also, I was like their big sister or aunt. I was the one that they came to with problems and issues. Their moms trusted me to handle them."

* * *

Many of the male coaches and athletic officials interviewed for this story believe a female coach could win Division I men's basketball games.

"If you took any of the women's coaches and you put them on the court in between the lines, they would be very, very competent," Donovan says.

Hall of Famer Pat Summitt, who won eight women's basketball national championships at Tennessee, is a name that's often been brought up over the years as someone who could have broken barriers on the men's side. C. M. Newton, the Kentucky athletic director who hired Pitino in 1989, admits that he thought about hiring Summitt instead.

"Pat Summitt was one of the seven people that I wrote down when I took the athletic director job at Kentucky that could do the Kentucky job," Newton says. "I'd known Pat, and I've never felt that women can't coach men."

On Feb. 13, 2003, Tennessee State athletic director and former women's coach Teresa Phillips became the first woman to coach a men's Division I basketball team, filling in for her coach who had to serve a one-game suspension. The Phillips-led Tigers lost, 71–56, at Austin Peay. At the time, Phillips downplayed the significance of what she did, telling reporters that women won't truly make history until one is hired to run a men's team. She called herself a pinch-hitter.

If the question is not, *Can women do it?*, it must be, *Why aren't they doing it?*

Start with the so-called "good ol' boys" club, Newton says, an explanation echoed by many others. Male coaches know and work with other male coaches. When they become head coaches and hire assistant coaches, they hire who they're familiar with. The same goes for male athletic directors.

"People just don't like to take that gamble," Mitchell says. "Men are men. A lot of times, they feel comfortable around men. It's the same (thought) I've had where there aren't a lot of African-American coaches. People feel comfortable with certain types of people."

Mitchell, who doubled as Coppin State's athletic director at the time, was willing to gamble on Ready because she'd played at the school and he'd seen her coach the women's volleyball team. Kampe gambled on Johnston because he was familiar with her as a player, knew her college coach and had to fill an introductory level, low-paying job as Oakland moved from Division II to Division I. Despite blowback from his administration, Kampe hired Johnston. In addition to her knowledge of the game, he gained some positive publicity from the hire (just as Pitino did, which was sorely needed while Kentucky was recovering from a scandal under former coach Eddie Sutton that kept the Wildcats off TV and out of the postseason).

Other forms of networking matter in coaching, too. Mainly, in recruiting. Though men have jumped into the women's game from scratch, some coaches think that would be too risky to hire a female assistant who had no prior experience recruiting men.

"If I were to go and take a women's head coaching job, I wouldn't know the AAU coaches, the high school coaches," Donovan says. "When you talk about bringing a woman over onto the men's side, a lot of times it has nothing to do with their knowledge or their ability to coach and teach and do those things.

"It's relationship-based, and it takes a long time to build those relationships."

Two of the women featured here—Mattox and Johnston—ended up coaching women's basketball after they left the men's game, illustrating what Kampe calls a "glass ceiling." There is no upward mobility for female assistants in the men's game; they have no shot at being hired as a head coach unless they coach women, he and other administrators feel.

After four seasons spent on Pitino's staff, Mattox stepped away from coaching to start a family. She became an assistant athletics director for one year, then accepted a head coaching job—with the Kentucky women's basketball program, a position she held until 2003. She spent the next decade as an assistant coach with the WNBA's Connecticut Sun.

Ready left Coppin State in 2001 and took an assistant coaching gig with the Greenville Groove, an NBA Developmental League team that would fold two years later after giving her the distinction of being the first female to coach in men's professional sports in the United States. Ready now works as a TV host and sideline reporter for the Charlotte Bobcats.

Johnston left Oakland in 2002 to take a job on the women's staff at the University of Toledo, a big pay increase. Four years later, she helped found Rauner College Prep, a charter school in Chicago, and launch its athletic department. These days, she remains its athletic director and physical education teacher. But Johnston still says her dream job was the one she got when she was 23.

The reminders are subtle near her desk at Rauner—a couple of photos from her Oakland days, a copy of an article from her hometown newspaper. When her students first noticed them a couple of years ago, they couldn't believe what their teacher had done a decade before.

"I tell them, but you know teenagers don't listen so well," Johnston says, laughing. "They really are interested in it. My students who are really into basketball will pick my brain, make me play with them, stuff like that."

She pauses.

"I don't think they realize how unique of a situation I was in."

Open-Access Harassment: Science, Technology and Women

The Working Cultures and Structures of Science and Technology May Be Different, but They Both Feed Sexist Myths of Meritocracy

By Georgina Voss and Alice Bell
The Guardian, October 24, 2013

These are not happy times for gender equality in science and technology. The past two months alone have offered up the truly grim "Titstare" app (no less awful for being a joke) and the *Scientific American* blogging network sexual harassment accusations. One minute we're reading a Storify documenting the #ripplesofdoubt that women in science experience as a result of institutional sexism; the next, we're looking at an invitation for a "Hackers and Hookers" Halloween party.

Many aspects of science and technology have long been male-dominated. Numerous projects have been set up to encourage more women to study science and engineering and learn to code, understand barriers and image problems, and recognize institutions which demonstrate commitment to this cause.

Science and technology is not a homogenous entity though. As well as huge differences between the physical and biological sciences, the private sector tech industry operates under different paradigms to academic science in terms of funding, knowledge landscapes, geographies, labor practices and attitudes towards openness and public engagement. These distinctions contribute to notable differences in the way that sexism and harassment are publicized and discussed.

We want to focus here on the different labor dynamics and work cultures. These issues are not restricted to gender but are symptomatic of wider issues around power, access and abuse across science and technology as a whole. Both academic science and the private tech sector have shoddy track records around hiring practices and supportive workplace environments for racial and sexual minorities.

First up, publicly funded academic science, whose labor markets tend to embody a steep, closed, pyramid-type hierarchy. At the peak are permanent lecturers and professors who hold stable and often well-paid positions, run their own labs, and who are valued for both their contribution to science and scholarship, but also for the large research grants which they are able to pull in from a decreasing pool of public money. At the bottom are the temporary workers who prop it all up: growing numbers of PhD students undertaking the doctoral research necessary for entry to the whole shebang; and early career researchers suffering through "postdocalypse", moving between numerous short-term contracts scattered wide across the few departments which focus on specific sub-disciplines. As many have argued, this disproportionally impacts upon women, especially as it is likely to hit during a period of their life where they may choose to have children.

Power is concentrated at the top with the few, in a structure which PhD Comic's Jorge Cham described as a "Profzi Scheme" (after the Ponzi Scheme). Or as the *Economist* put it, the disposable academic. Many senior academics were shocked by an infographic in the Royal Society's Scientific Century report in 2010, highlighting how few PhD students could make their way into permanent academic careers. It's not simply that some can't hack it: the jobs simply aren't there. The better senior academics have since been part of projects to diversify training to reflect the PhD diversity of post-doctorial career routes their students might take. The more clueless continue to parrot the line that there will always be good jobs for good people, with the unsaid implication that those who don't get jobs simply aren't worthy—any problems are those of the individual, not the surrounding infrastructure.

In this system, it is incredibly difficult for those at the bottom to have a publically critical voice without surrendering their careers. Further compounding the problem is a highly stratified system with little horizontal support networks. With a system built around reverence to superiors and a transient competitive workforce, postdoc-to-postdoc solidarity is hard to build. Melonie Fullick has described how under the apprenticeship framing of academia, it can be "risky practice" for junior scholars to enter into any form of public engagement—blogging, tweeting—which isn't explicitly approved by their institution; it is unlikely that institutions would grant approval for stories which openly describe their problems and politics. In many ways, this is a broader issue of workplace bullying which goes far beyond what men do to women, and is symptomatic of a broader pathology about power and its abuses.

As a result, harassment is kept closed-access which breeds at best behind-the-scenes networks which quietly warn women about staff with "wandering hands." Pipetting while female is still an unadvised activity in places and no matter how many inspirational videos get made, the odd quiet word from a cousin whose friend dropped out of her PhD program can do impossible-to-spot damage.

None of this is obvious, which is precisely its power. It's hidden because people are scared. It's frustrating, but pretending it doesn't happen just because we can't quote it won't get us anywhere.

By contrast, the tech scene would appear to be a more horizontal, open and welcoming environment. Several academics—both from the sciences and elsewhere—have openly spoken about their decision to move out of the ivory tower to the tech industry, citing how the sector allows them to continue to do intellectually challenging work but with improved work-life balance, a greater number of jobs in a more fluid labor market, and an opportunity to "make a difference." Yet an explicit discourse of open can breed its own forms of hidden inequalities—"open" to whom? and by what means?—and the tech sector carries its own pernicious brand of sexism.

While programming was originally "woman's work," it morphed into a male dominated field where hiring practices actively discriminate against women, setting up the straw man of the geeky, asocial male coder. The concept of "openness" was also valorized, filtering in as communities of developers worked together to freely share their expertise on collaborative open-source projects. Yet "open" does not automatically equate to accessible or equitable—only 3% of coders in free and open software are female.

In this space, notions of "culture fit" disproportionately affect women, who are less likely to be hired because they don't "match" extant (male) company culture. The industry's critics—who are often its members—describe the "brogrammer" culture prevalent in an industry which valorizes the well-paid young men who fill its ranks, reframing an idea of meritocracy as "the geek identity with a competitive frat house flavor."

Stories abound of how this culture embeds and is normalized, from "booth babes" at trade shows, to women being advertised as "perks" at hack events. Unlike academia however, many of these practices have happened in very public spaces and have also been addressed on public platforms by both junior and senior industry members. The "Titstare" debacle was documented on Twitter from the moment its creators went on stage. Essays about wider gender issues and harassment in the tech scene have sprung up on widely read platforms including *Medium* and *Gawker*, as well as on multiple personal blogs. Collective statements have also been released, such as that from the Ruby community in Berlin, which stated how they would re-think how they ran events as a way to combat sexism and racism.

Not of all these responses have been received well as their comment streams often stand testament to. Offering up the tech sector as a bastion of good practice around gender discrimination when such issues are ongoing and unresolved is incongruous, particularly given that pink-collar work is still prevalent in the industry. Making the call on whether to identify personal instances of harassment—and in particular, naming harassers—remains an impossible dilemma. However, academia's steep and closed ranks are lesser (although not absent), which means that more open conversations with larger groups of participants can take place. The people—mostly men—at the top of the tech world wield considerably more power than those below, but not to the gatekeeper extent of the senior academics who are both untouchable for the millions of pounds of grant money they bring in for their institutions, while acting as gatekeepers to the entire system. These might be small mercies, but mercies they remain.

One thing both science and technology communities share is an assumed neutrality combined with the mythos that career progression is egalitarian and meritocratic. Both academia's hierarchies and tech's allusions to freedom mean these go unquestioned. Moreover, this renders structural issues around sexism, racism and other areas of prejudice invisible, further disempowering those who find themselves at the receiving end.

Want to start solving gender problems in science and technology? Bugger Google Glass: build the spectacles which render visible the invisible inequalities of power, culture and mythologies of meritocracy. In the absence of such a techno-fix, we should call those myths and issues out for what they are. In doing so, we can address a swathe of other problems too and make the fields more inclusive, productive, safe and fun for everyone.

Meet the All-Male Team over at Tesla

By John Goreham
Torque News, November 18, 2013

All of the managers and all of the board of directors at electric car maker Tesla are men. If Tesla's future business plan is dependent on government credits, subsidies, and tax abatements, it may want to consider the other half of the population for key posts like its competitors do.

According to Tesla's website, all of the people at the company in a key decision making role are men. They might just be some of the world's smartest, hardest working men, but besides being good business, when it comes to bidding on contracts with the US government and state governments, having a few women on the team is law in some cases. Currently at Tesla, only men hold jobs like chief technical officer, chief financial officer, chief designer, vice president of human resources, and vice president of business development. Every director, and the non-director outside counsel, is a man as well.

Some might argue that Tesla is a car company, and that "cars are guy things, right?" Wrong. More than half of the cars sold in the US are bought by women according to most sources. Still, can't we agree that men are really the dominant gender when it comes to key automotive related STEM (science, technology, engineering, and math) type jobs? Sorry, but no. By example, let's look at what other automakers are doing with regard to gender diversity among top management.

At GM they are currently selling the car that Tesla has been promising to build since its inception. Chevy has an "affordable" little runabout that uses only electricity unless the driver wants more range. They call it the Volt and it is the leading electric vehicle in the US in terms of sales. The person in charge of all EVs at GM is Pam Fletcher, GM's Electrified Vehicles Engineering Chief.

If you think that Ms. Fletcher is the token gal over at the country club, think again. The person many point to as the next Chairperson of GM is Mary Barra. Her current title is Executive Vice President, Global Product Development and Global Purchasing and Supply Chain. She and Mark Reuss are the two top contenders for the job when Mr. Akerson finalizes his current retirement transition. Reuss would be perfect for the job in our opinion, except he has one huge thing holding him back. He came up through the ranks at GM as an engineer and is known as a "car-guy." As current Chairman Dan Akerson recently pointed out to *USA Today*, not a single US automaker is presently being run by a "car-guy." Before you start thinking in the back of your mind that women are only on the "clean side of the wall" over at GM, consider that when the Volt went into production GM made sure that the plant it was being built in was run by a person it knew it could trust. Ms. Teri Quigley.

Subsidies and mandates in states like California are a key part of every EV automaker's business plan and they are vitally important. Zero Emissions Vehicle (ZEV) credits are usually the difference between profit and loss in any given quarter at Tesla. In states like Massachusetts, which provides towns in the Commonwealth with up to $7,500 towards the purchase of an electric vehicle, not being a company with gender and ethnic diversity can mean being eliminated from the bidders list. Judy Habib, CEO of KHJ Brand Activation found that out the hard way. Even though she was a woman, and she owns her business in the Commonwealth, that was not enough. For some reason she did not include in her state contract application extension (she had done business with the state lottery in the past) the list of her minority- or woman-owned subcontractors. Since just being a woman and owning her business was not enough of a qualification to meet the state's diversity mandate, she was dropped from consideration for state contracts.

The Nissan Leaf is the other affordable "people's EV" currently in its second generation of sales in the US. Overall, Nissan USA is basically old-school, all-male, but there are two key women on the team. Carla Bailo is the Senior Vice President of Research and Development. The Vice President of Purchasing, Rebecca Vest is also female. Don't discount that job's significance at a car company. That was the job Carlos Ghosn, CEO of Nissan, had and where he got noticed before his legendary rise to the top job at one of the world's largest car companies.

It isn't just huge, successful car companies that see the value of having women in key posts. Or shall we say, hiring the best person for the job, regardless of gender. Over at little EV-maker GreenTech Automotive, Marianne McInerney, is (or was) the Executive Vice President, Sales and Marketing. She also worked at Smith Electric Vehicles USA, and is the former President of the American International Automobile Dealers Association. Tesla is fighting that organization in court all over the country right now. She might be a good person to have on the Tesla team. Things have turned for the worse recently over at GTA. Tesla should consider giving her a ring. She is also pals with Bill Clinton, perhaps the most influential American alive. That can't hurt if you are trying to get a government contract for electric cars.

Ford is making its big push into electric vehicles now. Like Nissan, it is pretty old-fashioned when it comes to hiring women. However, they do at least have a female human resources manager. This is like a hospital with all male doctors pointing to the head nurse as a female in a key position, but at least Ford has one female face for the group photo.

Tesla does give lip service to workplace diversity. In its mandatory code of ethics found on it investor's page it states under the discrimination section, "The diversity of the Company's employees is a tremendous asset. We are firmly committed to providing equal opportunity in all aspects of employment and will not tolerate any illegal discrimination or harassment of any kind." Being firmly committed to diversity is a great statement, but to walk the walk Tesla would need to actually have at least one female among its 14 managers and directors.

3

Women, Men, and Political Life

Women members of the Democratic Caucus pose for a group photo on Capitol Hill in Washington, D.C., on January 3, 2012, to highlight the historic diversity of the House Democratic Caucus in the 113th Congress and celebrate the increased number of women joining the Democratic Caucus.

Gender in the Realm of Politics

In a democratic environment, a shift in voting constituencies or a change in leadership can greatly alter the course of government. During the Reconstruction years following the Civil War, for example, federal laws permitting African American suffrage—at least temporarily—dramatically changed the political landscape in the former slave states of the South. During the 1920s, the ratification of the Nineteenth Amendment (which guaranteed women the right to vote) helped create a major political force that, among other legislation, helped pass laws providing federal funding for women and children's health care and protecting female workers.

The latter of these examples, women and gender politics, is of particular relevance to the twenty-first-century political landscape. The United States has long celebrated its diversity and yet has relatively rarely elected a woman to the US House, Senate or presidency. Since the Constitution was first ratified, 298 women have served in Congress, and none have reached the presidency or vice presidency. Even in 2013, of the 535 Representatives and Senators, only 102 were women. This trend is not simply evident in Washington, D.C., either: forty-five of the fifty states had male governors by 2014 (twenty-four states have never had a female governor), and only one of America's ten largest cities—Houston, Texas—has a female mayor.

Theories abound regarding the causes of this long-standing inequity among male and female politicians. One study, for example, suggests that women are simply less inclined than their male counterparts to endure the competitiveness and negativity that commonly occur during an election season. Other theories suggest that there remains a gender bias in Washington, one that is only worsened by the high-profile candidacies of liberal and conservative presidential candidates like Hillary Clinton and Sarah Palin.

The difference between men and women in American politics is significant. In a recent World Economic Forum study, the United States lagged far behind a number of other countries, including Cuba, in terms of gender equality in political leadership. This ranking (60 of 136 nations) was, to be sure, controversial. This study also ranked the United States number one in terms of women's educational attainment and sixth in terms of economic opportunity and participation for women. Nevertheless, such studies at the very least paint a profile of the United States as a nation in which political inequality has persisted.

The divide between men and women in American politics has existed for decades. In fact, as is the case in most nations, tradition has for centuries kept women in a position of political and economic disadvantage. One prominent theory, offered by Ester Boserup in 1970, suggests that the divide began in primitive society: men would venture out on the hunt, while women would toil in the fields. When tools such as the plough (which make agriculture easier and yet require greater physical strength) were introduced, however, men assumed responsibility for the fields as well. Women, according to Boserup, were relegated to household duties, a position that has persisted for centuries.

Over time, women have asserted themselves to effect economic and political change, such as the aforementioned achievement of suffrage in 1920. However, the "women's liberation" period that began in the 1960s helped lift women out of the traditional housewife role, and into a position of greater political leverage. Large-scale marches and other forms of political activism facilitated the passage of the Equal Pay Act and Title VII of the Civil Rights Act (outlawing gender-based discrimination in the workplace) in 1964. By the 1970s, more and more women were entering positions that had been traditionally occupied by men.

During the last several decades, however, the presence and influence of women in the political realm has been inconsistent. In the latter 1970s, women began to win elections, and the trend continued through the 1980s. During the early 1990s, however, women began running for seats at the local, state, and federal levels in much greater numbers. By the end of the twentieth century, that trend came to a plateau; come 2010, fewer and fewer women were pursuing federal and state positions.

One of the most well-known concepts associated with the difference between American men and women in the workplace is the so-called glass ceiling. Introduced into the American lexicon during the 1980s, the glass ceiling refers to the idea that women may have the ambition or will to pursue elected office but are often kept from doing so by artificial barriers resulting from long-standing, institutional bias. In other words, the traditionally male-dominated political machinery that has been in place since long before women's suffrage is—to a large degree—still alive in the American political system. In order to break through this glass ceiling in US politics, women must assert themselves with greater intensity than men.

While the disparity between the number of male and female elected officials in the United States remains somewhat wide, the intensity of women's political strength outside elected office has neither slowed nor reversed. Women's political causes often benefit from media exposure and the subsequent public awareness and support. In 1991, for example, Supreme Court nominee Clarence Thomas was about to be approved by the Senate when law professor Anita Hill, a former employee of Thomas's, came forward and accused him of sexual harassment. For days, the American television viewing public watched as Hill detailed Thomas's alleged behavior before a predominantly male Senate panel. Thomas's appointment was ultimately approved, but only barely—by a vote of 52–48. The public backlash was significant. Activists decried the overwhelming presence of men in Congress; and many believed that Thomas's appointment was made possible by the sexism of the male-dominated legislature. During the first election year after the Thomas hearings, a record number of female candidates ran for public office. Four women reached the Senate, and nineteen were elected to the House.

The dominating presence of women in higher education has also played a part in bolstering the political pull of women in America. As female voters have become more educated over the years, their ability to participate and influence change in the political system has increased. In one study, male and female respondents were asked for their knowledge of a wide range of issues in 1984 and 1996. In 1984, males were consistently more informed on the US political system and issue than women. By 1996, however, this gender "information gap" was considerably narrower, with a much greater number of female respondents demonstrating greater understanding of the wide range of issues facing the country.

In the twenty-first century, one of the primary sources of information about government and politics is the Internet. Today, countless websites offer information about elected officials, issues, candidates, and political trends. Such information empowers those who may have previously been unable to access it due to socioeconomic factors or a perceived glass ceiling.

American political opinion is often divided along gender lines. The consequences of this split in opinion have become more pronounced as the female voting constituency asserts an ever-growing influence on local, state, and national politics. As such, political candidates and incumbents are consistently courting women's groups for support.

Recent presidential elections provide evidence of this trend. During the 2000 presidential race, both Democrat Vice President Al Gore and Republican Governor George W. Bush actively pursued the female vote. However, Gore enjoyed a considerable advantage on this front, as he shared women's overwhelming opinion regarding a growing national issue: gun control. Although 70 percent of Americans were in favor of gun control in general, women were the strongest voices on a number of specific measures. More than 90 percent of women, for example, advocated for mandatory child safety locks for handguns, even in households without children. Additionally, 78 percent of women favored stricter handgun laws, compared to 62 percent of men. Although Bush would prevail in that election, women were not the ones to put him over: only 43 percent of women voted for the Texas governor in 2000.

Evidence dating back to the 1980s shows that women consistently align themselves with the Democratic Party in presidential elections, with the noted exception of Ronald Reagan's 1984 run. In 2008, men were largely split over Senator Barack Obama's campaign against Republican candidate Senator John McCain, but 56 percent of female voters cast a ballot for Obama. In the 2012 presidential election—despite the efforts of former Massachusetts governor Mitt Romney to secure the women's vote—55 percent of women voted for Obama.

The political gender divide manifests itself in some of today's most controversial policy issues and heated ideological debates. In 2013, for example, the interparty congressional battle over the federal budget led to a temporary government shutdown. Millions of Americans lost access to government services, while government employees themselves were laid off. Voter rancor over perceived Republican and Democratic unwillingness to compromise was at an all-time high. In the aftermath of that shutdown, an indicator of great importance to 2014's midterm elections became evident: men and women demonstrated different attitudes about the shutdown and the health of the economy in the near future. According to one poll, 38 percent of men believed the shutdown would not hurt the economy, while 58 of women thought the economy had been damaged. Furthermore, women largely put their trust in President Obama, a Democrat, to manage the economy, while a majority of men placed confidence in Republicans to maintain the country's economic health.

The ideological gap between men and women is also evident in a number of other issues of relevance to the 2014 midterm elections and beyond. For example, 45 percent of women believe that President Obama's landmark health care reform law, the Affordable Care Act, was a bad idea (compared to 54 percent of men). However, while a large percentage of those men who disagree with the law would prefer its outright elimination, most women who oppose the law would rather see Congress and the President fix the law's problem areas while keeping the law on the books.

Gender politics in the United States has evolved dramatically over the last century, driven by increased access to education, information, and the political process. The Nineteenth Amendment opened the doors for women to become more involved in American government, enabling them to find equal political footing with men. The number of women entering public service has been relatively slow to grow, but the significance of women's political support cannot be understated. Indeed, the ideological gap between male and female voters on a wide range of key issues is an important factor candidates must consider if they hope to find success at the polls.

—Michael P. Auerbach

Bibliography

Alesina, Alberto F., Paola Giuliano, and Nathan Nunn. "On the Origin of Gender Roles: Women and the Plough." *Quarterly Journal of Economics* 128.2 (2011): 496–530. Print.

"CBS Poll: The Gender Gap on Guns." *CBS News*. CBS Interactive, 14 May 2000. Web. 12 Feb. 2014.

Coffé, Hilde, and Catherine Bolzendahl. "Same Game, Different Rules? Gender Differences in Political Participation." *Sex Roles* 62.5–6 (2010): 318–33. Print.

The Global Gender Gap Report 2013. Geneva: World Economic Forum, 2013. Print.

Kurtz, Annalyn. "US Lagging Behind on Gender Equality." *CNN Money*. Cable News Network, 24 Oct. 2013. Web. 12 Feb. 2014.

Lawless, Jennifer L., and Richard L. Fox. *Men Rule: The Continued Under-Representation of Women in U.S. Politics*. Washington, DC: Women and Politics Institute, 2012. Print.

Lee, Barbara. "Women Running for Governor: Three Things to Watch for in 2014 Races." *Huffington Post*. TheHuffingtonPost.com, 25 Jan. 2014. Web. 12 Feb. 2014.

Manning, Jennifer E., and Ida A. Brudnick. *Women in the United States Congress, 1917–2013: Biographical and Committee Assignment Information, and Listings by State and Congress.* Washington, DC: Congressional Research Service, 2013. Print.

Moore, Martha T. "Women Still Struggling to Win Big-City Mayoral Jobs." *USA Today.* USATODAY, 9 Sept. 2013. Web. 12 Feb. 2014.

Newport, Frank. "Women More Likely to Be Democrats, Regardless of Age." *Gallup Politics.* Gallup, 12 June 2009. Web. 12 Feb. 2014.

Seib, Gerald F. "Mind the Gender Gap in American Politics." *Wall Street Journal.* Dow Jones, 17 Dec. 2013. Web. 14 Feb. 2014.

Siegel, Joel. "Clarence Thomas–Anita Hill Supreme Court Confirmation Hearing 'Empowered Women' and Panel Member Arlen Specter Still Amazed by Reactions." *ABC News.* ABC News Internet Ventures, 24 Oct. 2011. Web. 12 Feb. 2014.

Tolleson-Rinehart, Sue, and Jyl J. Josephson. *Gender and American Politics: Women, Men, and the Political Process.* 2d ed. Armonk: Sharpe, 2005. Print.

Zamfirache, Irina. "Women and Politics—The Glass Ceiling." *Journal of Comparative Research in Anthropology and Sociology* 1.1 (2010): 175–85. Print.

Bridging the Gender Gap in Politics
Leads to Greater Consensus

By Glenn Davis
Independent Voter Network (*IVN*), December 20, 2013

In October of 2013, a group of Senate women brought their cooperative and consensus-building skills to the table and succeeded where men failed. At the time, there was well-deserved focus on the role of women in negotiating the bipartisan plan which resulted in bringing the 16-day-long government shutdown to an end.

More recently, Senate Budget Committee chair, Patty Murray, has received great praise and attention for her no-nonsense, consensus-building style in budget negotiations with her House counterpart, U.S. Representative Paul Ryan. In their announcement of the deal reached with Ryan, Murray said of their relationship: "We cheer for a different football team, clearly. We catch different fish, but we agree that our country needs some certainty."

She was given a job no one else wanted, yet as it turned out, she was successful because of her unique negotiating skills that run counter to the stereotypical male ego.

The expanding influence of women in politics, however, did not start in October nor did it end in December. It is an ongoing topic which deserves renewed attention and serious analysis.

The concept of gender gap in politics is primarily conveyed to describe the differences between men and women in their behavior at the polls and in their respective attitudes toward issues. Disproportionate gender representation in our political leaders signifies this as well. Yet a different type of gender gap is also emerging, one which relates to how gender differences are involved in the actual *practice* of politics.

The numbers as well as the impact of women in the political arena are clearly increasing. The question of whether women, by their very nature, are better able to reach compromise and consensus in negotiating the challenges which our country faces is an equally important one. The ongoing efforts and notable successes speak loudly to support this premise, even if only on an anecdotal basis.

Another perspective to consider is whether the negative political climate which is so pervasive in American politics can be turned around as the number of women in politics continues to increase. Murray's comments about working with Ryan exemplify her efforts to rise above the negativity. In fairness to Ryan, this was a two-way street; perhaps men also will show a more positive focus when they increasingly must deal and negotiate with their women counterparts.

There are currently 78 women in the US House of Representatives and 20 in the Senate—a total of 20 percent of Congress. Over the 15-year period since 1998, this has increased from 12 percent.

At the same time, women are increasing their national representation in the presidential cabinet, on the Supreme Court, as candidates for executive office, as well as on state and local levels. Hillary Clinton, if she seeks and is successful in securing the Democratic Party nomination in 2016, would be the first woman running as a major party candidate for president. It remains to be seen whether America is ready for this.

Ongoing efforts lead to change, whether predicted or not.

Are women by nature more cooperative, better at compromise, and more skilled in consensus building? If so, the growing trend toward female leaders may very well result in less partisanship in Congress and other branches of government.

One plausible theory supporting this premise may be what has been called "The Jackie (and Jill) Robinson Effect." Women in politics, like early minority athletes, need to achieve greatness to gain respect. Average performance is not enough; they must excel to be noticed, and thus may work harder than men to solve the most complex and thorny problems.

Initiatives abound providing research, support, and promotion of women in politics. The Center for American Women and Politics (CAWP) is a leading source of research, whose mission is: "to promote greater knowledge and understanding about women's participation in politics and government and to enhance women's influence and leadership in public life." CAWP's research suggests that the inclusion of women in elective office has led to change.

One of these changes is greater legislative emphasis of issues important to women: families, education, health and welfare, and women's reproductive rights.

Differing leadership styles and views of power versus their male counterparts have also led to greater participation, with an emphasis on cooperation and teamwork. Women in particular seem to recognize that to make a contribution, they must work together to achieve common goals. Greater visibility of women in politics also serves to provide role models for young girls who aspire to become future leaders themselves.

The Bipartisan Policy Center recently hosted a Women as Leaders forum featuring former Senators Olympia Snowe and Blanche Lincoln, as well as other women in national politics. They spoke of the importance of staying positive, knowing the facts, and keeping one's eye on the issues, as opposed to the destruction of the opposition.

Snowe claimed that: ". . . listening is half the battle in understanding where somebody else is coming from."

Senate women have met for monthly dinners for 20 years, with the express purpose of getting to know one another on a personal level. The formation of personal relationships has led to renewed respect for one another, despite deep political and ideological differences. Such an emphasis on relationship building is not a perspective one traditionally expects from male leaders. Yet it is crucial in finding common ground to work through difficult issues.

Another new group, a PAC called More Women in Congress, was started this past year by activist Shannon Meade of Portland, Oregon. Her goals include giving women a stronger voice by supporting bipartisan female candidates to public office. Regarding differences in leadership styles, Meade claims: "women in leadership are much more likely to be team builders and engaged listeners," and "women tend to be more pragmatic in their approach and that, along with the willingness to listen, can add up to strong leadership."

Women in politics strive not just to be equals to male leaders but also to bring new perspectives and different views to the political forum. Reconciling the gender gap is not just a numbers game where equal representation is the goal; instead, it is an effort to optimize how male and female leaders can contribute in different ways to the political process. New highs may be reached in how our elected leaders interact and achieve results. Hopefully this trend will accelerate.

Looking Ahead

Opportunities and Challenges for
Women's Political Participation in 2014

By Catherine M. Russell
US Department of State, December 12, 2013

Thank you, Ken, for opening up NDI [National Democratic Institute] to us today, and thank you, Lorne, for your kind introduction.

I'd like to thank IRI [International Republican Institute] and NDI for the work that you do every day—promoting democracy, supporting democratic institutions and practices, safeguarding elections, and promoting citizen participation. Your work is critical. It also showcases our bipartisan, mutual commitment to democracy, to peaceful democratic transitions and to the engagement of women and men in shaping the futures of their countries.

I'd like to congratulate IRI and NDI for doing this hard and important work every day for 30 years. I know that you each had events earlier this week to mark those anniversaries and I'd like to add my personal congratulations on this important anniversary.

Finally, I'd like to thank you for your commitment to women's political participation, and the amount of time, resources and staff that you devote to achieving women's full participation in politics.

You both have well-respected and effective programs that help women acquire the tools they need to participate successfully in all aspects of the political process.

Let me commend specifically the important work that you are doing in the hard places. To IRI, thank you for the work you have done with your Women's Democracy Network—to build the capacity of Syrian women in negotiation, leadership, advocacy, and other skills at this critical time for their country.

To NDI, thank you for the work you are doing in Afghanistan to help Afghan women be competitive in the upcoming elections—through women's campaign schools, one-on-one consultations with women candidates and developing policy working groups.

My job as Ambassador-at-Large for Global Women's issues is to promote the status of women and girls as a critical element of our diplomatic efforts. We believe that peace, security, prosperity, and economic growth cannot be achieved without the full participation of women, and that men and boys are important partners in this effort.

Whether we are striving to advance women's political or economic participation; end the scourges of gender-based violence, sexual violence in conflict, or human trafficking; or reduce the rates of maternal and child mortality—we must work together, at all levels, and across all sectors, to protect the rights of women and girls and achieve lasting gender equality.

We know that investing in women and girls—helping them unleash their potential—is the right thing to do morally—and the wise thing to do strategically.

I've seen firsthand how women's involvement in public and political life makes a difference.

Last month, I traveled to Afghanistan, where I met with women in government at both the provincial and national levels. I spent time with women leaders in Kabul and Mazar-e-Sharif, and discussed a number of issues, including their critical role in the upcoming elections—as voters, and as candidates, searchers and observers. They were all committed to an increased role for women.

I've also just returned from a trip to Japan, where the current government is working to increase the percentage of women in leadership roles across society from single digits to 30 percent. There seems to be a growing recognition that the only way to ensure Japan's emergence from its decades-long recession is to ensure that women are finally given the tools to participate in the political, economic and social spheres.

This is a daunting challenge, given long established cultural norms that result in the majority of women to leaving the workplace after starting families. Just 2.6 percent of managers in Japan's civil service, about 8 percent of the members of the country's lower house of the Diet, and 18 percent of the members of the upper house are women. But I met with some dynamic Japanese women members of parliament and government ministers who are committed to the effort to increase those figures. I met with the female mayor of Yokahama (just 1 percent of mayors in Japan are women) who in the space of a few short years managed to reduce the child care waiting list in her city from several thousand to zero.

Despite comprising over 50 percent of the world's population, women continue to be underrepresented in every aspect of political and public life. Today, as you all well know, only 21 percent of the world's parliamentarians are women. There are 21 women either serving as head of state or head of government. Only 17 percent of government ministers are women, with the majority serving in the fields of education and health. Since 1992, women have represented fewer than 3 percent of mediators and 8 percent of negotiators to major peace processes. These numbers are too small. These are the places where decisions get made, and simply put, there aren't enough women in them.

There is still much work to be done, and what IRI and NDI do is critical to progress in this arena, and to ensuring that this progress moves quickly.

All of my work is based on our belief that countries are more peaceful and prosperous when women are accorded full and equal rights and opportunity. All around the world, people and countries are beginning to accept this very basic truth. There is increased focus by policy makers and governments on the need for women's participation and contribution to build stronger societies.

My office is one example of the U.S. government's commitment to women's central role in foreign policy. So is USAID's Senior Coordinator for Gender Equality and Women's Empowerment. Through initiatives like the Equal Futures Partnership we are encouraging other countries to expand the political and economic participation of women and girls. And women across the globe are rightfully demanding their place in public life.

Increasing women's meaningful participation in political and public life is about changing cultural norms about women and changing the culture of politics. It's about building and sustaining representative societies. It is essential to ensuring that laws, regulations and policies reflect the reality of women's everyday lives. Women often raise issues that others have overlooked, reach out to constituencies that others ignore and have unique knowledge that stems from their societal roles and responsibilities. For my office, the goal of parity in political participation is an integral underpinning to our other goals in the arenas of women/peace/security, economic empowerment and key development outcomes, especially in the areas of education, health, climate change and food security. We see women's political participations as one of the key foundations for women's overall empowerment and inclusion across sectors. We know that women's expertise, experiences and knowledge must be brought into every decision making table, and to every forum. Women's participation affects the types of policy issues that are debated and decided in parliaments, local councils and government ministries. It also affects the solutions debated and decided. Women's experiences and expertise—and men's experiences and expertise—must both inform policy.

An OECD study of 19 countries found that when countries had an increase in the number of women legislators, there was an increase in funds spent on education in those countries. In India, research showed that West Bengal villages with greater representation of women in local councils called *panchayats* (pan-chai-ats) saw an investment in drinking water facilities double that of villages with fewer women on local councils.

Finally, we know that women's unique perspective is critical to peace-building and post-conflict reconstruction. Women often suffer disproportionately during armed conflict. They often advocate most strongly for stabilization, reconstruction and the prevention of further conflict. Peace agreements, post-conflict reconstruction and governance have a better chance of long-term success when women are involved.

According to research conducted by the International Crisis Group in Sudan, Congo and Uganda, women who participate in peace talks often raise issues like human rights, security, justice, employment, education and health care that are fundamental to reconciliation and rebuilding and therefore to lasting and sustainable peace.

So we know the path forward. We only need to keep committing ourselves and recruiting others to join us. Martin Luther King, Jr. famously said that the arc of the moral universe is long, but it bends toward justice . . . I believe this is true for women worldwide. Our work, and the work we do together, is integral in these efforts. Thank you.

Why I'm Voting for Her

In 2016, I'm Casting My Vote for a Woman. Not Because She's Guaranteed to Be the Most Feminist Candidate, but Because I'm Fed Up.

By Jessica Valenti
The Nation, June 3, 2013

In 2008, I was one of the young feminist whippersnappers who voted for Barack Obama over Hillary Clinton in the Democratic primaries—or as many of my older counterparts called me at the time, a traitor. I didn't believe there was (as Jen Moseley, my then-colleague at *Feministing*, put it) a "vagina litmus test." I wanted to vote for the most feminist candidate, regardless of gender.

Next time around, though, I'm voting for a woman. Not because I believe that the female Democratic candidate (and I think we all have a good idea who that will be) is guaranteed to be the most feminist, but because I'm just too fed up to do anything else. I've made a full transition from youthful idealism to jaded orneriness, and my vote will be just as angry as I am.

EMILY's List has just launched a more optimistic appeal: "Madam President," a campaign to put the first woman in the White House. Stephanie Schriock, the president of EMILY's List, said in a statement that enthusiasm for women's leadership is at historically high levels: "It is clear that this is our time."

"Americans are not only ready for a woman president, but—this is the best part—they see women's leadership as a positive," Schriock told me. "We are in a new time, and I can feel this bubbling everywhere. We're seeing more women step up and run for office. And we've quintupled our size in two years."

The organization's polling tells the same story: 90 percent of voters in battleground states would vote for a qualified woman candidate from their party, and 86 percent believe that America is ready to elect a female president. At least some of that sentiment has to come from a place of frustration with the all-male status quo—not just the presidency, but so many places of power. The popular "100 Percent Men" Tumblr, for example, shines a light on those "corners of the world where women have yet to tread"—from the list of the top twenty highest-paid American CEOs to the all-male leadership at companies like T-Mobile. And if the firestorm surrounding Sheryl Sandberg's bestseller *Lean In* is any indication, women aren't just ready to see more of their gender in power—they're champing at the bit.

Voting for a woman with the sole purpose of breaking the most important political glass ceiling in the country—possibly the world—does give me pause. The belief that a female politician is inherently more woman-friendly is the same misguided notion that allowed even Sarah Palin—who, as mayor of Wasilla, made women pay for their own rape kits and, as governor of Alaska, cut funding for a shelter for teen moms—to call herself a feminist. And the insistence on putting gender above all other identities often means that white women take the lead. I'll never forget being told by a representative of a mainstream women's organization that they were looking for a panelist for an election-related event who "wouldn't trump race over gender." I still believe that my 2008 vote was the right one, and that expecting women to vote for a female politician simply because they share the same gender is cynical and shortsighted.

But I'm also absolutely exhausted. Why?

Because campus rapists are being "punished" by research papers, not prison. Because the man in charge of curbing sexual assault in the Air Force was himself charged with sexual battery. Because the leading cause of death for pregnant women is murder by a partner. Because the Obama administration would rather play politics than make emergency contraception available to all women. Because of "legitimate rape."

It's not that these intractable problems would magically disappear if we had a woman president. But it just might make the relentless sexism easier to bear. Maybe, despite the seemingly endless misogyny and the daily offenses, a female president would be a hopeful reminder of progress made. Because right now, I don't see any.

It's no exaggeration to say that feminists have been stuck in the same defensive crouch for decades. We've been so busy trying to hold on to the ground already won that imagining a feminist future has been a luxury we haven't had the time, money or energy for. Maybe the way to kick the movement into forward motion is with a bang: the presidency. Schriock believes that having a female president would cause reverberations around the world, and that when it comes to the power of role models, "sometimes you have to see it to understand."

"Will it end sexism as we know it?" she adds. "No, but it starts changing the conversation rapidly."

I don't have any illusions about women's "innate goodness" or think that a woman president would transform the United States into a feminist utopia. (Birkenstocks for everyone!) Like most politicians, a woman president could be just another disappointment. So why not a female disappointment? Equal representation of jerks is still equality.

But there is something to be said for the power of figureheads. After Hillary Clinton became secretary of state, a record number of countries posted female ambassadors to the US—some of whom have dubbed this "the Hillary effect." In 2010, Mozambique's ambassador to the United States, Amélia Matos Sumbana, told the *Washington Post*: "Hillary Clinton is so visible. She makes it easier for presidents to pick a woman for Washington." In the same way, seeing a woman serve as president of the United States could be the proverbial game-changer.

I don't know that my course of action is the one I'd recommend for others—in many ways, it's a marker of my dying idealism. But I do know that seeing a woman hold the nation's highest office would bring me great joy, and that if there's anything American women need right now, it's a win.

Immigrants' Greatest Potential Ally—
American Women

By Elena Shore
New America Media, May 2, 2012

A new report by the Pew Hispanic Center documents a trend that reporters have been covering anecdotally for several years: we are now seeing net-zero immigration from Mexico to the United States.

The factors that may have contributed to this change—high U.S. unemployment, a Mexican economy that is recovering more rapidly, a low Mexican birthrate, and increased immigration enforcement—all point in one direction: The number of people moving to Mexico from the United States is equal to—or greater than—the number of people coming into the country from Mexico.

But with a record number of state and local laws cracking down on undocumented immigrants, this hardly means an end to the anti-immigrant sentiment that has taken root in America.

That's because, as blogger Mario Solis-Marich of the blog MarioWire once said, immigration restriction has never really been about border enforcement; it's about brown people living in their towns and communities.

And with the Mexican American population booming—through birth, not immigration—the new target of anti-immigrant and anti-Latino hysteria is now the pregnant mother.

By 2050, Latinos will represent an estimated 30 percent of the U.S. population, according to census figures. The majority of this population growth, especially for Mexican Americans, is not from immigration but from U.S.-born children.

The Latina mother—who has the power to change the demographics of this country through childbirth—has replaced the male immigrant worker as the new threat for many nativist Americans.

She also has become the target of a new wave of legislation.

2011 saw a record number of laws cracking down on immigrants—and a record number of laws limiting reproductive rights. At the center of these attacks are immigrant women, who are struggling to keep their families together amid record detentions and deportations, and fighting for reproductive health care even as their access to basic health services is becoming more and more restricted.

The push to repeal the Fourteenth Amendment of the U.S. Constitution, to ban birthright citizenship for the children of undocumented immigrants, is the latest example of the use of anti-immigrant laws to attack women. This movement, which is expected to make a comeback after the presidential elections, isn't likely to succeed—after all, changing the Constitution is extremely difficult to do—but it already has been successful in changing the conversation around immigration and giving anti-immigrant hardliners a platform in the public discourse.

Laws limiting reproductive rights have also been used to attack immigrants. Last month, Nebraska Gov. Dave Heineman vetoed a bill that would give undocumented immigrant mothers access to prenatal care. The Nebraska state legislature ended up overriding his veto—but to do this, they essentially argued that fetuses had more rights than their mothers, a bizarre debate that reflected the way we as a country devalue and dehumanize immigrant mothers.

Nowhere is this dehumanization more evident than in the shackling of women immigrant detainees during childbirth. New America Media reported on the practice in Arizona's immigration detention centers in January 2010. Just this year [2012], Arizona became the 15th state to outlaw the practice.

Meanwhile, immigrant women and their families are impacted every day by an immigration enforcement policy that separates families through detention and deportation, and sometimes causes mothers to lose parental rights over their own children. In the first six months of 2011, Immigrations and Customs Enforcement (ICE) deported 46,000 parents of U.S.-citizen children. And at least 5,100 children currently living in foster care are prevented from uniting with their detained or deported parents, according to a report by Applied Research Center.

In 2009 New America Media commissioned a multilingual poll of women immigrants in the U.S., and found that the majority of respondents said they came to this country "to keep their families together." This reality stands in stark contrast to the image of the lone male worker who left his family to find work in the United States.

But there was something even more surprising that we discovered as a result of our poll.

As we traveled across the country presenting the findings of our poll, we found that there was an enormous untapped audience for whom the story of women immigrants had a special resonance: American women.

That's because immigration is, at its heart, a women's issue.

Immigrant women are struggling to protect their rights as mothers—from access to prenatal care to keeping their parental rights. They are fighting for their rights as workers—from equal pay to fair working conditions free from sexual harassment and assault. They are fighting to keep their families and communities together, despite an immigration enforcement policy that is making this simple desire a Herculean task.

The struggles of immigrant women in America today are the struggles of all women.

And as soon as they are able to make this connection, to see immigration as "our" issue, not "theirs," American women could very well be game-changers in the way our country deals with immigrants.

This year, New America Media has been meeting with women leaders across the country to help foster this conversation.

After organizing Alabama's first ethnic media gathering last year, we returned to Birmingham this year in partnership with the We Belong Together campaign to bring together women's rights and immigrants' rights leaders to oppose Alabama's HB 56 and other unjust laws.

We are also working to expand reporting on the intersection of immigration and gender.

Last month we brought 10 journalism fellows from ethnic and mainstream media news outlets across the country to Washington, D.C., where they met with experts in immigration, women's rights, human trafficking and reproductive rights. Reporters learned how to apply a gender lens to immigration, and activists discussed how the immigrant rights and women's rights movements—too often working in silos—could join together to work toward common goals.

Little by little, we hope that the work being done by New America Media and other organizations will help persuade American women that violations against the rights of immigrants are violations against all women.

From the shackling of women immigrant detainees to the effective kidnapping of American-born children whose parents are deported, we are witnessing a humanitarian crisis in our country being carried out against women immigrants.

And American women from all backgrounds have the power to stop it.

The Feminist Factor

By Eleanor Smeal

Ms. Magazine, Winter 2013

As we move forward after the elections of 2012, it's time to acknowledge that it wasn't just women who made a critical difference in reelecting President Barack Obama, but feminists.

I've been thinking about the gender gap since the early 1970s, when I was doing graduate work on women's political attitudes. And in 1980, I proved its existence while analyzing job-approval polling, segmented by gender, for President Ronald Reagan, who opposed the Equal Rights Amendment (ERA). Women approved of him less than men—a statistic borne out in the election, in which there was an 8-point gap between women's votes for Reagan and men's. A team of us at NOW (the National Organization for Women), who were campaigning hard for the ERA, named it the gender gap, and we even had a ditty that we chanted toward politicians we opposed: "The gender gap will get you if you don't watch out!"

The gap—the measurable difference between the voting behavior and political attitudes of women and men—has grown considerably since then. It was decisive in November, both in the presidential race and in maintaining a Democratic majority in the U.S. Senate.

To begin with, women (53 percent of all voters) cast some 8 million more votes for the president than men did. And 55 percent of those women chose Obama, compared to just 45 percent of men—for a 10-percent gender gap. If only men had voted, Mitt Romney would have won the presidency, 52 percent to 45 percent.

The gender gap and women's votes were also decisive in some key Senate races in which the Democratic candidate won, including Elizabeth Warren's in Massachusetts (a 12-percent gender gap) and Chris Murphy's in Connecticut (11 percent). If only men had voted in each of these races, the Republican candidate would have won.

Most importantly, this gender gap was crucial in the battleground states in which the presidential election was determined: In Ohio and Wisconsin, for example, the gender gap was 10 percent pro-Obama, and 8 percent and 10 percent, respectively, in favor of Democratic senatorial candidates Sherrod Brown and Tammy Baldwin. Even in states in which the gap was smaller, such as Virginia and Florida, it was large enough for Democrats to win the presidential and Senate contests.

But now it's time to add another metric beyond the gender gap to our postelection analysis: the "feminist factor." While there were many reasons for President Obama's decisive victory, the feminist factor may be one of the most significant.

We dubbed it that after analyzing an in-depth poll *Ms.* commissioned with the Communications Consortium Media Center and the Feminist Majority Foundation. Conducted Nov. 4–6, 2012, by Lake Research Partners, it found that 55 percent of women voters and even 30 percent of men voters consider themselves feminist.

These results are generally 9 points higher than they were in 2008, when the same question was posed to voters, and this upward trend is likely to continue given the strong identification with feminism by younger women and women of color.

Speaking of younger women, a solid majority of them (58 percent) identify as feminists—as did 54 percent of older women, nearly three-quarters (72 percent) of Democratic women and a respectable 38 percent of Republican women. The feminist factor cuts across race and ethnic lines, with a majority of Latina, African American and white women voters considering themselves feminists.

Most importantly, voters' views on feminism correlated with their choice of candidates. Among feminist women, some two-thirds (64 percent) voted for Obama, as did 54 percent of feminist-identified men. Looking at voters who identified as pro-choice, 61 percent cast their ballot for Obama.

While the votes of women—especially feminist women—were crucial in re-electing the president and a Democratic-majority Senate, they were not successful in electing a Democratic House majority. However, they probably could have done so if it weren't for severely gerrymandered districts that underrepresent Democrats (60 percent of whom are women), Latina/os, African Americans and women. Overall, Americans cast some 1.3 million more votes for House Democrats than House Republicans, but because of gerrymandering, they would need to win the popular vote in House elections by more than 7 percent just to barely gain a House majority. (Thanks to Ian Millhiser of ThinkProgress for that analysis.)

Although feminists feel that the election was a victory for us in the War on Women—the term now commonly used by feminists and the media to describe initiatives in state legislatures and Congress that severely restrict women's rights in such areas as reproduction, violence and pay equity—we can't savor it for long. The 2012 election wins have prevented some of the worst attacks on women's rights from succeeding, but we won just a battle: The opposition to women's rights, especially at the state level, is certainly not going away. We have much to do if we are to realize the pro-choice, pro-women's rights agenda upon which President Obama and other candidates ran—an agenda that will move women and the nation forward.

Now is the time for feminists and feminist organizations to gear up and mobilize, making sure that the message we delivered in the 2012 election is actually received and results are delivered. We must work to prevent a backslide, as happened in the congressional and state elections in 2009 and 2010, and instead build for further victories in the 2013 and 2014 elections.

Here is what we must do:

FIRST We must work to avert an economic crisis. As I write this, we just faced a "fiscal cliff," with another fight looming in Congress about raising the debt limit. Conservatives in Congress keep demanding benefits cuts in Social Security, Medicare and Medicaid—programs that women, especially, desperately need—so we cannot let this happen.

Congress must not balance the federal budget on the backs of the poor, the disabled or the elderly. There are plenty of cuts that can be realized without slashing benefits for programs that women rely upon. Just one example: The Affordable Care Act cuts some $716 billion out of Medicare over 10 years, but does so by reducing administrative costs and insurance company subsidies rather than cutting benefits to older recipients.

SECOND We must work to pass a series of other critical measures in Congress. For one, there's the federal Paycheck Fairness Act—filibustered by Senate Republicans in 2012—which increases protections for workers who sue employers for sex discrimination or even discuss their pay with coworkers. And we still must pass the reauthorization of the Violence Against Women Act (VAWA), which House Republicans blocked in 2012 by rolling back coverage the Senate had voted on for students, immigrants, Native Americans and the LGBT community.

We also must urge Congress to increase access to family planning and abortion, and keep intact the Affordable Care Act. Plus, we repeat: In these tough economic times, we must insist on keeping the protections of Medicare, Social Security and Medicaid.

But the next set of battles is not just at the national level.

THIRD We must organize to stop attacks on women's rights in many state legislatures, which are often led by their governors. We hardly had time to analyze the election results before those attacks started up again. One of the more egregious examples was when the lame-duck Michigan Legislature passed, and the governor signed into law, an extreme TRAP law (Targeted Regulations against Abortion Providers) in an effort to close abortion clinics.

Ohio's Legislature also used its lame-duck session to attack women's rights, introducing a very restrictive abortion law—which, fortunately, was withdrawn. But in Mississippi, the state is defending a newly passed TRAP law designed to close the only remaining abortion clinic in the state. And in Texas, a law that went into effect earlier this year is preventing Planned Parenthood—because it provides abortion services—from receiving any funding from the new Texas Women's Health Program, even though the health-care provider's services other than abortion aid some 50,000 women.

Clearly, the message of the gender gap and feminist factor weren't heard in Virginia, either. That state is in the process of implementing its new TRAP law, which the Republican anti-choice governor signed in late December, even though state voters favored President Obama and prochoice Democratic Senate candidate Tim Kaine (Kaine's gender gap was 7 percent, by the way). This action by the state just continues the extreme anti-abortion and anti-family-planning measures that seemed to dominate the Virginia Legislature in 2012.

FOURTH We must help build upon the wins in the equal-marriage movement for gay men and lesbians. Feminists were thrilled that four states voted in favor of same-sex marriage (with the gender gap being decisive in each state), and we eagerly await the outcome of the Supreme Court cases concerning the Defense of Marriage Act (DOMA) and California's Proposition 8. But, of course, we can't become complacent, and must still work to make equal marriage available in all 50 states.

FIFTH Feminists must seize the opening to push for more-stringent gun control. Considering the nationwide horror of the Sandy Hook massacre, there's probably no better time than now to bring this issue to congressional and state attention and support President Obama's gun-control initiatives. Too often women and children are the victims of gun violence, so it's no surprise that there is a massive gender gap on this issue, with women more strongly in favor of gun control. We cannot be ignored any longer on this issue: Enough is enough.

SIXTH We can't forget the women around the globe fighting against violence— from the girls in Pakistan such as Malala Yousafzai, battling the Taliban for the right to be educated; or the Pakistani women health-care workers assassinated just for doing their jobs; or Afghan girls and women bravely going to school and work or seeking health care despite threats and assassinations; or the women in India, victims of brutal gang rapes and facing everyday hostility.

One of the things we can do is work hard for the Senate to ratify the United Nations Convention on the Elimination of Discrimination Against Women (CEDAW) and pass the International Violence Against Women Act. It is disgraceful that the U.S. is one of only seven nations that has not ratified CEDAW, which requires a two-thirds vote, so the Democratic Senate must keep bringing it up until it is passed. The women of the world fighting horrific violence deserve our nation's full and unqualified support, and we feminists must demand it.

Finally, we'll keep pressing for the ratification of the Equal Rights Amendment to the U.S. Constitution. How can women and feminists accept anything less than full equality for women in the supreme law of our nation? Recognizing the power of the gender gap and the feminist factor, we can and must make it happen. Our strategy will be to increase cosponsors of the ERA in the new Congress and fight for its passage in the unratified states.

Full equality and full respect, nothing less and nothing more. We take that as the message of the 2012 elections as we continue to push forward.

House of Cads

The Psycho-Sexual Ordeal of Reporting in Washington

By Marin Cogan
New Republic, March 11, 2013

"We've all done it," begins one of the spicier dialogues in the new Netflix political thriller, *House of Cards*. Janine Skorsky, a veteran political reporter, is revealing to her young colleague, Zoe Barnes, how female journalists in Washington snag their scoops. "I used to suck, screw, and jerk anything that moved just to get a story." She runs through her carnal C.V.: the communications director on a Senate race, a staffer in the Department of Defense, her "very own" White House intern. "I even had a fling with a congressman," she says, with a hint of pride.

In popular fictions of Washington, everyone is a prostitute in one way or another; when it comes to female journalists, though, the comparison is often tediously literal. "I can play the whore," Barnes later tells her very own congressman, House Majority Whip Francis Underwood. It's not that sex never happens between political reporters and their sources, as David Petraeus's affair with his biographer, Paula Broadwell, recently reminded us. It's not even that women (and men) don't sometimes flirt in the process of news gathering. It's just that the notion of sexy young reporters turning tricks for tips is not how news is usually made in the nation's capital. For every Judith Miller, the ex–*New York Times* reporter who would sometimes quote her live-in lover, former Representative and Defense Secretary Les Aspin, there are dozens of female journalists for whom the power of appropriations is not an aphrodisiac. We have not "all done it," as Skorsky claims. And yet, the reporter-seductress stereotype persists, in part because some men in Washington refuse to relinquish it.

As a political reporter for *GQ*, I've been jokingly asked whether I ever posed for the magazine and loudly called a porn star by a senior think-tank fellow at his institute's annual gala. In my prior job as a Hill reporter, one of my best source relationships with a member of Congress ended after I remarked that I looked like a witch who might hop on a broom in my new press-badge photo and he replied that I looked like I was "going to hop on something." One journalist remembers a group of lobbyists insisting that she was not a full-time reporter at a major publication but a college coed. Another tried wearing scarves and turtlenecks to keep a married K Street type from staring at her chest for their entire meeting. The last time she saw him, his wedding ring was conspicuously absent; his eyes, however, were still fixed on the same spot. Almost everyone has received the late-night e-mail—"You're incredible" or "Are you done with me yet?"—that she is not entirely sure how to handle. They're what another lady political writer refers to as "drunk fumbles" or "the result of lonely and insecure people trying to make themselves feel loved and/or important."

These are the stories you don't hear, in part because they don't occupy the fantasies of the mostly male scriptwriters of Washington dramas and in part because women reporters are reluctant to signal to any source—past, present, or future—that they might not be discreet or trustworthy. Such stories tend to fall on the spectrum somewhere between amusing and appalling. Sometimes they reach the level of stalking: One colleague had a high-profile member of Congress go out of his way to track down her cell-phone number, call and text repeatedly to tell her she was beautiful, offer to take her parents on a tour of the Capitol, and even invite her to go boating back home in his district.

"I think journalism schools should have workshops for young female reporters on managing old men who have no game and think, because you're listening to them intently and probing what they think and feel, that you're romantically interested, rather than conducting an interview," says Garance Franke-Ruta, a senior editor at *The Atlantic*. "Every female reporter I know has had this issue at one time or another."

Sometimes it's enough to turn a reporter off from her source permanently. "I can't bring myself, at least for a while after such an incident, to call them again, mostly because I find this behavior presumptuous and then I can't help but find these people revolting, even as sources," according to one Washington reporter, who says men have interrupted national security discussions to call her pretty and have invited her to movies. "It's just a totally visceral thing. I also think women reporters don't talk about it because we don't want to seem presumptuous or full of ourselves. Complaining makes it seem like you're humble-bragging or that you're delusional."

This is to say nothing of the idea that we might prostitute ourselves for a communications director, a Department of Defense staffer, or—for the love of God!—a White House intern. One woman reporter who covers national politics remembers going out with a regional Obama fund-raiser who seemed particularly impressed with himself. Over a round of overpriced margaritas at Washington's Lauriol Plaza, the fund-raiser turned to the reporter and asked suggestively, "Would you ever sleep with a source for a story?" She replied: "If I did, it would be with someone much higher up the command chain than you."

Studies suggest that men are more likely than women to interpret friendly interest as sexual attraction, and this is a constant hazard for women in the profession. The problem, in part, is that the rituals of cultivating sources—initiating contact, inviting them out for coffee or a drink, showing intense interest in their every word—can often mimic the rituals of courtship, creating opportunities for interested parties on either side of the reporter-source relationship to blur the line between the professional and personal. A source may invite you to meet at the bar around the corner from your apartment. If you agree, he might offer to pay for the drinks and walk you home. One Washington climate reporter remembers an environmentalist stroking her leg at one such outing and noting, disapprovingly, that she hadn't shaved.

"I always remind young female reporters to be wary about falling victim to the 'source-date,'" says Shira Toeplitz, politics editor at *Roll Call*. "You're on a second glass of something, and it occurs to you, he may be misinterpreting this as a date. I advise them to drop an obvious clue along the lines of, 'I'm going to expense this.'"

This sort of behavior was probably worse in the days when Americans tolerated more skirt-chasing from their politicians; but back then, there were also fewer women political reporters to target. The high-water mark for male politicians behaving badly toward their female interviewers may have been in 1994, when Lisa DePaulo (who sometimes writes for this magazine) profiled Philadelphia Mayor Ed Rendell and wrote that he told her "in raw and alliterative terms, how he presumes I am in bed." Rendell had to call a press conference to address the media maelstrom, but DePaulo—who was nicknamed the "lady in red," because she wore a red suit the day her story broke—faced the bigger backlash. The press corps questioned her relationship history and wondered why anyone would bother to waste ink on the mayor's well-known licentiousness. But few politicians have been eager, after Rendell's media blowup, to repeat his mistakes—some even seem reluctant to converse alone with women reporters for fear it might be misconstrued.

What all of this obsession with political power and sex might overlook is that the majority of reporter-source interactions are exceedingly polite and professional. But not always. Which is why there is one line Barnes delivers on *House of Cards* that is so relatable you might just hear it on the tongues of some women reporters. "Oh Brian, you're so sweet, really," Barnes tells a hopeful suitor as they reach her apartment after a night out. "But if I was going to f—k you, you'd know."

Take Their Wives, Please

Huma, Silda, and the Fallacy of Understanding Candidates through Their Spouses

By Isaac Chotiner
New Republic, August 19, 2013

We've obsessed over political wives for years—searching for meaning and drama in the ambition of Hillary Clinton, the privilege of Cindy McCain, and the travails of Elizabeth Edwards—but the press conference that Anthony Weiner and Huma Abedin gave on the state of their union felt like the moment when our obsession officially went overboard. "I love him, I have forgiven him, I believe in him," Abedin said in heartfelt, halting tones, following her husband's confession that he'd continued to sext with strangers after resigning from Congress two years ago in disgrace. "It took a lot of work and a whole lot of therapy to get to a place where I could forgive Anthony," she went on. "But I do very strongly believe that that is between us and our marriage."

The absurdity of an accomplished woman explaining her marriage to the world—while also declaring her marriage to be private territory—was lost in the torrent of over-analysis that gushed forth. Was Abedin a victim, an opportunist, or an empowered woman? "Huma comes from the Clinton school of forgiveness—power is more important than dignity," a media strategist, that most dignified of professionals, told *The New York Post*. In *The New York Times*, Maureen Dowd suggested that Abedin's loyalty to her husband could be attributed to her upbringing in patriarchal Saudi Arabia. Even her attire was mined for clues to her psychological state. "Her nondescript black sweater over a throwaway floral sundress was the outfit of someone who had been through a lot and someone who was beginning to come undone," a *New York* magazine blogger opined.

By now this phenomenon has become a dreary cliché: As a politician apologizes for his particular combination of sexual dysfunction and arrogance with practiced, lip-biting "sincerity," we can't seem to take our eyes off his wife, standing to one side and looking a little shell-shocked. It's her reaction that largely determines whether her husband is perceived to have a shot at redemption. As an added bonus, she is graded on her contribution to feminism: Has she single-handedly advanced the cause of women or dealt it a mortal blow? After Silda Wall Spitzer endured one of these ordeals several years ago, an ABC newscaster called her decision to do so a "syndrome," comparing her unfavorably with Jenny Sanford, who had refused to attend her husband Mark's public admission of adultery and had thus "[kept] her dignity." In *The Washington Post*, Sally Quinn described Abedin's press conference as "a setback for women everywhere." But the truth is that we know almost nothing about these women or the decisions they've made in their marriages. And the fact that we even pretend to understand them exposes an ugly fallacy at the heart of the political process.

One reason we're so captivated by political spouses is that we—that is, voters—don't really know what we're doing. Americans want to elect competent, morally upstanding people to high office but are unsure of how to do so. Politicians tend to mouth the same bromides about faith, country, and honor; policy-making can be an impenetrable business. So voters take an intuitive shortcut: We look to candidates' families and especially—since most politicians are men—their wives. Michael Douglas recently observed that one of the hardest parts of being an actor is doing sex scenes, since "everyone has had sex—which means everyone has an opinion on how it should be done." In politics, everyone has an opinion on marriage, because it's something we understand, or at least we understand it better than Obamacare's application of medical loss ratios. That's how the wife, smiling and coiffed, becomes the symbolic shorthand for her husband's authentic character.

But it's not just the voters' fault. Ever since politics entered the TV age, campaigns have exploited our fascination with the spouses relentlessly. When Al Gore planted a long kiss on his (now estranged) wife, Tipper, at the 2000 Democratic National Convention, the show of affection was thought to have done wonders for his starchy reputation. Last year, Romney campaign staffers repeatedly boasted of their plans to deploy Ann Romney to battleground states in order to "humanize" Mitt. In 2007, after much chatter that Michelle Obama's jokes at her husband's expense were, as Dowd put it, "emasculating," her public persona became less outspoken and more "relatable." The underlying logic at work here is depressingly retrograde: The wife is an extension of her husband, not a person in her own right. And when the rosy picture of a politician's marriage gets shattered, who is used to tell the narrative of his redemption? The political wife, again.

The final culprit is—no surprise here—the media, which loves to dissect political spouses as avatars of feminism, working motherhood, or modern marriage, but almost never as real people. The press coverage of wronged wives can be downright fawning. Abedin was described in a recent *New York* magazine profile as "quite possibl[y] . . . the most cosmopolitan human being on Earth." The *New York Times* devoted a front-page story to Silda Spitzer last month, presenting her as almost supernaturally devoted to long workweeks and charitable endeavors. After the news of Mark Sanford's affair broke, Jenny released a statement saying she loved her husband and wanted to reconcile. A *Newsweek* editor gushed: "It's loving. It's forgiving. It is pious. And she really kicks some butt." These portraits of noble victims may be sympathetic, but they also reek of condescension. Their subjects are not complicated human beings who make difficult, sometimes messy decisions, but reassuring cardboard cutouts: If the man is a scoundrel, then the woman must be a saint.

What's most grating about the fixation on the wives, by practically everyone involved in politics, is that it's based on a fundamentally misguided assumption. No matter how often the connection between effective public service and family values is disproved, we insist on seeing one. (The irony is that we do so while simultaneously regarding politicians as only slightly more ethical than gangsters.) The three great exemplars of moral leadership over the past century are generally considered to be Mohandas Gandhi, Martin Luther King Jr., and Nelson Mandela, none of whom were models for marital best practices. Gandhi loftily informed his wife after two decades of marriage that he would henceforth be celibate and periodically tested his resolve by sleeping nude with his 18-year-old grandniece. King had numerous extramarital affairs, causing his wife great pain. During his first marriage, Mandela conducted a brazen affair with his secretary. As for American politicians, Franklin Roosevelt and John F. Kennedy remain the two most popular, respected presidents of the last 100 years, and both were legendary philanderers.

Some say that, when wives choose to fund-raise or lobby for their husbands' campaigns, as Abedin did, they are opening themselves up to scrutiny, just like any other surrogate. And, of course, if a wife's involvement raises questions of conflicts of interest, it's a legitimate area of inquiry. But Abedin is not running for office, and her personal life is just not that relevant to the future of New York City. There was once a time when a woman's only role in society was thought to be as a complement to her husband or, at best, a useful accessory. That time is long gone, and yet in the realm of politics, we cling to it. In many countries, the families of politicians are barely even public figures, let alone stars in a neverending national morality tale.

So here's an idea. Let's try and get through the 2016 campaign cycle without focusing on spouses. If politicians bandy them around, let's refuse to participate in the charade. If a candidate is caught with his pants down in a Starbucks restroom, let's skip the mass mind-reading of his wife. It's time for this gruesome ritual to end.

Where Are Politics' Interracial Couples?

More Americans Are Open to Mixed Marriages, but Few Government Officials Marry outside Their Race

By Keli Goff

The Root, August 28, 2012

The furor that erupted over coverage of Republican vice-presidential candidate Paul Ryan's admission that he once dated a black woman raises an interesting question, with few easy answers. If society is becoming increasingly multiracial, then why don't those leading society, or running for office to do so, reflect that? Why aren't there more interracial couples in American politics and government?

According to political consultant Michael Goldman, who has advised the late Ted Kennedy and current Massachusetts Governor Deval Patrick, the lack of multiracial families in politics is not that surprising. The reason, he explained, is that having a spouse of a different race still represents a political liability. "To be as ordinary as possible is the goal for a candidate," Goldman said, adding that most voters feel comfortable voting for someone they can relate to. Since most people still marry people of the same race, for many voters a candidate with a spouse of a different race is simply less relatable. He drew comparisons to the struggle faced by candidates who practice a different religion than the majority of their constituents.

New York public advocate Bill de Blasio has not allowed such concerns to deter him from a career in politics. He is mounting a campaign to become New York City's mayor. Should the Democrat win, he and his family would make history. [[De Blasio was elected mayor in 2013.]] De Blasio is white. His wife Chirlane is black. De Blasio admitted, however, in an interview with *The Root*, that the unique challenges multiracial families, including his own, have faced, can be a deterrent to entering politics. "If you're an interracial family you're still dealing with a certain amount of challenge from society around you just in having that family and in trying to make that family work." He explained that the glare of the public eye that politics brings could make coping with those challenges even tougher.

Echoing Goldman's sentiments, he said, "Society as a whole is not totally acclimated to interracial families yet." He added, "We can't think of another black-white couple active in politics."

They are out there, but to de Blasio's larger point they are few and far between. The highest profile mixed-race couples include former Secretary of Defense William Cohen, who is white, and his wife Janet Langhart, a former Ebony Fashion Fair model and news anchor, who is black. They wrote of the challenges they faced early in their relationship in a memoir titled *Love in Black and White*. The only black justice currently on the Supreme Court, Clarence Thomas, is married to Tea Party activist Virginia Thomas, who is white.

It is worth noting, however, that neither of these couples faced the scrutiny of a campaign. Both men are best known for appointed positions, which means they did not have to defend their unions before voters. In Cohen's case, though, he and his wife married while he was still a Republican member of the U.S. Senate, in the last year of his final term. He has previously acknowledged that the relationship gave some of his supporters pause, meaning their union could have become campaign fodder had he run for re-election.

Studies show that interracial relationships are gaining increasing acceptance with younger generations and that nearly all millennials do not take issue with such unions. Many observers noted that Rep. Paul Ryan is the first member of a major party ticket to disclose an interracial relationship, and at age 42, he also happens to be the first member of a major party ticket who is a member of Generation X. (Some have mentioned in comparison that President Obama had a white girlfriend at one time, but since his mother was also white, it doesn't make such a disclosure quite as noteworthy.)

Ryan is not alone. Thirty-seven-year-old Republican mayor-turned-GOP congressional candidate Mia Love, who is speaking at this week's Republican National Convention, is also a member of Generation X and has also dated interracially, and subsequently married. Love is black, while her husband is white.

Basil Smikle, a New York–based political consultant who once worked for Hillary Clinton, speculated that couples like Love's and de Blasio's may have an easier time than others, and not just because the public is growing more open-minded. Smikle theorized that black men with white spouses are likely to have the toughest time of all mixed race matches in a campaign. "I think for an African-American male candidate with a white spouse there is a credibility hurdle that he will need to overcome with black voters that another candidate would not face," he said.

He explained that while black voters may look at a black woman married to a white man and assume perhaps she simply did not meet the right black man, they see an accomplished black man married to a white woman and assume perhaps he married a trophy wife. This makes visiting black churches and other locales to which black candidates often go a challenge. For instance, as a candidate for the senate in Tennessee, Rep. Harold Ford was the target of an ad featuring a white woman suggestively telling him to "call me," which many viewed as a racially coded reference to his interracial relationships. Ford later explored running for the senate in New York, but by that time his white girlfriend had become his wife.

Though New York is not Tennessee, it still would have presented a challenge for him, Smikle explained. "I don't think it is something he could not have overcome," he added. Yet Smikle did conclude that "If Obama had a white wife it is unlikely he would be president."

Despite the challenges their unique family may bring in the political sphere, de Blasio and his wife are optimistic about where our country is headed when it comes to race. They recalled that they met weeks after the racially charged Crown Heights riots in New York, and it was love at first sight. Yet after the Spike Lee film *Jungle Fever* was released that year they were harassed by a group of teens that cornered them while shouting, "jungle fever."

Now, two decades later they are preparing to possibly become New York's first family. "Today we feel broadly respected and embraced with a few exceptions," he said. His wife pointed out, though, that there are still times when people see their family together and treat them like they couldn't possibly be a family, what both of them referred to as "awkwardness."

"The day I look forward to is when we are a country without awkwardness, where people just accept people in every configuration," de Blasio said. "You would think that by having a biracial president that would be the end of the chapter and we could all go home now, but nothing could be further from the truth. We have a long way to go."

4

Media and the Sexes

Jason Pohuski/CSM /Landov

Rashard Mendenhall, number 34, is interviewed by Fox reporter Laura Okmin after he scores the game-winning touchdown during the Steelers versus Falcons game in Pittsburgh at Heinz Field. The Steelers won 15–9 in overtime.

Women in the Media: On Screen and Off

The relationship between media and gender representation is complex and in a constant state of flux. The media *creates and maintains* gender stereotypes, by displaying men and women in stereotypical gender roles and by promoting characters or media personalities that represent certain gender norms to new generations of viewers. At the same time, the media *reflects* changing attitudes about gender in the broader environment by tailoring entertainment and news media to the tastes of viewers and by attempting to remain "modern" in their depictions of gender.

Studies of American mass media reveal that women are more often the subject of stereotyped depictions and sexualization than men. Men, while portrayed in a far more diverse manner, are also often presented with standards of masculinity that misrepresent the diversity of male interests and behavior. Male executives, writers, and producers dominated both news media and the entertainment industry in 2013, with women holding less than 30 percent of media jobs across all industries. Despite an overwhelming male bias and the continuing marginalization of women in both popular media and the media industry, pioneering female broadcasters, journalists, publishers, and content creators have the potential to affect the balance of gender representations in the media.

Sex Balance in Media

Women constitute half the population and nearly half of the American workforce, and yet women are underrepresented in many key industries, including every facet of American media. According to 2013 estimates from the USC Annenberg School for Communication and Journalism, only 7 percent of media writers, 13 percent of directors, and 20 percent of media producers are women. Men outnumber women in high-level media management and production positions by a margin of five to one, and this ongoing imbalance translates to bias within the industry, maintaining a media environment in which both entertainment and news media disproportionately target male audiences.

In the news media environment, women have had greater success in front of the camera, as approximately half of local television news anchors were women in 2008. However, data from the Radio-Television News Directors Association indicates that only 28 percent of local news directors and 16 percent of managers at television and radio stations are women. In print news, more than two-thirds of editors, columnists, and reporters are white men. Similarly, data from the radio industry indicates that women account for less than 25 percent of managers and local radio news directors across the country. Statistics from the Pew Foundation in 2013 indicated that approximately one-third of newsroom managers across all fields are women and that the number of women working in news media has declined since 1998.

When it comes to sex representation in entertainment, research indicates that male characters outnumber female characters in film and television three to one, including children's television and family film productions. Moreover, research from the Geena Davis Institute on Gender in Media found that the percentage of characters that are women has not changed significantly since World War II, and has in fact declined slightly in the late twentieth and early twenty-first centuries.

Even when television and film casts are balanced in terms of male and female characters, male characters are far more likely to have speaking roles and garner a disproportionate amount of screen time overall. Research from the Geena Davis Institute indicated that women receive just over 31 percent of screen time in prime-time comedy programs, 40 percent in dramas, and 30 percent in children's programming. Women's participation in feature films follows a similar pattern, with few films featuring primary female leads. In 2011, the Motion Picture Association of America noted that only 33 percent of characters in the top-grossing films were female.

Researchers have noticed similar indications of gender bias across nearly all facets of the media industry. For instance, a 2012 article in the *Huffington Post* reported statistics indicating that 77 percent of notable deaths reported in newspapers and magazines were about men. Statistics gathered by the media research project 4th Estate regarding the 2012 presidential election indicated that men were also more likely to be interviewed and quoted in print and television journalism, even in stories focusing on women's issues. For instance, the study found that, in stories focused on women's rights, 52 percent of quotes were from men, versus 31 percent from women (the other 17 percent were from organizations); the disparity was even starker in stories about abortion, in which men were quoted 81 percent of the time and women 12 percent of the time. In *New York Times* articles, 65 percent of quotes overall were from men, versus 15 percent from women.

Researchers have also examined how the demographics of the production and content creation industries affects the representation of female characters, finding that the addition of a single female writer to a program increased female character screen time by more than 10 percent. Critics of the media industry have argued that the lack of women both behind and in front of the camera serves to create gender bias and stereotypes, especially as these patterns are present in children's programming. While women are underrepresented in the industry, data from Nielsen ratings and television network reports indicate that women make up the majority of prime-time television viewers and constitute nearly half of motion picture audiences, even when the majority of films are targeted at male viewers.

Gender Depictions in Film and Television

In addition to being underrepresented in the media industry, women are consistently marginalized and sexualized in media depictions. Examinations of female and male characters in film, family programming, and prime-time television programming indicate that women are five times more likely than men to be depicted wearing revealing or sexualized attire and to be shown with exposed skin or body parts. Female characters are also far more likely to be referred to as "attractive" or "sexy" by other characters. The American Psychological Association's (APA) Taskforce on the Sexualization of Girls has identified media depictions of women as one of the factors promoting unhealthy gender values to young girls and maintaining sexist attitudes among men. The APA argues that depicting women as sex objects teaches young girls to focus on their appearance and sexuality as their most valuable characteristics, thus training young women to enact marginalized gender roles.

The relationship between media depictions of gender and body image is affected by the tendency to display thin body types among female characters. For instance, in prime-time television programming, approximately 14 percent of male characters are depicted having thin bodies, as opposed to more than 37 percent of female characters. Children and older women are less likely to be depicted as thin, while women who are teenagers and young adults are nearly always depicted as thin and sexualized. Sociologist Sarah Murnen's research has shown that the prevalence of the thin, highly sexualized ideal in media depictions of women may be a contributor to high levels of body image issues among American women and girls.

Another issue indicative of the imbalance of gender representation in the media is the disparity in occupational depictions of men and women in film and television. According to the Geena Davis Institute, more than 80 percent of working characters in films and television are male, which contrasts sharply with the professional world, in which nearly half the workforce consists of women. Looking specifically at family films, which have a greater potential to influence gender concepts among children, the Geena Davis Institute could not identify a single female doctor, politician, or business leader depicted in any American G-rated film between 2006 and 2009.

While professional women are now more regularly depicted in films and television, women are rarely depicted as political or business leaders. Women are also rarely depicted taking part in STEM fields (science, technology, engineering, and mathematics) and, when they are, women are nearly always depicted as being subordinate to men. For instance, on prime-time television, women only hold 21 percent of the roles depicting STEM scientists, and less than 1 percent of engineers and computer scientist characters are women. The lack of women in leadership and STEM roles reflects the reduced participation of women in these sectors of the professional environment, but critics argue that media depictions also teach viewers to accept this imbalance as a normal facet of American society.

While women are far more likely to be depicted in a stereotypical way in popular media, research also indicates that men suffer from media stereotyping as well. Research from Break Media in 2012 indicated that men feel that media portrayals limit the behavioral and social range of men, most often depicting men as chasing women, overly "macho" in behavior, and inept at parenting and intimate relationships. Break Media has created the concept of a "Normal Gap" to represent the breakdown between media representations of masculinity and normal modes of behavior among modern American men. Keith Richman, CEO of Break Media, said in a 2012 interview with *Forbes* magazine that he feels the changing realities of the American workforce and economy are altering the career and life goals of men and that these changes are making common media depictions of men obsolete.

Women Leaders in the Modern Media

Media analyses indicate that gender bias and gender-role stereotypes in the media decrease when women take part in management and content creation. To cite one example, filmmaker and actress Lena Dunham, creator of the popular HBO television series *Girls*, has been credited with transcending numerous gender-role stereotypes with her depictions of both men and women. Media reviews often contrast the characterizations of women in *Girls* to those found in *Sex and the City*, which was predominantly created, written, and produced by men and was often criticized as promoting and maintaining feminine stereotypes.

Despite advances of women in media leadership, a number of feminist scholars have noted that women leaders are still subject to gender bias and gender-role stereotypes that discourage other women from aspiring to leadership positions. A Gallup Poll study in 2013 indicated that most Americans still prefer a male boss to a female one. While Americans continue to believe that men are more capable leaders in general, Pew Research indicates that Americans rank women leaders higher than men in key leadership qualities. Studies also indicate that female leaders are more likely to be judged by a different set of criteria from their male counterparts.

An example of this phenomenon can be found in the case of Jill Abramson, executive editor of the *New York Times*, who is considered one of the most powerful and influential women in American media. A 2013 article from journalist Dylan Byers on the website *Politico* reported, citing anonymous sources, that Abramson was "difficult to work with" and "condescending" to her employees. Emily Bell, writing for the *Guardian*, called the *Politico* article an example of the "sexist narrative" about women in power positions. Bell argues that the criticisms of Abramson are biased, focusing on her personality rather than her job performance, while male executives who are seen as unlikeable or tough are more likely to be praised for their effectiveness. In a 2012 article for the *Washington Post*, journalist Jena McGregor argued that, no matter how valid the criticisms of Abramson, the fact remains that women leaders are "judged twice": first by their performance and second by how well they fit into their masculine roles.

—Micah Issitt

Bibliography

Bell, Emily. "Jill Abramson and the Wholly Sexist Narrative of the Woman in Power." *Guardian*. Guardian News and Media, 24 Apr. 2013. Web. 4 Feb. 2014.

Carli, Linda L., and Alice H. Eagly. "Women and Leadership." *The Sage Handbook of Leadership*. Ed. Alan Bryman, David Collinson, Keith Grint, Brad Jackson, and Mary Uhl-Bien. Thousand Oaks: Sage, 2011. Print.

Casserly, Meghan. "Are Men the Latest Victims of Media Misrepresentation?" *Forbes*. Forbes.com, 14 Nov. 2012. Web. 4 Feb. 2014.

Guskin, Emily. "5 Facts about Ethnic and Gender Diversity in US Newrooms." *Pew Research Center*. Pew Research Center, 18 July 2013. Web. 4 Feb. 2014.

McGregor, Jena. "The Double Bind for Jill Abramson and Other Women at the Top." *Washington Post*. Washington Post, 25 Apr. 2013. Web. 4 Feb. 2014.

Mirkinson, Jack. "Men Dominate Discussion of Women's Issues in Media." *Huffington Post*. TheHuffingtonPost.com, 5 June 2012. Web. 4 Feb. 2014.

Newport, Frank, and Joy Wilke. "Americans Still Prefer a Male Boss." *Gallup*. Gallup, 11 Nov. 2013. Web. 4 Feb. 2014.

Papper, Bob. "The Face of the Workforce." *Radio-Television News Directors Association*. RTNDA, July/Aug. 2008. Web. 4 Feb. 2014.

"Silenced: Gender Gap in the 2012 Election Coverage." *4th Estate*. GNI, 2012. Web. 4 Feb. 2014.

Silverstein, Melissa. "Memo to Hollywood: Women Go to the Movies Too." *Washington Post*. Washington Post, 29 June 2012. Web. 4 Feb. 2014.

Smith, Stacy L., Marc Choueiti, Ashley Prescott, and Katherine Pieper. "Gender Roles and Occupations: A Look at Character Attributes and Job-Related Aspirations in Film and Television." *Geena Davis Institute on Gender in Media*. Geena Davis Inst. on Gender in Media, 2012. Web. 4 Feb. 2014.

Smith, Stacy L., and Crystal Allene Cook. "Gender Stereotypes: An Analysis of Popular Films and TV." *Geena Davis Institute on Gender in Media*. Geena Davis Inst. on Gender in Media, 2008. Web. 4 Feb. 2014.

Examining Media's Socialization
of Gender Roles

By Warren J. Blumenfeld
The Huffington Post, August 8, 2013

Do the media create, or maintain, or reflect the gender-based roles that saturate our environment? If you picked "All the Above," you and I would have filled in the same oval on our imaginary multiple-choice bubble answer sheets.

Promoted very consciously and carefully taught to us throughout our lives, "gender roles" (sometimes called "sex roles") include the set of socially defined roles and behaviors assigned to the sex assigned to us at birth. This can and does vary from culture to culture. Our society recognizes basically two distinct gender roles. One includes the "masculine," having the qualities and characteristics attributed to males, and the other, the "feminine," having the qualities and characteristics attributed to females. A third gender role, rarely condoned in our society, at least for those assigned "male" at birth, is "androgyny," combining assumed male (andro) and female (gyne) qualities.

A fairly simple way to remember the differences between "sex" and "gender" is to consider "sex" as a noun and "gender" as a verb (a repeated action). According to social theorist Judith Butler in her 1990 book, *Gender Trouble: Feminism and the Subversion of Identity:*

> The act that one does, the act that one performs, is, in a sense, an act that has been going on before one arrived on the scene. Hence, gender is an act, which has been rehearsed, much as a script survives the particular actors who make use of it, but which requires individual actors in order to be actualized and reproduced as reality once again. (p. 272)

So back to the media, which comprises a social institution that casts actors in performances on this stage who rehearse, learn, "actualize and reproduce" the gendered scripts handed to them long before they entered the scene.

Let's investigate two companies, for example, analyzing how the actors perform their scripted television commercial roles.

I am particularly struck by the relatively recent series of commercials created by the La Quinta Inns and Suites chain. All of the four scenarios profile businessMEN who, after spending a comforting stay at La Quinta, perform exquisitely well in their respective business presentations by "getting his ducks in a row," or by "taking out all the stops," or by "thinking outside the box," or by "bringing home the bacon." In the latter scenario, the businessman literally bowled over and buried his waiting and expectant wife with an enormous truckload of bacon.

Another series of commercials that particularly caught my attention was produced by Depend Shields and Guards for Men. A brawny Tony Siragusa shouts out over the television screen that for men "who leak a little," using Depend Shields and Guards for Men will "guard your manhood." Siragusa reminds us that he "has been around some of the toughest guys in football," and advises the leaking men in the audience to use "man-style protection" and to create "man space" in their bathrooms replete with a dart board and darts, bowling ball, free-standing weights, poker chips, table ice hockey set, and a humungous sports trophy. For further training by the former football star, guys need to connect to the web at "guardyourmanhood.com."

As one scrolls down, a series of objects jump to the fore (a set of billiard balls, guitar, boxing gloves, and, of course, boxes of Depend Shields and Guards. Tony's video "Know Your Gear" appears for the viewer to begin the "training."

Using his deepest of deep voices, "First, let's talk about the tools of the trade." Reminding the guys that "Ladies have their own stuff," while he grabs and lifts a white flowered basket filled with brightly colored, primarily pink, products, he sternly warns: "See this? This is for girls. This is NOT for you!," as he forcefully hurls it to the floor. Pointing firmly with both hands (no hint of a limp wrist showing) to the boxes of Depends: "This is for guys. . . . This is made for men! You don't see any pink do you? No girly package."

In a following "training" video, he helps guys determine which type of Depend to depend upon. Picking up a golf ball and crashing it into the bathroom glass window, "If you've got a little leakage, like this, you probably want to go with the Shields. . . . If there's more than a little bit . . ." Siragusa flings darts at a dart board, ". . . like that, you probably want to hit up the Guards."

Scrolling down further, a couple of darts fly across the screen on their own (symbolic?), table tennis paddles, and, of course, various balls (symbolic?) appearing interspersed with additional videos for viewing in sequence, picking up where the last left off.

The television commercials for Depend for Women, on the other hand, emphasize primarily appearance by demonstrating that this form of "protection" transforms virtually undetectably under women's garments, including a stunning red evening gown, and even beneath a tightly fitting dance outfit while the dancer performs a wild cha cha cha.

A number of critical questions need addressing in these two series of commercials. In the first, why does the company and advertising agency project men only as representatives of business travelers? What does this indicate about gender-based roles constructed by our society? What messages does it covertly as well as overtly send to boys and men, and also to girls and women? What impact may it have on boys and men, girls and women's self-esteem and decision making? What implications does this have on women in the workplace in terms of hiring, advancement, and levels of salaries compared to men?

The second series, while seemingly more like *Saturday Night Live* parody of television commercials, raises a number of issues as well. Upon this humanly devised and regulated binary, then, how does our society determine or define so-called "manhood" and "womanhood"? How are these constructed? How are they maintained? How are they measured? What does it mean to "Man Up," or to "Take it like a man," or to "Be a man," or to "Talk man-to-man"? What does it mean to "Act like a lady," or to "Be ladylike"? Is one considered to have lost one's "manhood" if one leaks from either of the two orifices inside one's underpants? Is one considered "unladylike" by displaying a visible panty line? What are the rewards for upholding our socially scripted roles, and what are the penalties and punishments doled out for those who transgress unintentionally or willingly?

No matter how we respond to these questions, the fact remains that we as individuals and as a society should be expected to critically, reflectively, and creatively investigate and analyze the media rather than simply absorb them at face "value." Not only must our schools help equip students with communication literacy skills but also they must actively teach skills of media literacy to empower students in deconstructing, analyzing, and reflecting upon the media images and messages that bombard them like atmospheric microwaves on a daily basis.

Maybe then will we all exhibit proficiency in "thinking outside the box."

Combine Equal Parts Oprah and Martha

The New Domestic Ideal Owes More
Than a Little to the Fading Moguls

By Lisa Miller
New York Magazine, November 30, 2012

Apart from their plainest similarities—you can count the living women's-media ty-coons who are also lifestyle icons on two fingers—Martha Stewart and Oprah Win-frey would seem to come from different planets. One is blonde, thin, tall, chilly, ex-acting. The other is brown, sometimes plump, warm, accepting. In the hypothetical event that your piecrust failed to cohere, Martha might scold, instructing you to use colder butter next time. Oprah would hand you a Kleenex, tell you about her own piecrust catastrophes, and lay a soothing arm around you.

With layoffs and other contractions at Martha Stewart Living Omnimedia and turbulence at Oprah's OWN network and O magazine, both moguls now face di-minishing profiles. And as Martha (at 71 years old) and Oprah (approaching 60) fight off involuntary retirement to one of their many mansions, it's worth noting the key thing they had in common at their peaks. The products of a white Polish-Catho-lic family and a poor black one, respectively, the two shared an outsider's clear view of the twentieth-century American woman's obsession with feminine and domestic perfection. Way back in the eighties, they understood that goal for the fantasy that it is. Martha and Oprah built dynasties on the insight that millions of women like them had their noses pressed up against the dream of the domestic goddess; their genius was to dismantle the myth.

Martha and Oprah attacked their target from opposite flanks. Martha assaulted perfection by giving every woman a guidebook on how to attain it. Unsentimental, unembellished, her instructions were lab manuals leading step-by-step from sugar and cocoa powder to bûche de Noël. Oprah, in contrast, simply said to hell with it. Life is a mess. The goddess is within; embrace her and get on with it.

It may be that American women don't need Oprah and Martha anymore only because they've absorbed their lessons so well. On mommy blogs and Facebook walls, today's home-front strivers pursue their individual domestic obsessions, each crocheted baby hat and Thanksgiving-leftovers sandwich a monument to famil-ial love and self-expression. At the same time, there's a new liberty to leave other chores half-done. "It's getting easier and easier not to be perfect," says Anne-Marie Slaughter of Princeton and not-having-it-all fame. (She's now working on a book expanding on her widely read *Atlantic* essay.) "Walk into my house, you will see in three seconds that I am not perfect. How am I supposed to do all this and have a perfect house?"

In the new ethos, the ideal is to be at once a little Martha and a little Oprah, aiming for ever-higher domestic prowess but always with a dose of self-deprecating self-forgiveness. On her blog, Dinner: A Love Story, Jenny Rosenstrach posts photos of her adorable kitchen and her perfect three-layer cake, then confesses that it can take her weeks to change a lightbulb and that preparing breakfast for her children threatens to make her weep. "From a food perspective, 'perfect'—a word I associate with white linens and the word 'fussy'—is not what it's about anymore," she said in an e-mail. "Now it seems like everyone is just entertaining in their kitchens. This trend is great, because it's so simple." There is a catch, though: Without a darling centerpiece to deflect attention, your cooking better be good. "It introduces a whole new pressure to deliver," Rosenstrach says. The perfection imperative is not dead. It's just been precisely chopped and amiably bear-hugged down to a more manageable size.

Changing the Portrayal
of Women in the Media

By Susan Bulkeley Butler
The Huffington Post, February 8, 2013

The *Wall Street Journal* chronicles America's best practices which provide the pipeline for business innovation.

So why, then, does the *Journal* seem so stuck in the past in the way it portrays women in the workplace and in advocating for equality in the business world?

I recently perused the *Wall Street Journal* and it really struck a nerve. Here's some of what I saw in a single issue:

- Under the headline "Innovators of the World to Convene in Singapore" were pictures of 21 people. Only one was a woman. Does the *Journal* really think there is only one woman in the world who is an innovator, has the most cutting-edge ideas in business and technology today?

- A house advertisement for an upcoming edition of *WSJ Money* featured an older woman with gloves seated round a table; a woman who was scantily dressed; another younger woman who was dressed in a sexy and seductive way . . . and a man who was obviously in charge. The house ad seeks advertisers for the upcoming special section described as sophisticated and engaging financial advice on how to grow your investments, keep it and pass it on.

- A story with the headline "Juicers Invade Kitchen Counters" features a mother with two young girls, like a 1950s advertisement for refrigerators or ovens, but with an expensive juicer to get more vegetables into their diet. Does this mean the *Journal* wants us to believe that a woman's place is (still) in the kitchen—or that real men don't use juicers?

Of course the *Wall Street Journal* isn't alone in the media world when it comes to portraying women poorly.

In a comprehensive study, the Global Media Monitoring Project found that only 24 percent of the people interviewed, heard, seen, or read about in mainstream broadcast and print news in 2010 were women. In other words, in a world where the population is basically split 50-50 between men and women, nearly three-quarters of all people mentioned in the media in 2010 was a man.

Moreover, only 13 percent of the stories that appeared that year focused specifically on women, and only 6 percent focused on issues of gender equality or inequality, according to the Global Media Monitoring Project.

In a separate study by the American University School of Public Affairs Women and Politics Institute, women represented just under one-fifth—about 22 percent—of guests on Sunday morning news shows on the major networks in 2011.

Hollywood isn't any better. According to the Geena Davis Institute on Gender in Media, men outnumber women 3 to 1 in family films. Remarkably, that ratio is about the same as it was in 1946, according to the institute.

Women are almost four times as likely as males to be shown in sexy attire on television and movies, according to the Geena Davis Institute. Maybe that's because only 7 percent of directors, 13 percent of writers and 20 percent of producers are women.

Here's what this all adds up to: There is simply no equality when it comes to the portrayal of women in the media—whether it's on the news pages, in advertisements, on the airwaves or on the Big Screen. We need to think about what the underrepresentation of women and stereotyping means to the society that relies on the media.

The editors and reporters of august publications like the *Journal* need to remember the power of their pages when they're planning stories, writing headlines and mocking up ads.

And we all need to work to advance equality in the workplace—including on the movie sets of Hollywood, and in the newsrooms of America's publications and the studios of our television stations.

Only when we have more women making decisions in the media can we expect the media to be more reflective of the population as a whole.

YouTube's Most-Viewed Videos

Where the Girls Aren't

By Mary Tucker-McLaughlin
Women & Language, Spring 2013

This media report examines the results of a journey into user-generated content on You-Tube from the perspective of gender representation. The findings point to two areas of concern expressed both in mass communication and feminist scholarship: (1) the lack of representation of women as generators and agents of technology, and (2) the representation of women in misogynistic ways within user-generated content.

Mass communication and feminist studies scholars have often blamed traditional media for the misrepresentation and underrepresentation of women (Kohrs, 1998; Larson, 2001; Lawless, 2009; Parry-Giles, 2000; Rhode, 1995; Simpson, 2000; Tuchman, 1979; Tucker-McLaughlin & Campbell, 2012). Yet as technology advances—granting users the ability to generate their own media content—there are parallels that can be drawn between this user-generated content and the "symbolic annihilation" of women as pointed out by mass communication scholars in traditional media (e.g., Tuchman, 1979). In my 2010 study of YouTube's most-viewed videos, what was most striking was the lack of female participation. As I looked at the most-viewed videos in terms of the content and who was generating and posting them, I wondered, "Where are the girls?"

In order to address such representative discrepancies, women will need to embrace and use technology to give themselves voice, improve their lives economically, and provide an alternate dialogue in multimedia and social media platforms.

YouTube as a Form of Self-Expression

From its emergence in April 2005 with a 19-second video of one of its founders standing in front of the elephant exhibit at a zoo talking about the elephant's long trunks (Costello, 2009), YouTube is now used in multiple ways including posting videos, viewing videos, commenting on videos, video journaling or vlogging, and promotion (Lange, 2007). It is one of the most visited Internet sites in the world, with over 800 million unique visitors watching four billion hours of video each month (YouTube.com, 2012). Five hundred years of video are watched each day on Facebook alone, with over one million advertisers using the Google advertising platform to reach the YouTube audience (YouTube.com, 2012).

From *Women & Language* 36.1 (Spring 2013): 43–49. Copyright © 2013 by Organization for the Study of Communication, Language & Gender. Reprinted with permission. All rights reserved.

For some users, YouTube may function primarily as a simple source of video entertainment, but for others, it is an outlet of self-expression and a means of establishing an identity through the creation and sharing of video (Lange, 2007). Patricia Lange categorizes video sharing habits in two ways. Some users practice "publicly private" video sharing in which they reveal their identities but share only with whom they wish by limiting access to the videos. The second category of video sharing—"privately public"—involves the unlimited sharing of video but with little information regarding the creator's identity. The majority of the videos analyzed in this study can be defined by the second category, "privately public," in which creators are willing to provide their video content to anyone who will watch. I also found that an additional category—"publicly public"—revealed itself in this study where the creators provided disturbing content openly, while revealing their faces, names, and the identities of others in the video.

Assessing YouTube Video Content

In this study, the lack of female representation found in YouTube's most-viewed videos section merits discussion as part of a larger picture of how women are engaging in our technological society. This particular set of videos was collected every day over a two-week period from October 12, 2010, through October 25, 2010. A total of 67 videos were analyzed.

YouTube's most-viewed video section is located on YouTube's home page. Little has been written about the inner-workings of YouTube; however, social media blogger Mark Claser (2010) published a blog stating that YouTube is responsible for choosing the videos that appear in the most-viewed section and that the video posters do not pay for this privilege, nor do they meet with YouTube staffers to promote their videos. The choice of the most-viewed videos seems to rely on a combination of how topical the video appears to be, and an algorithm that calculates the number of views videos receive.

Because it is impossible to assess whether males or females viewed the videos, I instead analyzed the videos based on the content of the video and the gender of the primary actor in the video. The primary actor often disclosed that he or she had made and posted the video to the site or there were nuances in the video (audio or verbal discourse) that supported the assumption that the video poster was either male or female. Prominent themes in the videos included escapism, male entertainment at the expense of others with misogynistic discourse and violence, and information gathering. I used a set of several criteria in determining where the videos fell on the gender spectrum. All videos that had a man as a primary actor were characterized as representing male gender representation. Videos that featured a primary female actor were characterized as female videos. Gender neutral videos contained no human actors.

Escapism

The most prevalent theme in the videos was escapism. Fifty-five percent of the YouTube videos viewed had an escapism theme, representing favorite pastimes including sports, music, and non-offensive comedy. Gender representation in these videos was neither misogynistic nor violent. However, there was a distinct *lack* of female representation for both actors in the videos and user-generators of the videos: of the 35 videos categorized as escapism, 65 percent contained mostly male gender representation with a male primary actor and male nuances. Only one of the sports videos contained a female athlete as the primary actor. The video text was in a foreign language, making it indiscernible; however, the footage focused on the female player's apparent trip to the restroom during a tennis match (Pausoon, 2010). A female music video produced by teen rocker Willow Smith, "Whip my Hair," had over one million views in 2010 at the time of the analysis and 11 months later had garnered over 61 million views (Smith, 2010). Three of the videos concerned hair and make-up (Chic, 2010; HouseofGlam, 2010; Makeupgeek, 2010); in two of these videos the primary actors were female (HouseofGlam, 2010; Makeupgeek, 2010). Other videos in this category were considered neutral.

Male Entertainment at the Expense of Others: Misogynistic Discourse and Violence

Nearly 25 percent of the 67 videos analyzed had representations of misogynistic discourse, violence, or both. These videos all had one thing in common: the primary actor or actors were male. Statements in some of the videos were so offensive as to afford the label of obscene.[1] Three of the videos referred to the molestation of a female child, while others used offensive language referring to female genitalia, referring to women and girls as bitches, and sexualizing and objectifying women and girls.

All of the videos posted by two vloggers who regularly post on YouTube, Shane Dawson and Three Equal, contained both obscene material and large amounts of profanity (Dawson, 2010b; Equal, 2010). The Three Equal video "Go Supreme" had over seven million views 11 months after it had premiered on YouTube's most-viewed video section. The "Go Supreme" video used misogynistic language to reference Japanese actors calling them, ". . . hot lesbians who look hot but have no acting skills." When talking about actress Miley Cyrus, the host said, "B—ch, extinguish your crotch and go back to Disney Channel" (Equal, 2010). In another reference in the video, the host says, "[I]t seems like they're saying supreme vagina" (Equal, 2010).

All of vlogger Shane Dawson's videos made obscene sexual references. Two videos that were particularly offensive involved a puppet named "Milly." The videos , called "Ask Milly" and "The Perverted Puppet," both feature Milly, who is supposed to be an 8-year-old girl. Milly talks with the host about how she is molested by her parents, makes slang sexual references about her genitalia, and talks about how actress Miley Cyrus had sex with a stuffed animal (Dawson, 2010a, 2010b). She then tells the host, "I hope that I grow up to be a whore" (Dawson, 2010a). Both videos had over 100,000 views at the time they were downloaded and 11 months later were approaching 1 million views each. As of December 2012, Dawson had nearly one million four hundred thousand subscribers.[2]

One of the most common vlogs, Failblog, contained mild violence and was characterized by entertainment at the expense of others. The primary actors in these videos were all male with the exception of one video, where an older woman is the victim of a man who trips her in the turnstile of a subway (Failblog, 2010). The apparent point of these videos is to catch some misfortune of another person where they are embarrassed and mildly injured.

Information Gathering

Approximately 14 percent of videos (nine) were gathered from news sites or were news related. Of these nine, two of the videos addressed the issue of gay teen bullying (Burns, 2010; House, 2010). Although the videos did not distinguish between male and female gay teens, both primary actors in the video were male, and the anecdotal references concerned the bullying of male gay teens. One of the information gathering videos was a taped radio debate between Senator Christine O'Donnell and her opponent. Although O'Donnell is a primary actor in the video, the representation of her is negative. Her opponent laughs at her several times when she asks, "Where is the separation of church and state in the Constitution?" (FameAppeal, 2010).

Absent Voices

Gender identity may play a role in the early, late, or never adoption of technology (Demiray, 2010), and there is some concrete evidence that women are not participating in technology at the same rate as men. In 2009, the National Center for Women in Technology (NCWIT) reported that only 25 percent of information technology (IT) positions were held by women (NCWIT, 2008). Of these 25 percent, only 2 percent were African American, revealing an entire segment of women who are not playing a role in technology (NCWIT). By 2018, there will be over 1.4 million computer science positions available, and technology will play a critical role in almost every sector of the U.S. economy. Without intervention through exposure to technology at early ages and encouragement to explore technological careers, women will be left out of these critical roles. According to NCWIT, "Because so few women are inventing the technology upon which our society increasingly depends, we cannot know what problems they would solve or what products they would conceive" (p. 3).

Both feminist and career-oriented scholarship support the premise that women are not sharing equally with men in the technological revolution (Demiray, 2010; Molyneaux, O'Donnell, Gibson, & Singer, 2008; NCWIT, 2008; Thornham & McFarlane, 2011). This technological divide illustrates a "virtual" domestic versus public (Rosaldo, 1980). According to Demiray (2010), women still are not the builders and designers of technology. Thornham and McFarlane (2011) found in interviews with women that women and teenagers across generations "are actively excluding themselves from (technological) activities using gendered discourses of sociability and incompetence" (p. 68).

In this way, Judith Butler's (1988) description of gender performance may now transcend into the technological world. Research has shown that women's uses of technologies are primarily passive and consumptive (Demiray, 2010). This precept may help to explain why user-generated content appears, in this investigation, to be primarily male in orientation. Only five of the videos found in the most-viewed section during the duration of the study had primarily female actors, with gender representations of a female nature (HouseofGlam, 2010; Makeupgeek, 2010; Pausoon, 2010; Smith, 2010; Sugarland, 2010). These videos fell into two specific categories including personal appearance (i.e., hair or make-up tips) or commercial music videos. While the personal appearance tips videos appeared to have been created by the women who functioned as their primary actors, the music videos were commercially produced. This begs the question again, "Where are the girls?"

A Canadian study of vlogs in 2008 showed men exceeded women in vlog viewing by 25 percent, and none of the women surveyed in the study had ever posted a video to YouTube (Molyneaux, O'Donnell, Gibson, & Singer, 2008). The lack of female posters as compared to male posters may help to explain the proliferation of male-oriented videos in this study. The performance of gender in society clearly has implications for women's ability to succeed, and technology awareness should begin at an early age when girls are introduced to computers, computer games, and even social media like YouTube (Bray, 2007; Demiray, 2010).

My brief journey into YouTube's most-viewed videos provoked questions of both women's exposure to misogynistic content and their seeming lack of interest in generating video themselves. For example, what are the potential effects of young women viewing most-viewed videos that underrepresent women or contain misogynistic material? Only five of the 67 videos analyzed in this study contained women as primary actors, which speaks loudly of underrepresentation. Of the male-generated videos, nearly 25 percent of the 67 videos contained violence, misogyny, obscenity, or a combination of the three.

As male-generated content continues to dominate the realms of media platforms such as YouTube, alternative voices need to enter into the exchange. Without a robust and equitable dialogue in these spaces, the imbalance of power in communication spaces like YouTube's most-viewed videos section will continue to misrepresent women. Women need to challenge the existing voices in this technological conversation and enter this realm as equals. It is critical that we continue to explore the reasons why women are being marginalized in all realms of technology including education, careers, and social media, and keep asking ourselves, "Where are the girls?"

Notes

1. The nature of the Internet allows free speech to the extreme. YouTube vloggers are free to use offensive language and refer to otherwise unspeakable acts without fear of censorship. Obscenity is not protected by the First Amendment of the Constitution and is defined by the Supreme Court in a three-pronged test:

    • An average person, applying contemporary community standards, must find that the material, as a whole, appeals to the prurient interest;

- The material must depict or describe, in a patently offensive way, sexual conduct specifically defined by applicable law; and

- The material, taken as a whole, must lack serious literary, artistic, political, or scientific value. (Federal Communications Commission, 2011)

The Federal Communications Commission utilizes the above Supreme Court definition in determining what can and cannot be broadcast on radio and television, but does not regulate the Internet. In analyzing the videos, this three-pronged Supreme Court test was used to identify obscene materials in the videos.

2. Although YouTube may appear on the surface as a form of leisure, it is also a money-making enterprise representing millions of dollars. A survey of top grossing YouTube creators in 2010 reflects a deep technological divide between genders. Shane Dawson, whose videos in this study reflected the most misogyny and violence towards women, is reported to have made over $315,000 in advertising revenues from his videos (O'Neill, 2010). Of the top ten highest earners, nine were male, with the tenth being Vietnamese-Australian Natalie Tran who made $101,000 (O'Neill, 2010).

Bibliography

Bray, F. (2007). Gender and technology. *Annual Review of Anthropology*, 36(1), 37-53. doi:10.1146/annurev.anthro.36.081406.094328

Burns, J. (Writer). (2010). Gay teens: It gets better [Internet]. USA: YouTube.

Butler, J. (1988). Performative acts and gender constitution: An essay in phenomenology and feminist theory. *Theatre Journal*, 40(4), 519-531.

Chic, H. (Writer). (2010). Hippy chic [Internet]. USA: YouTube.

Costello, J. (2009, October 17). Why we're all going down the tube. *Irish Independent*, p. 1.

Dawson, S. (Writer). (2010a). Ask Milly [Internet]. USA: Youtube.

Dawson, S. (Writer). (2010b). The perverted puppet [Internet]. In S. Dawson (Producer). USA: YouTube.

Demiray, E. (2010). Information technologies and women. *Distance Learning*, 7(1), 1-15.

Equal, T. (Writer). (2010). Go supreme [Internet]. USA: YouTube.

Failblog (Writer). (2010). Wrong way [Internet]. USA: YouTube.

FameAppeal (Writer). (2010). Christine O'Donnell on the constitution [Internet]. USA: YouTube.

Federal Communications Commission. (2011). Obscenity, indecency and profanity. Retrieved from http://www.fcc.gov/guides/obscenity-indecency-and-profanity

Glaser, M. (2010). YouTube explains the mystery of home page picks. *MediaShift*, 9. Retrieved from http://www.pbs.org/mediashift/2006/12/youtube-explains-the-mystery-of-home-page-picks347

House, T. W. (Writer). (2010). President Obama: It gets better [Internet]. USA: YouTube.

HouseofGlam (Writer). (2010). Electric zoo [Internet]. USA: YouTube.

Kohrs, C. K. (1998). The discursive performance of femininity: Hating Hillary. *Rhetoric & Public Affairs*, 7(1), 1-19.

Lange, P. C. (2007). Publicly private and privately public: Social networking on YouTube. *Journal of Computer-Mediated Communication*, 13(1), 361-380.

Larson, S. C. (2001). American women and politics in the media: A review essay. *Political Science and Politics*, 34(2), 3.

Lawless, J. (2009). Sexism and gender bias in election 2008: A more complex path for women in politics. *Politics & Gender*, 5(1), 70-81.

Makeupgeek (Writer). (2010). Angelina Jolie makeup [Internet]. USA: YouTube.

Molyneaux, H., O'Donnell, S., Cibson, K., & Singer, J. (2008). Exploring the gender divide on YouTube: An analysis of the creation and reception of vlogs. *American Journal of Communication*, 10(2), 14.

NCWIT. (2008). Evaluating promising practices in informal information technology education for girls (No. 2013). Boulder, CO.

O'Neill, M. (2010). How much money do the top grossing YouTube stars make? Retrieved from http://socialtimes.com/money-youtube-partners_b21335

Parry-Ciles, S. J. (2000). Mediating Hillary Rodham Clinton: Television news practices and image making in the post-modern age. *Critical Studies in Mass Communication*, J7(2),21.

Pausoon (Writer). (2010). Ana Ivanovic Zahovava tennis match [Internet]. USA: YouTube.

Rhode, D. L. (1995). Media images, feminist issues. *Signs*, 20(3), 685-710.

Rosaldo, M. Z. (1980). The use and abuse of anthropology: Reflections on feminism and cross-cultural understanding. *Signs*, 5(3), 389-41.

Simpson, P. A. (2000). Covering the women's movement. *Nieman Reports*, 53/54(4/1), 6.

Smith, W. (Writer). (2010). Whip my hair [Internet]. USA: YouTube.

Sugarland (Writer). (2010). Stuck like glue [Internet]. USA: YouTube.

Thornham, H., & McFarlane, A. (2011). Cross-generational gender constructions. Women, teenagers and technology. *The Sociological Review*, 59(1), 64-85. doi:10.1111/j.l467-954X.2010.01992.x

Tuchman, C. (1979). Women's depiction by the mass media. Signs, 4(3), 528-542.

Tucker-McLaughlin, M. & Campbell, K. (2012). A grounded theory analysis: Hillary Clinton represented as voiceless and innovator in TV news. *Electronic News*, 6(1), 3-16.

YouTube.com. (2012). *Statistics*. Retrieved from http://www.youtube.com/t/press_statistics

Sex Sells Sex, Not Women's Sports

So What Does Sell Women's Sports?

By Mary Jo Kane
The Nation, August 15, 2011

"The newest kid on the women's sports block is finding that the old formula for atten-tion-getting is as robust as ever. 'Sex sells,' says Atlanta Beat defender Nancy Augustyn-iak, who was astonished to learn she finished third in a Playboy.com poll of the sexiest female soccer players."—Wendy Parker, Atlanta Journal-Constitution

Last winter, champion alpine skier Lindsey Vonn won the downhill gold medal at the Vancouver Winter Olympics, the first American woman to achieve gold in this prestigious event. From 2008 to 2010, Vonn also won three consecutive World Cup championships, the first US woman and second woman ever to accomplish such a feat. For her unprecedented achievements, Vonn was named Sportswoman of the Year by the US Olympic Committee.

Even *Sports Illustrated*—notorious for its lack of coverage of women's sports—couldn't ignore this historic moment and devoted its cover to Vonn. *SI*'s cover, how-ever, blatantly portrayed Vonn as a sex object and spoke volumes about the rampant sexual depictions of women athletes. Rather than emphasize her singular athletic talent, the magazine depicted Vonn in a posed photograph, smiling at the camera in her ski regalia. What was most noticeable—and controversial—about the pose was its phallic nature: Vonn's backside was arched at a forty-five-degree angle while superimposed over a mountain peak.

Offensive as this portrayal may have been, it came as no surprise to sports-media scholars. Over the past three decades we have amassed a large body of empirical evidence demonstrating that sportswomen are significantly more likely to be por-trayed in ways that emphasize their femininity and heterosexuality rather than their athletic prowess. Study after study has revealed that newspaper and TV coverage around the globe routinely and systematically focuses on the athletic exploits of male athletes while offering hypersexualized images of their female counterparts.

These findings are no trivial matter. Scholars have long argued that a major con-sequence of the media's tendency to sexualize women's athletic accomplishments is the reinforcement of their status as second-class citizens in one of the most pow-erful economic, social and political institutions on the planet. In doing so, media images that emphasize femininity/sexuality actually suppress interest in, not to mention respect for, women's sports.

Many of those charged with covering and promoting women's sports take an entirely different view. As the quote beginning this article makes clear, the "sex sells" strategy remains deeply embedded among sports journalists and marketers, who also believe that reaffirming traditional notions of femininity and heterosexuality is a critical sales strategy. This approach, or so the argument goes, reassures (especially male) fans, corporate sponsors and TV audiences that females can engage in highly competitive sports while retaining a nonthreatening femininity.

The widely held assumption that sexualizing female athletes is the most effective way to promote women's sports creates cognitive dissonance. To begin with, marketing campaigns for leagues like the WNBA also emphasize the wholesome nature of women's sports, highlighting the connection between fathers and daughters. The underlying message is that women's sports embrace traditional "family values" and that their appeal cuts across generational lines. Given this message, a "sex sells" strategy is counterproductive. How many fathers would accept the notion that support for their daughters' sports participation would be increased by having them pose nude in *Playboy*? And should we buy the argument that what generates fan interest is how pretty athletes are versus how well they perform when a championship is on the line?

I don't disagree that when *SI* publishes its swimsuit issue males are quite interested in buying that particular issue of the magazine. It does not automatically follow, however, that their interest in women's sports has increased. On the contrary, I would argue that what males are interested in consuming is not a women's athletic event but sportswomen's bodies as objects of sexual desire.

To investigate empirically whether sex truly sells women's sports, I conducted a series of focus groups based on gender and age (18–34; 35–55) with a colleague at the University of Minnesota. Study participants were shown photographs of female athletes ranging from on-court athletic competence to wholesome "girls next door" to soft pornography and asked to indicate which images increased their interest in reading about, watching on TV and attending a women's sporting event.

Our findings revealed that in the vast majority of cases, a "sex sells" approach offended the core fan base of women's sports—women and older men. These two groups rated the image that portrayed athletic prowess as the one most likely to influence their interest in women's sports. Said one younger female: "This image [of a WNBA player driving toward the basket] really sucked me in. I want to be there. I want to be part of that feeling." In contrast, younger and older females, as well as older males, were offended by the hypersexualized images. One older male said: "If she [Serena Williams in a sexually provocative pose] were my sister I'd come in, slap the photographer, grab her and leave." Even when younger males, a prime target audience, indicated that sexually provocative images were "hot," they also stated that such images did not fundamentally increase their interest in women's sports, particularly when it came to attending a sporting event. The key takeaway? Sex sells sex, not women's sports.

So what *does* sell women's sports? The answer lies with women's college basketball and the coverage it receives on ESPN. Each year during the NCAA's March Madness tournament, women's hoops garner record attendance and TV ratings. Coverage of the women's Final Four bears a remarkable resemblance to that of the men's—a focus on great traditions, conference rivalries (Duke versus North Carolina), legendary coaches (Pat Summitt vs. Geno Auriemma)—and, most important, showcasing sportswomen as physically gifted, mentally tough, grace-under-pressure athletes.

Millions of fans around the globe just witnessed such media images and narratives during coverage of the Women's World Cup in Germany. Perhaps such coverage will start a trend whereby those who cover women's sports will simply turn on the camera and let us see the reality—not the sexualized caricature—of today's female athletes. If and when that happens, sportswomen will receive the respect and admiration they so richly deserve.

Women Still Have Long Way to Go in Sports Journalism

By Scarlett McCourt
The Daily Wildcat, November 19, 2013

One of my favorite people in the world is Robin Roberts.

In the 1990s, when men dominated sports journalism, Roberts made her way in and shattered the glass ceiling. A black woman, Roberts came to ESPN as an anchor on "SportsCenter" and won the respect of her colleagues and viewers. And she did so with poise and elegance.

Fast forward to today.

Erin Andrews. Pam Oliver. Rachel Nichols. Sam Ponder. Women are all over the sports broadcast scene. They're on the sidelines, they're anchors, they're doing in-depth investigative pieces.

But the truth is, there is a long way to go until women are truly accepted in the sports journalism world.

The women I just mentioned? They're all in sports broadcast. They're on camera as the pretty face of sports. Erin Andrews was even voted America's Sexiest Sportscaster by *Playboy Magazine* in 2008 and 2009.

Thanks for acknowledging her journalistic talents.

People tell me I have the face for broadcast. I have the personality for broadcast. But what if I don't want to do broadcast?

What if I want to sit in the press box and write stories on deadline? What if I enjoy writing columns and features and having a byline in the paper? Is that just for men?

According to a 2012 study from The Institute for Diversity and Ethics in Sport, at 150 newspapers and websites around the country, 90.4 percent of sports editors were men and 88.3 percent of sports reporters were men.

I have often found myself one of the few, if not the only, women at practices, at press conferences and in the press box.

In other markets, it's different. There might be handfuls of women covering sporting events. But there's no question: Women are the minority.

Look, I can hang with the boys, not a problem. But really, it's 2013. Where are the women sports writers?

I'm not asking anyone to acknowledge the fact that I'm one of the only women around. I want to blend in—I want everyone to look at each other as equals. And I'm lucky that I've been treated with respect by my male colleagues.

But it's obvious that there are some differences between myself and my male counterparts.

Student chapter coordinator for the Association for Women in Sports Media Gina Mizell, who is also the Oklahoma State football beat writer for *The Oklahoman*, said that in response to her pre-game story for the Oklahoma State/Texas game, a Texas fan wrote her an email that closed by calling her "sweetie."

"Seriously, really, we're going to go there?" Mizell said.

That Texas fan wouldn't have called a male writer "sweetie," would he?

Although that might not be hugely offensive, it's telling of the ways men are treated differently than women in the business.

A man wouldn't be accused of flirting to get a story, nor would he be ogled by athletes as he walks off the practice field.

The problem is that if a female reporter makes a mistake, her gender becomes a target of scrutiny.

Recently, an editor of mine wrote a blog that sparked a lot of outrage.

It was football trash talk, not her most well-written piece, and maybe it was an error in judgment. But the backlash against the piece has been relentless, and quite frankly, repulsive.

The comments and the tweets derailed from football itself—they became personal attacks.

People attacked her gender with comments that were both disgusting and degrading in nature.

"Get back in the kitchen," they said. "Become a housewife."

"Assume the position. #KNEES," they said. "Suck my d—k." And of course, the classic: "Women and sports don't mix."

Sure, sports fans are passionate. Columnists, male or female, open themselves up to vitriol whenever they express an unpopular opinion. But the insults thrown at a male writer are different than those female writers have to face.

"You'll deal with heat no matter if you're a man or a woman; I just think it's a different type of heat," Mizell said. "It goes from stuff like, 'You're an idiot' to 'Get back in the kitchen,' or stuff about your appearance that I don't think my male counterparts necessarily have to deal with."

It's 2013. Haven't we gotten past the stereotype that women belong in the kitchen? Haven't we accepted that women can, indeed, talk about sports? Haven't we gotten past the fact that women are equal to men in this country and shouldn't be treated differently in the workplace?

It might not be the 1990s, but we sure have a long way to go.

Girls Talk

What Lena Dunham's Smart HBO Series Says about 21st-Century Womanhood

By Katelyn Beaty
Christianity Today, April 13, 2013

There's a spate of new television shows with the word *girl* in the title—even though the girls in view are all decidedly over age 21. There's *New Girl*, the Fox comedy where doe-eyed Zooey Deschanel plays a klutzy teacher living with three guys, a *Three's Company* for the 21st century. There's the Bravo reality show *Gallery Girls*, a vapid and catty look at seven young women clamoring their way into the art scene of New York City. And *2 Broke Girls* is like the all-female counterpart to *Two and a Half Men*—a raunchy half-hour comedy about men ogling women's breasts, but see, it's written by women instead of men. Ah, the sweet liberation we've waited for.

Though they differ in tone, these new shows share a common thread: They focus on unmarried women (or *girls*, if we must) in their 20s and 30s trying to land a career, and a meaningful way to live, in a time of tricky economic realities for many young Americans, and of choices previously unknown for women. That is also the theme of the smartest and most divisive show of them all, the 2012 HBO series *Girls*.

Written and directed by 26-year-old Lena Dunham (with help from executive producer Judd Apatow), *Girls* follows the postcollege travails of Hannah Horvath (also played by Dunham), an aspiring writer culling material for her forthcoming memoir, four chapters of which are written—"the rest I kind of have to live," she tells her concerned parents in the pilot episode. Guided by a mantra of feeling and experiencing everything she can, she's busy "trying to become who I am"—either obnoxiously self-centered or simply too introspective for her own good, depending on whom you ask.

Hannah, her three girlfriends, and their boyfriends and lovers live in Greenpoint, Brooklyn, a place where NYU grads can open a business that will take your normal-sized ties and turn them into skinny ones (this is true), and where the population of young, wealthy 30-year-olds has doubled since 2000. It's a place of well-camouflaged privilege: Hannah and company lack secure jobs, hopping from unpaid internship to barista gig. Yet somehow they pay the rent, party, and wear stylish if awkward ensembles, trendy in a disheveled way—which neatly sums up Hannah's whole way of life.

Girls is a fitting title, then, because it portrays four women teetering on the verge of adulthood, not knowing which way they will or should fall. The coming-of-age story is an old faithful, and *Girls* follows in this sturdy tradition. What's new about the show is that these women, like many real-life ones, are working from a rough script. The lines that signal "womanhood" are absent, coming later or not at all, or look quite different from the lines our mothers followed.

Girls is Dunham's attempt to offer a new script, one that diverges from the chick-lit comedies her generation grew up on. As she told NPR host Terry Gross in 2012, "I don't see any of myself in [chick flicks and chick lit]—none of my actions have ever been [determined] by the search for a husband, or wondering if I was going to have a family someday, or wanting to live in a really great house, or thinking it would be really great to have a diamond .... [T]here's a kind of female character that doesn't make sense to me."

So, what does this new script for womanhood look like? And is it worth taking to the stage?

A Tall Order

One thing is for sure: The new script includes a lot of sex and graphic talk of sex, both as commonplace in the characters' universe as the weather or dinner. Herpes, abortion, sexting, and the fear of virginity all appear within the first few episodes, and Hannah is frequently naked, whether in bed or walking around her apartment. But this is not the perfectly toned bod of *Sex in the City*'s Carrie Bradshaw or that show's glamorous Manhattan sexcapades. Rather, the sex scenes in *Girls* are uncomfortable, for both the female characters and the viewer—a disturbing look at relationships in a pornified culture, where many young men take their sexual cues from fantasy and have never learned how to date a real woman.

For all her nakedness and crass talk, Hannah is at heart traditional in one sense: She wants a boyfriend. And she's willing to subject herself to the weird and degrading sexual preferences of Adam, her simian kind-of boyfriend in season one, in hopes that the hookups will turn Adam into a monogamous partner. Her "breakup" speech to him is telling: "I just want someone who wants to hang out all the time, and thinks I am the best person in the world, and wants to have sex with only me." In the world of *Girls*, this is a tall order to fill.

It's apparently a tall order to fill in the world of Lena Dunham, too. Speaking with *New York Times* columnist Frank Bruni last year, the daughter of acclaimed NYC artists bemoaned the "empowered" sexual expectations placed upon her female peers: "I heard so many of my friends saying, 'Why can't I have sex and feel nothing?' It was amazing: that this was the new goal."

"It's painful when sex, which is supposed to be the most intimate form of communication, is the least intimate form of communication," she told Gross. In the middle of season two, Hannah spends two days with a 42-year-old doctor in his lovely brownstone, tasting the comforts of monogamy and economic security. At the end of their time together, Hannah makes an astonishing admission, almost despite herself: "What I didn't realize is that I was lonely in such a deep, deep way. I want what everyone wants, to be happy."

This is a crucial turn in the series, and a crucial admission for the church to hear from an influential voice in our culture. For all the vast economic and cultural changes that have rewritten the script of womanhood, there is one truth we can't shake: We are made for relationship. In fact, we cannot fully exist without relationship. We discover our truest selves only in connection to others, in the bonds of friendship, family, marriage, and civic and faith communities. Hannah struggles to "become who I am" in part because so many of her relationships are broken: By the middle of season two, she has dumped Adam, has driven two close friends to move out of their apartment, and is reduced to trying to make out with the former crack addict who lives in the apartment below hers. She is lonely by her own making, but lonely nonetheless.

Hannah is decidedly not the archetype for every young American woman. (Dunham winks at this in the pilot episode with this line: "Mom and Dad, I don't want to freak you out, but I think that I may be the voice of my generation. Or at least *a* voice … of *a* generation.") But she is one significant archetype, and with two Golden Globes under her belt and a third season coming, her voice will become more pronounced and influential. Are our churches places where women like Dunham can know and be known? Where their ambitions and dreams are encouraged, not squelched or made to fit into old scripts of womanhood that don't speak to them? Where a story is told and retold that speaks to their deepest desires and orients them toward wholeness and self-giving instead of self-gazing?

Since *Girls* majors in embarrassing revelations, here's one: I secretly hope to meet Lena Dunham some day. For all the ways we are worlds apart, we are nonetheless both single, white women in our 20s who like to write and make others laugh. At some point in the conversation, I imagine, the whole Jesus thing would come up, and I could tell of the ways he and his people have kept me deeply rooted in an uncertain decade. But then I would thank her for shaking things up, for creating a show that captures how confusing it can be to be girls in this postfeminist generation—or at least to be *a* girl, in *a* generation.

Difficult Women

How "Sex and the City" Lost Its Good Name

By Emily Nussbaum
The New Yorker, July 29, 2013

When people talk about the rise of great TV, they inevitably credit one show, "The Sopranos." Even before James Gandolfini's death, the HBO drama's mystique was secure: novelistic and cinematic, David Chase's auteurist masterpiece cracked open the gangster genre like a rib cage, releasing the latent ambition of television, and launching us all into a golden age.

"The Sopranos" deserves the hype. Yet there's something screwy about the way that the show and its cable-drama blood brothers have come to dominate the conversation, elbowing other forms of greatness out of the frame. It's a bias that bubbles up early in Brett Martin's otherwise excellent new book, *Difficult Men: Behind the Scenes of a Creative Revolution: From "The Sopranos" and "The Wire" to "Mad Men" and "Breaking Bad,"* a deeply reported and dishy account of just how your prestige-cable sausage is made. I tore through the book, yet when I reached Martin's chronicle of the rise of HBO I felt a jolt. "It might as well have been a tourism campaign for a post-Rudolph Giuliani, de-ethnicized Gotham awash in money," Martin writes of one of my favorite shows. "Its characters were types as familiar as those in 'The Golden Girls': the Slut, the Prude, the Career Woman, the Heroine. But they talked more explicitly, certainly about their bodies, but also about their desires and discontents outside the bedroom, than women on TV ever had before."

Martin gives "Sex and the City" credit for jump-starting HBO, but the condescension is palpable, and the grudging praise is reserved for only one aspect of the series—the rawness of its subject matter. Martin hardly invented this attitude: he is simply reiterating what has become the reflexive consensus on the show, right down to the hackneyed "Golden Girls" gag. Even as "The Sopranos" has ascended to TV's Mt. Olympus, the reputation of "Sex and the City" has shrunk and faded, like some tragic dry-clean-only dress tossed into a decade-long hot cycle. By the show's fifteen-year anniversary, this year [2013], we fans had trained ourselves to downgrade the show to a "guilty pleasure," to mock its puns, to get into self-flagellating conversations about those blinkered and blinged-out movies. Whenever a new chick-centric series débuts, there are invidious comparisons: don't worry, it's no "Sex and the City," they say. As if that were a good thing.

But "Sex and the City," too, was once one of HBO's flagship shows. It was the peer of "The Sopranos," albeit in a different tone and in a different milieu, deconstructing a different genre. Mob shows, cop shows, cowboy shows—those are formulas with gravitas. "Sex and the City," in contrast, was pigeonholed as a sitcom. In fact, it was a bold riff on the romantic comedy: the show wrestled with the limits of that pink-tinted genre for almost its entire run. In the end, it gave in. Yet until that last-minute stumble it was sharp, iconoclastic television. High-feminine instead of fetishistically masculine, glittery rather than gritty, and daring in its conception of character, "Sex and the City" was a brilliant and, in certain ways, radical show. It also originated the unacknowledged first female anti-hero on television: ladies and gentlemen, Carrie Bradshaw.

Please, people, I can hear your objections from here. But first think back. Before "Sex and the City," the vast majority of iconic "single girl" characters on television, from "That Girl" to Mary Tyler Moore and Molly Dodd, had been you-go-girl types—which is to say, actual role models. (Ally McBeal was a notable and problematic exception.) They were pioneers who offered many single women the representation they craved, and they were also, crucially, adorable to men: vulnerable and plucky and warm. However varied the layers they displayed over time, they flattered a specific pathology: the cultural requirement that women greet other women with the refrain "Oh, me, too! Me, too!"

In contrast, Carrie and her friends—Miranda, Samantha, and Charlotte—were odder birds by far, jagged, aggressive, and sometimes frightening figures, like a makeup mirror lit up in neon. They were simultaneously real and abstract, emotionally complex and philosophically stylized. Women identified with them—"I'm a Carrie!"—but then became furious when they showed flaws. And, with the exception of Charlotte (Kristin Davis), men didn't find them likable: there were endless cruel jokes about Samantha (Kim Cattrall), Miranda (Cynthia Nixon), and Carrie as sluts, man-haters, or gold-diggers. To me, as a single woman, it felt like a definite sign of progress: since the elemental representation of single life at the time was the comic strip "Cathy" (*ack! chocolate!*), better that one's life should be viewed as glamorously threatening than as sad and lonely.

Carrie Bradshaw herself began as a mirror for another woman: she was the avatar of the New York *Observer* columnist Candace Bushnell, a steely "sexual anthropologist" on the prowl for blind items. When the initial showrunner, Darren Star, and his mostly female writing staff adapted Bushnell's columns, they transformed that icy Carrie, pouring her into the warm body of Sarah Jessica Parker. Out popped a chatterbox with a schnoz, whose advanced fashion sense was not intended to lure men into matrimony. For a half dozen episodes, Carrie was a happy, curious explorer, out companionably smoking with modellizers. If she'd stayed that way, the show might have been another "Mary Tyler Moore": a playful, empowering comedy about one woman's adventures in the big city.

Instead, Carrie fell under the thrall of Mr. Big, the sexy, emotionally withholding forty-three-year-old financier played by Chris Noth. From then on, pleasurable as "Sex and the City" remained, it also felt designed to push back at its audience's wish for identification, triggering as much anxiety as relief. It switched the romantic comedy's primal scene, from "Me, too!" to "Am I like *her*?" A man practically woven out of red flags, Big wasn't there to rescue Carrie; instead, his "great love" was a slow poisoning. She spun out, becoming anxious, obsessive, and, despite her charm, wildly self-centered—in her own words, "the frightening woman whose fear ate her sanity." Their relationship was viewed with concern by her friends, who were not, as Martin suggests, mere "types" but portrayals of a narrow slice of wealthy white thirty-something Manhattanites: the Waspy gallerina, the liberal-feminist lawyer, the decadent power publicist.

Although the show's first season is its slightest, it swiftly establishes a bold mixture of moods—fizzy and sour, blunt and arch—and shifts between satirical and sincere modes of storytelling. (It's not even especially dated: though the show has gained a reputation for over-the-top absurdity, I can tell you that these night clubs and fashion shows do exist—maybe even more so now that Manhattan has become a gated island for the wealthy.) There is already a melancholic undertow, full of foreshadowing. "What if he never calls and three weeks from now I pick up the *New York Times* and I read that he's married some perfect little woman who never passes gas under his five-hundred-dollar sheets?" Carrie frets in Episode 11. In a moment of clarity, she tells Miranda that, when she's around Big, "I'm not like me. I'm, like, Together Carrie. I wear little outfits: Sexy Carrie and Casual Carrie. Sometimes I catch myself actually *posing*. It's just—it's exhausting."

That was the conundrum Carrie faced for the entire series: true love turned her into a fake. The Season 1 neurotic Carrie didn't stick, though. She and Big fixed things, then they broke up again, harder. He moved to Paris. She met Aidan (John Corbett), the marrying type. In Season 3, the writers upped the ante, having Carrie do something overtly anti-heroic: she cheated on a decent man with a bad one (Big, of course), now married to that "perfect little woman," Natasha. They didn't paper over the repercussions: Natasha's humiliation and the way Carrie's betrayal hardened Aidan, even once he took her back. During six seasons, Carrie changed, as anyone might from thirty-two to thirty-eight, and not always in positive ways. She got more honest and more responsible; she became a saner girlfriend. But she also became scarred, prissier, strikingly gun-shy—and, finally, she panicked at the question of what it would mean to be an older single woman.

Her friends went through changes, too, often upon being confronted with their worst flaws—Charlotte's superficiality, Miranda's caustic tongue, Samantha's refusal to be vulnerable. In a departure from nearly all earlier half-hour comedies, the writers fully embraced the richness of serial storytelling. In a movie we go from glare to kiss in two hours. "Sex and the City" was liberated from closure, turning "once upon a time" into a wry mantra, treating its characters' struggles with a rare mixture of bluntness and compassion. It was one of the first television comedies to let its characters change in serious ways, several years before other half-hour comedies, like "The Office," went and stole all the credit.

So why is the show so often portrayed as a set of empty, static cartoons, an embarrassment to womankind? It's a classic misunderstanding, I think, stemming from an unexamined hierarchy: the assumption that anything stylized (or formulaic, or pleasurable, or funny, or feminine, or explicit about sex rather than about violence, or made collaboratively) must be inferior. Certainly, the show's formula was strict: usually four plots—two deep, two shallow—linked by Carrie's voice-over. The B plots generally involved one of the non-Carrie women getting laid; these slapstick sequences were crucial to the show's rude rhythms, interjecting energy and rupturing anything sentimental. (It's one reason those bowdlerized reruns on E! are such a crime: with the literal and figurative fucks edited out, the show *is* a rom-com.)

Most unusually, the characters themselves were symbolic. As I've written elsewhere—and argued, often drunkenly, at cocktail parties—the four friends operated as near-allegorical figures, pegged to contemporary debates about women's lives, mapped along three overlapping continuums. The first was emotional: Carrie and Charlotte were romantics; Miranda and Samantha were cynics. The second was ideological: Miranda and Carrie were second-wave feminists, who believed in egalitarianism; Charlotte and Samantha were third-wave feminists, focused on exploiting the power of femininity, from opposing angles. The third concerned sex itself. At first, Miranda and Charlotte were prudes, while Samantha and Carrie were libertines. Unsettlingly, as the show progressed, Carrie began to glide toward caution, away from freedom, out of fear.

Every conversation the friends had, at brunch or out shopping, amounted to a "Crossfire"-like debate. When Carrie sleeps with a dreamy French architect and he leaves a thousand dollars by her bed, she consults her friends. "Money is power. Sex is power," Samantha argues. "Therefore, getting money for sex is simply an exchange of power." "Don't listen to the dime-store Camille Paglia," Miranda shoots back. The most famous such conversation took place four episodes in, after Charlotte's boyfriend asked her to have anal sex. The friends pile into a cab for a raucous debate about whether her choice is about power-exchange (Miranda) or about finding a fun new hole (Samantha). "I'm not a hole!" Charlotte protests, and they hit a pothole. "What was that?" Charlotte asks. "A preview," Miranda and Samantha say in unison, and burst out laughing.

The show's basic value system aligns with Carrie: romantic, second-wave, libertine. But "Sex and the City" 's real strength was its willingness not to stack the deck: it let every side make a case, so that complexity carried the day. When Carrie and Aidan break up, they are both right. When Miranda and Carrie argue about her move to Paris, they are both right. The show's style could be brittle, but its substance was flexible, in a way that made the series feel peculiarly broad-ranging, covering so much ground, so fleetly, that it became easy to take it for granted.

Endings count in television, maybe too much. "The Sopranos" concluded with a black screen: it rejected easy satisfaction and pissed off its most devoted fans. (David Chase fled to the South of France.)

Three years earlier, in 2004, "Sex and the City" had other pressures to contend with: while a mob film ends in murder, we all know where a romantic comedy ends. I'll defend until my dying day the sixth-season plot in which Carrie seeks respite with a celebrity like her, the Russian artist Aleksandr (Mikhail Baryshnikov), a chilly genius she doesn't love but who offers her a dreamlike fairy tale, the one she has always longed for: Paris, safety, money, pleasure. It felt ugly, and sad, in a realistic way. In one of the season's, and the show's, best episodes, she saw other older women settling (Candice Bergen) or falling out of windows (the hilarious Kristen Johnston, who delivered one of "Sex and the City" 's best monologues: "When did everybody stop smoking? When did everybody pair off? . . . I'm so bored I could die"). The show always had a realpolitik directness about such social pressures; as another HBO series put it recently, winter was coming.

And then, in the final round, "Sex and the City" pulled its punches, and let Big rescue Carrie. It honored the wishes of its heroine, and at least half of the audience, and it gave us a very memorable dress, too. But it also showed a failure of nerve, an inability of the writers to imagine, or to trust themselves to portray, any other kind of ending—happy or not. And I can't help but wonder: What would the show look like without that finale? What if it were the story of a woman who lost herself in her thirties, who was changed by a poisonous, powerful love affair, and who emerged, finally, surrounded by her friends? Who would Carrie be then? It's an interesting question, one that shouldn't erase the show's powerful legacy. We'll just have to wait for another show to answer it.

On Overlooking Female Chefs and the *Time* "Gods of Food" Issue

By Kate Dries
Jezebel, November 12, 2013

There's nothing like a list to get people angry. That much was clear last week, when *Time* Magazine put together their "Gods of Food" issue and featured almost no women, inflaming food lovers the world over, as these inadequate breakdowns of "The Best" tend to do. So why do them at all?

In the US, the *Time* issue was controversial because of a cover that heavily implied New Jersey Governor Chris Christie was fat (Headline: "The Elephant in the Room."). Around the rest of the world, it featured three famous male chefs: David Chang of Momofuku, Alex Atala of D.O.M. and René Redzepi of Noma. As *Eater* extensively covered, inside the magazine wasn't much better: a tree of influencers in the food world included no women, a list of 13 "Gods of Food" had a few—though none of them were female chefs—and a small sidebar about pastry chefs featured two women.

Eater's Hillary Dixler interviewed editor Howard Chua-Eoan about how the issue came together and his responses about the issue were frustrating. He dismissed women Dixler suggested who could have been included by saying "they don't have that. . . ." (What? *Je ne sais quoi?*) while admitting that yes, there's a gender imbalance in the food world:

> Why are there no female chefs on the chef family tree?

Well I think it reflects one very harsh reality of the current chefs' world, which unfortunately has been true for years: it's still a boys club. There are of course very good and terrific female chefs: Carme Ruscalleda, Elena Arzak, April [Bloomfield] of course, Anita Lo of course, and of course Alice [Waters]. But it's very strange, the network of women, as Anita herself has been saying for so many years now, isn't as strong as the network of men. And when you look at this chart it's very clear. It's all men because men still take care of themselves. The women really need someone—if not men, themselves actually—to sort of take care of each other. The thing about the women I named, they are all spectacularly good chefs. But they also had to force their way to where they are now, they are almost their own creations. It's unfortunate, the women who are there are very good, but very few of them actually benefitted from the boys club, as you can see from the chart.

"At this point, rather than have someone on the list who other people will say 'fills a quota,' we did not want to fill a quota of a woman chef just because she's a woman, Chua-Eoan added, essentially admitting that their ranking system was based on old school ideas of success, and therefore ultimately flawed. "We wanted to go with reputation and influence."

The *New York Times* tried to explore the question of why female chefs get overlooked in their Room for Debate section, featuring short essays from male and female chefs in the industry. But none came up with anything other than what's commonly known, and what Chua-Eoan has already said here. Anita Lo of Annisa wrote, "'The Gods of Food' represents an old world point of view. Let's make it the last vestige. And let's use the conversation it started as an opportunity for change."

That's one argument for the continuation of these lists: that *their total* inadequacy sparks a conversation about what's missing and what should change in industries that have power imbalances (most industries). On one hand, editors know this, and sometimes purposefully shape lists so they'll be controversial and spark conversation, i.e., sales and clicks. On the other hand, some editors like Chua-Eoan do believe that they have only the responsibility to represent the "truth" of an industry and not diversify these lists for diversity's sake. As Chua-Eoan explained:

What role does the media play, if any, in the gender gap among famous chefs?

I think the media covers the industry. I don't think the media has to advocate for anything. Of course, if chefs advocate for things and make news about it, as Anita [Lo] has for years, talking about the gender divide among chefs, then I think it's worthwhile to cover them. But bring the subject up? I think we need someone to tell us, someone there who has an opinion that we can then reflect.

You don't think that the media has a role?

No, I think it does. Especially if the chefs talk about it, then we can cover it. If the female chefs talk about it, we'll cover it. But this story, this package is about influence. It's not about the social and gender roles in the world of haute cuisine. If there had been someone who had made a huge stir this year about how terrible it is, then perhaps. But even then we'd have to consider it against everyone else we want to include.

Here is an argument that it is not the media's job to change things. Which is one that's been made for television as well, or the movies; when criticism about the lack of diversity on *Girls* first came out, some argued that the show didn't need more black characters because it was unrealistic that the women on that show would be hanging out with people who weren't white. Here, Chua-Eoan argues the same thing: that it would have been a misrepresentation for *Time* to have included females based on the parameters of their issue and the realities of the food industry.

"Waiting to get on a list, working to get on a list—this is a time- and soul-suck with no good end," wrote Gabrielle Hamilton of Prune. Hamilton's opinion on how she lives her life fits right in with what we know about female behavior in many fields; that they keep their heads down, do good work and don't seek the praise that, in the culinary industry, for example, male chefs, many of whom are considered highly egotistical, do. We know this already, though apparently, we have to be reminded.

A Best XX list works in that it does what it's supposed to: it inflames the readers who would pay attentions to these issues in the first place and sometimes brings attention to people who deserve it. It doesn't often spark the minds of the casual readers of *Time*; they're much more likely to—however smart they are—walk away thinking subconsciously that there are no real female influencers in the food world. If we are to take *Time* at their word that it would have been disingenuous to include more women, then perhaps we should also be honest about the fact that the conversation after the fact has been lacking. No solutions have been put forward. No woman suddenly got drastically more due.

The best argument for continuing these lists actually comes from Chua-Eoan himself, when he said of the issue, "It's not about the social and gender roles in the world of haute cuisine. If there had been someone who had made a huge stir this year about how terrible it is, then perhaps." *Time* inadvertently made that stir themselves, proving how responsible the media is for shaping the narratives we read about what and who is important, made more meaningful by the fact that they seem to think they're outside it all. The lesson learned here isn't about the food industry, though we clearly need continual reminders about the injustices there. It's that even the information spreaders don't get what they're doing.

How Using Sexy Female Avatars in Video Games Changes Women

By Eliana Dockterman
Time, October 14, 2013

A new Stanford University study looks at the connection between hyper-sexualized gaming characters and the way female players view rape and their own bodies.

It's not "just a game."

The debate over whether we should worry about little boys playing violent video games never seems to die down. But maybe we should be fretting just as much about little girls playing those same games. Women who used sexy avatars to represent themselves in video games were more likely to objectify themselves in real life. Not only that, they were more likely to accept what's called rape myth—i.e., the idea that a woman is in some way to blame for her rape—according to a Stanford study published on October 11 [2013] in *Computers and Human Behavior*.

We've known for a long time that the oversexualization of women has a negative impact on the female psyche: one experiment asked women to try on either a bikini or a sweater; those who tried on a bikini reported feeling shame about their bodies and performed more poorly on a math test than their sweater-wearing counterparts. And studies have shown that sexualization of women in the media can negatively impact young girls' body image. It's for that very reason that moms worry about their daughters watching the Video Music Awards.

But playing Lara Croft—the wasp-waisted, impossibly large-breasted protagonist in the *Tomb Raider* video-game series who fights bad guys in an ever-so-practical tight tank top and short shorts—might be worse than watching Miley Cyrus twerking in a bikini. Researchers have demonstrated that embodying characters in virtual worlds has a stronger effect on gamers than just passively watching a character; game play can influence off-line beliefs, attitudes and action thanks to a phenomenon called the Proteus effect in which an individual's behavior conforms to their digital identity.

And if your avatar resembles you (i.e., you're playing with a dopplegänger), the game can make an even greater impression. Previous studies have shown playing with a dopplegänger can lead the user to replicate the dopplegänger's eating patterns, experience physiological arousal or prefer a brand of product endorsed by the dopplegänger. Given that connection, this new study looked at whether embodying sexualized female avatars online changed women's behavior.

The Stanford researchers asked 86 women ages 18 to 40 to play using either a sexualized (sexily dressed) avatar or a nonsexualized (conservatively dressed) avatar. Then, researchers designed some of those avatars to look like the player embodying them.

Those women who played using sexualized avatars who looked like them were more accepting of the rape myth, according to the study. After playing the game, women responded to many questions with answers along a five-point scale (from "strongly disagree" to "strongly agree"), including, "In the majority of rapes, the victim is promiscuous or has a bad reputation." Those who played sexy avatars who looked like themselves were more likely to answer "agree" or "strongly agree" than those women who had nonsexy avatars who did not look like them.

Participants were also asked to freewrite their thoughts after the study. Those with sexualized avatars were more likely to self-objectify in their essays after play.

Though this is a small study and certainly not a definitive answer to the question of how video games affect female players, the results do raise concerns. As many as 46% of gamers are women, and according to this research, in many of the most popular games, their options for female avatars are mostly ones with absurdly exaggerated, busty body types. And many of those female gamers are young girls: 31% of girls ages 8 to 18 report playing video games on any given day.

But even as more researchers study issues around women in gaming and protests against sexism in gaming grow, it's unlikely that video-game companies are going to change their character-design strategy anytime soon. Last year, US consumers spent $16.6 billion on video games, according to the Entertainment Software Association.

And while the makers of this fall's record-breaking hit, *Grand Theft Auto V*, have gotten complaints about the fact that you can't play as a female character in the game (even though you can play as a man and kill prostitutes), maybe it's better that way—at least until someone gives the women in these games a real makeover.

One Weird Old Trick to Undermine the Patriarchy

By Michelle Nijhuis
The Last Word on Nothing, December 18, 2013

My five-year-old insists that Bilbo Baggins is a girl.

The first time she made this claim, I protested. Part of the fun of reading to your kids, after all, is in sharing the stories you loved as a child. And in the story I knew, Bilbo was a boy. A boy hobbit. (Whatever that entails.)

But my daughter was determined. She liked the story pretty well so far, but Bilbo was definitely a girl. So would I please start reading the book the right way?

I hesitated. I imagined Tolkien spinning in his grave. I imagined mean letters from his testy estate. I imagined the story getting as lost in gender distinctions as dwarves in the Mirkwood.

Then I thought: What the hell, it's just a pronoun. My daughter wants Bilbo to be a girl, so a girl she will be.

And you know what? The switch was easy. Bilbo, it turns out, makes a terrific heroine. She's tough, resourceful, humble, funny, and uses her wits to make off with a spectacular piece of jewelry. Perhaps most importantly, she never makes an issue of her gender—and neither does anyone else.

Despite what can seem like a profusion of heroines in kids' books, girls are still underrepresented in children's literature. A 2011 study of 6,000 children's books published between 1900 and 2000 showed that only 31 percent had female central characters. While the disparity has declined in recent years, it persists—particularly, and interestingly, among animal characters. And many books with girl protagonists take place in male-dominated worlds, peopled with male doctors and male farmers and mothers who have to ask fathers for grocery money (Richard Scarry, I'm looking at you). The imbalance is even worse in kids' movies: Geena Davis' Institute on Gender and Media found that for every female character in recent family films, there are three male characters. Crowd scenes, on average, are only 17 percent female.

More insidiously, children's books with girl protagonists sometimes celebrate their heroines to a fault. Isn't it amazing that a *girl* did these things; they seem to say—implying that these heroines are a freakish exception to their gender, not an inspiration for readers to follow. Children's lit could benefit from a Finkbeiner Test. (Well-intentioned kids' media can, ironically, introduce their youngest listeners and viewers to gender barriers: The first time my daughter heard the fabulous album *Free to Be ... You and Me*, she asked "Why *isn't* it all right for boys to cry?")

So Bilbo, with her matter-of-fact derring-do, was refreshing. With a wave of my staff I turned Gandalf into a girl, too, with similarly happy results. I started to fool around with other books and their major and minor characters, sometimes by request and sometimes not. In *The Secret Garden*, Dickon, the animal-loving adventurer who rescues Mistress Mary, became Mary's best friend Diana. In the Finn Family Moomintroll books, the Snork Maiden and her brother the Snork traded genders. In the Narnia series, Peter Pevensie and his sister Susan made the pronoun switch. (That was a nice fix for the infamous line about Susan's abandoning Narnia for "nylons and lipstick and invitations.")

Friends tell me they pull similar tricks while reading to their sons and daughters: Women who farm become not "farmer's wives" but "farmers." Boy animal characters become girls, and vice versa. Sleeping Beauty goes to MIT. Their kids, boys and girls alike, get to hear about a world as full of women as the real one—and as free of stereotypes as we'd like ours to be. Kidlit may be catching up to our kids, but we don't have to wait for it.

My daughter might forget all about the heroines and heroes she helped create. But she might not. I hope that years from now, when she has a chance to take her own unexpected journey, she'll remember the story of Bilbo—and be a little more inclined to say yes.

5

Gender Roles in America

Leisa Thompson/Newhouse News Service/Landov

David Rice prepares dinner as his son, Caleb, 4, supervises. Rice is a self-proclaimed stay-at-home father while his wife, Shannon, works full-time at the University of Michigan.

Shifting Gender Roles in the Home and Workplace

Gender roles are patterns of behavior that are associated with individuals of a particular sex within specific cultures. The study of gender roles is complex because gender emerges from the murky territory between innate and learned behavioral patterns. In America, gender roles are changing, as both men and women increasingly inhabit roles that challenge traditional concepts of femininity and masculinity. Historical American gender roles envisioned domestic maintenance and childrearing as feminine activities. Today, men are increasingly taking on historically feminine duties as more women begin working outside the home, and in careers once considered appropriate only for men.

Changes in gender roles are the result of many converging variables and influences, including the ongoing feminist and women's rights movements, generational shifts affecting overall attitudes about gender, and the economic environment of America, which increasingly requires individuals of both sexes to work outside the home. Though gender roles are changing, women and men are not equal in American society. Women continue to suffer institutionalized disadvantages in the occupational environment, including gender bias in advancement, pay rate, and hiring. The blending of gender roles is also complicated by the need to balance work and family, and the sex-specific challenges of childbirth and childrearing faced by women in America and around the world.

Marriage and Family

Studies of American families in the twenty-first century indicate that the roles of parents, mothers, and families are in a state of flux. The institution of marriage itself has changed significantly over the last thirty years, with an increasing number of young people opting for cohabitation or nontraditional relationships as opposed to marriage. This trend is increasingly evident among individuals in lower socioeconomic sectors, where marriage rates have declined precipitously over the last three decades. A *Time* magazine survey conducted in 2010 found that 39 percent of Americans believe that marriage is becoming obsolete, and more than 34 percent of respondents said that the growing number of family types was a beneficial societal change. Even among older Americans (age fifty-five and up), attitudes about nontraditional families seem to be changing. According to a Gallup Poll data reported in 2013, 57 percent of older Americans now accept having children outside marriage, as compared to 29 percent in 2002.

One way that families are changing is through the growing acceptance of single-parent family structures. The Pew Research Foundation found in 2013 that 80 percent of Americans believed a single parent and child constituted a legitimate family. Although 64 percent of Americans in 2013 believed that single women having children is a negative social trend, this percentage had decreased from 71 percent in 2007. Traditional gender roles continue to hold sway in certain key areas. For instance, Pew data indicates that in 2013, half of Americans believed that children are better off with stay-at-home mothers, while only 8 percent said the same thing about stay-at-home fathers.

Research indicates that the changing nature of the American family has not followed a consistent trajectory. A comparison of data from the Census Bureau, public polling, and sociological research indicates that attitudes about marriage have strengthened since divorce rates peaked in the 1960s, and that satisfaction with marriage has increased despite the increase in nontraditional relationships and cohabitation. A 2010 Pew Research report indicated that 76 percent of Americans continue to rate family as the most important aspect of their lives. However, since the 1960s, reasons for marriage have shifted, with fewer men and women choosing to marry for financial security or having children and a greater number citing personal fulfillment and love as their primary reasons for getting married.

When it comes to the decision to have and care for children, American attitudes have also moved gradually toward an egalitarian approach. Increasingly, Americans believe that men and women should contribute equally to both childcare and home maintenance. In a 2011 study from Boston College, more than 65 percent of fathers said that men and women should contribute equally to childcare. A 2010 study from Pew Research produced similar results, revealing that as many as 72 percent of Americans between 18 and 29 believe that men and women should contribute equally to household labor and child rearing.

Women continue to provide the majority of domestic work and childcare, though domestic equality is gradually increasing. In 2011 the Families and Work Institute noted that 66 percent of women in 2008 reported taking on the majority of childcare responsibilities, as opposed to 73 percent in 1992. Similarly, Pew Research data from 2013 indicated that fathers in 2011 spent an average of 10.5 hours per week more on childcare and domestic duties than fathers in 1965. However, the increase in male involvement with children and home care is less than the increase in female involvement in working outside the home. Pew Research indicates that between 1965 and 2011, women with children increased their time working outside the home by an average of thirteen hours per week.

Careers and Gender

Career advancement has become an increasing focus for women, and a 2012 study from Pew Research found that 66 percent of women ages eighteen to thirty-four listed having a high-paying career among their life goals, compared with 59 percent of men. Statistics from the Bureau of Labor Statistics indicated that women (both married and unmarried) made up approximately 47 percent of the workforce in 2011, and had reached near-parity with men in many occupations that were considered "masculine" professions in the 1960s and 1970s.

Women have also become more successful in their careers, contributing more to household income. In 2010, for instance, 29 percent of married women earned more than their husbands, compared to just 18 percent in 1987, according to the Bureau of Labor Statistics. In 2011, Census Bureau statistics indicated that mothers were the sole or primary income providers in a record 40 percent of families with young children. The study also found that 65 percent of women with children were working outside the home in 2011, as compared to 37 percent in 1968.

Numerous studies have shown that women have a more difficult time moving into leadership and management positions in many industries. In a March 2012 blog post on the *Harvard Business Review* site, leadership consultants Jack Zenger and Joseph Folkman proposed that subtle gender bias in many industries made it more difficult for women to acquire skills that contribute to success in leadership roles. The authors found that more than 64 percent of business leaders in America were men, and that this percentage increased as the study focused on the upper echelons of the corporate environment.

A Gallup Poll study from November 2013 indicated that 35 percent of Americans would prefer a male boss, compared to 23 percent who chose a female boss and 41 percent who claimed that the gender made no difference. Despite greater difficulty getting into leadership positions, the Zenger/Folkman study indicated that women leaders ranked as superior to men in many key leadership characteristics, including traits that have been traditionally considered masculine, such as taking initiative and being results-driven.

Cycles of Change

In a 2011 article published in the *American Journal of Sociology*, authors David Cotter, Joan M. Hermsen, and Reeve Vanneman report on a long-term study of gender role attitudes suggesting that the most drastic shifts in American gender roles occurred during the 1970s and 1980s. Two primary factors affected this shift in gender values. First, a generational shift occurred resulting in the gradual removal of "traditional" gender norms from society due to age-cohort replacement. Second, women increased their participation in the education system, eventually surpassing men in secondary and higher education attainment and therefore playing a greater role in the education and professional environments.

Cotter, Hermsen, and Vanneman argue that twenty-first-century gender roles are not a reversal of traditional values, but represent the emergence of a new set of gender norms, which the authors refer to as "egalitarian essentialism," in which support for stay-at-home mothering and feminine domesticity is blended with feminist and postfeminist ideals of equality and freedom of choice. In essence, the preferred gender model has become one of total choice, in which women expect to have the freedom to choose from among the entire range of human activity, even if they choose to enact roles that might be considered stereotypically feminine or antifeminist.

However, while an increasing number of millennials gravitate toward egalitarianism in gender roles, some feminist scholars believe that women must continue pursuing an aggressive feminist agenda to address institutionalized inequities in

American society. Census Department statistics indicate that women still suffer from a wage gap, with males earning 25 to 30 percent more in some occupational areas. Women professionals also continue to suffer more than men from their biological and traditional role in childbirth and childcare, in terms of interrupting advancement in their careers.

The Institute for Women's Policy Research (2008) ranked the United States last among twenty nations in adopting policies to help employees balance family life and career advancement. A lack of family-friendly employment policies is one of the primary issues identified in a 2013 Pew Research report indicating that the majority of Americans have significant difficulty balancing work and family.

Gender roles in America have become institutionalized in governmental and economic policies. The feminist movement has had significant success in changing attitudes among the populace, but less success in fostering a generation of women and men who demand equality in the economic and professional environments. In essence, current institutional concepts of gender continue to force women and men to strike a compromise between family and professional success, and this compromise is more difficult for women due to the biological constraints of maternity. In 2013, *New York Times* journalist Stephanie Coontz argued that gender equality requires Americans to recognize that work/family balance is a human rights issue rather than only a women's rights issue. Toward this end, policies and professional values will have to shift to reflect the changing gender attitudes of the public if true gender equality is ever going to be achieved.

—Micah Issit

Bibliography

Coontz, Stephanie. "Why Gender Equality Stalled." *New York Times* 16 Feb. 2013: SR1. Print.

Cotter, David, Joan M. Hermsen, and Reeve Vanneman. "The End of the Gender Revolution? Gender Role Attitudes from 1977 to 2008." *American Journal of Sociology*. 117.1 (July 2011): 259–89. Print.

"The Decline of Marriage and Rise of New Families." *Pew Research Social and Demographic Trends*. Pew Research Center, 18 Nov. 2010. Web. 11 Feb. 2014.

Fry, Richard, and D'vera Cohn. "Women, Men, and the New Economics of Marriage." *Pew Research Social and Demographic Trends*. Pew Research Center, 19 Jan. 2010. Web. 11 Feb. 2014.

Harrington, Brad, Fred Van Deusen, and Beth Humberd. "The New Dad: Caring, Committed and Conflicted." *Boston College Center for Work and Family*. Boston College, 2011. Web. 11 Feb. 2014.

Hegewisch, Ariane, and Janet C. Gornick. "Statutory Routes to Workplace Flexibility in Cross-National Perspective." *Institute for Women's Policy Research*. U of California, 2008. Web. 11 Feb. 2014.

Leeder, Elaine J. *The Family in Global Perspective: A Gendered Journey*. New York: SAGE, 2004. Print.

Luscombe, Belinda. "Who Needs Marriage? A Changing Institution." *Time*. Time, 18 Nov. 2010. Web. 11 Feb. 2014.

Newport, Frank, and Joy Wilke. "Americans Still Prefer a Male Boss." *Gallup Economy*. Gallup, 11 Nov. 2013. Web. 11 Feb. 2014.

Parker, Kim, and Wendy Wang. "Modern Parenthood: Roles of Moms and Dads Converge as They Balance Work and Family." *Pew Research Social and Demographic Trends*. Pew Research Center, 14 Mar. 2013. Web. 11 Feb. 2014.

Patten, Eileen, and Kim Parker. "A Gender Reversal on Career Aspirations." *Pew Research Social and Demographic Trends*. Pew Research Center, 19 Apr. 2012. Web. 11 Feb. 2014.

Wang, Wendy, Kim Parker, and Paul Taylor. "Breadwinner Moms." *Pew Research Social and Demographic Trends*. Pew Research Center, 29 May 2013. Web. 11 Feb. 2014.

Wilke, Joy, and Lydia Saad. "Older Americans' Moral Attitudes Changing." *Gallup Politics*. Gallup, 3 June 2013. Web. 11 Feb. 2014.

Zenger, Jack, and Joseph Folkman. "Are Women Better Leaders Than Men?" *Harvard Business Review*. Harvard Business School, 15 Mar. 2012. Web. 11 Feb. 2014.

Alpha Women, Beta Men

By Ralph Gardner Jr.
New York Magazine, November 17, 2003

Wives are increasingly outearning their husbands, but their new financial muscle is causing havoc in the home.

After dropping off their children at their East Side private school one morning, Betsy and another mother shared a secret. "It was one of those things where you circle around each other," Betsy remembers. "I assumed they had a pretty conventional marriage."

By that she means, as with most of the other families at the school, the other woman's husband was a chest-beating breadwinner who set off for Wall Street each morning in his Town Car to bring home the six- or seven-figure bacon. Or, alternatively, both husband and wife slaved away at medium-to-high-powered jobs, neglecting their children, to pay for the August rental in the Hamptons and their $25,000-per-kid tuition bills.

The embarrassing truth the other mother confided to Betsy was that she was her family's sole support. She worked in advertising while her spouse, an "artist"—predominantly in his own imagination, since he had not a single gallery show nor even a commission to show for his talent—puttered around the house. "She kind of indicated they were living on her money, and I was surprised," Betsy says.

And perhaps a little relieved. Betsy thought she was the only mother in their grade supporting a stay-at-home husband—especially one who refused to polish the surfaces. "It's like one of those things," she says, "where you realize you're married to people who drink."

Well into feminism's second generation, there are finally a significant number of women reaching parity with the men in their fields—not to mention surpassing them—and winning the salary, bonuses, and perks that signify their arrival. (The Town Cars idling in front of their children's schools these days at morning drop-off are almost as likely to be Mom's as Dad's.) In 2001, for example, wives earned more than their spouses in almost a third of married households where the wife worked. Yet this proud professional achievement often seems to have unhappy consequences at home.

From *Buffy the Vampire Slayer* to *Alias* to *Kill Bill*, the culture has for some time been awash in fantasies of powerful women. Fetching as these female superheroes may be—and however potent at the box office and in the Nielsens—are these really the same chicks the average, or even above-average, guy wants to curl up next to in bed in real life? Perhaps not. As the wives grow more powerful and confident, their husbands often seem to diminish in direct proportion to their success.

Indeed, there's little evidence to show that as women acquire financial muscle, relations between the sexes have evolved successfully to accommodate the new balance of power. Neither the newly liberated alpha women nor their shell-shocked beta spouses seem comfortable with the role reversal.

For women, the shift in economic power gives them new choices, not least among them the ability to reappraise their partner. And husbands, for their part, may find to their chagrin that being financially dependent isn't exactly a turn-on. According to psychologists (and divorce lawyers) who see couples struggling with such changes, many relationships follow the same pattern. First, the wife starts to lose respect for her husband, then he begins to feel emasculated, and then sex dwindles to a full stop.

Anna, a public-relations executive, saw her relationship with her Web-designer husband collapse as she became more and more successful and he floundered. In the last year of their marriage, she earned $270,000 while he brought in $16,000.

"He never spent money that wasn't his in an extravagant way," she says while taking therapeutic sips of a Sea Breeze at Tribeca Grill on a recent evening. "But by not helping, he was freeloading."

She felt unable to confront him. "We were really dysfunctional," she admits. "We acted as if we were a two-income family. He was in denial, and I was sort of protecting him. He'd pay for groceries. He was running up credit-card debt to make it appear he had more money."

While they may have been able to avoid the truth while she was off at work during the day, it came back to haunt them at night. "Sexuality is based on respect and admiration and desire," says Anna. "If you've lost respect for somebody, it's very hard to have it work. And our relationship initially had been very sexual, at the expense of other things.

"Sex was not a problem for him," she goes on. "It was a problem for me. When someone seems like a child, it's not that attractive. In the end, it felt like I had three children."

"The minute it becomes parental, it becomes asexual," agrees Betsy. "A friend of mine who works and makes money and whose husband doesn't told me one day that he was taking $100-an-hour tennis lessons," she recalls. "She said to him, 'You are not in the $100-an-hour category.' She had to spell it out for him. It was totally parental."

There are, of course, happy exceptions: couples evolved enough to feel perfectly comfortable acknowledging that the wife is more driven to be the breadwinner, so it makes sense for everyone if he's giving junior his first feeding while she's off covering the presidential campaign.

"Kurt has never been someone who defines himself by his job," says Jami Floyd, a correspondent with ABC's *20/20*, of her stay-at-home husband, Kurt Flehinger. "Nor does he care much what people think about him. He's not a Master of the

Universe type. I am much more testosteronic. I'm much more driven, much more traditionally male."

But in many cases the role reversal is the work of market forces as much as force of personality; the husband's career is expected to take precedence, and initially it does, but it's overtaken by his wife's. Neither of them saw it coming—nor do they welcome it.

"Maybe the guy's industry changed and he lost his job," says Ken Neumann, a psychologist and divorce mediator who has seen his share of depressed dads lately. "Or the wife steps into the right place—something she couldn't fully have anticipated. The question is, how secure does the guy feel? When the woman earns more, we can't assume in our culture it's a nonevent. We're a long way off from a world where it doesn't affect the relationship."

"I think women earning more than men can be devastating to relationships unless the guy is doing something the wife regards as having cachet, such as academia," says Betsy, even though she still speaks fondly of her ex-husband and sends him the occasional check.

It's not as if these women ever expected their husbands to support them completely—at least a lot of them didn't. It's just that it never occurred to them that they might be the ones doing all the heavy lifting. And as hip and open-minded as they like to think they are, they were, after all, raised on the same fairy tale as the rest of us—the one where Prince Charming comes to the rescue of Sleeping Beauty.

"I didn't really give a damn where the money came from," says Betsy, an attorney. "That's not the gift I expected a husband to give me. I wanted a romantic figure." That was until she found him taking money from her wallet and leaving an IOU. "I just didn't want to be giving him spending money."

At first, her spouse, a composer, satisfied that fantasy. "It was about his artistic vision," she says. To this day, despite the fact that he's refused to make any of the compromises necessary to get ahead—and blamed Betsy for contributing to his failure by being too controlling—she continues to believe in his talent. "I think Tom's smarter than I am," she says. "He really gets excited by ideas."

'It's not a matter of how good you are," says Anna, still trying to fathom why she's successful and her former husband is not. "It's a matter of how you get work in this town. It's about connections and attitude and how you market yourself, and it's about confidence."

Among the reasons these women were originally attracted to their husbands—sex appeal, sense of humor, charisma—earning power may not have been high on the list. But that could be because it was a given. Unfortunately, the other qualities start to fade over time if the husband isn't adding something tangible to the equation.

"It was the artist thing I thought I was getting," says Anna, who met her husband when she hired him to design her company's Website. "Sexy was part of it. There was a huge physical thing. I'm not the kind of person to be attracted to a lawyer—maybe next time I will be.

"If he'd really been a starving artist, I'd have been fine with that," she adds. "But he wasn't a starving artist in the end. He wasn't driven to do his art."

The problem with living in a meritocratic culture such as New York's—and to the misfortune of those who consider moving the family car on alternate-side-of-the-street mornings a prolific day's work—is that there are objective ways to measure success, even in fields as traditionally unprofitable as literature and the arts. There are bylines and advances and gallery shows and paid commissions.

"The successful artist makes money," Neumann observes. "You're better off being an academic. People see through the artist shit.

"An academic person might get a 'waiver,' " he adds. "Or a serious, published writer. A primary-school teacher wouldn't get a waiver. We may think, *What a great thing we have men teaching!* However, we're not giving waivers yet for men teaching primary school."

When it works, it tends to be when the wife's respect for her husband remains intact. "Women need to admire their partner," says psychologist Harriette Podhoretz. "They need to find something that doesn't interfere with their passionate glue, that keeps the marriage charged up and alive."

One such relationship where the adhesive seems to be holding, against the considerable social stresses of Upper East Side living, involves Laura, an investment banker for a top Wall Street firm. Her husband, Jeff, is an actor, though one you haven't heard of. He has yet to land a role in anything, even a toothpaste ad.

But the relationship works well, they report, because Laura's admiration for Jeff, whom she met when they both worked in finance for a giant West Coast media conglomerate, seems complete. "Jeff was never laid off," his wife explains. "There's not that feeling that my husband is a loser. We made a conscious decision—he's got the creative talent—to play to each other's strengths.

"I know my husband could do my job with his eyes closed," she says. "He's really good at math. He's twice as smart as I am."

Sometimes it's the Alpha woman who needs reassurance that she's still feminine.

"When you're a big money earner and your husband isn't, it makes you question how feminine you are," says Barbara Corcoran, the ubiquitous real-estate broker. "I felt I was less feminine than if I was a supporting wife, or a second fiddle, or 'Mrs. Higgins.' The struggle was as much mine as Bill's."

Corcoran harks back to her husband Bill Higgins's glory days. Bill's career included a stint as an FBI agent—"He had more arrests than anybody ever," his wife boasts—and a top post in the Naval Reserve during the first Persian Gulf war. His last job was running his family's New Jersey real-estate company, which he sold in 1997. A teaching fellowship in the Bronx followed, but now he answers to "spouse," the title on his business card.

"My husband had a very strong identity and was successful in his life," Corcoran explains. "Thank God for that. There's no way I can control him. I wouldn't stay married to him if I felt I could. I can readily take my business personality into the home. But he forces me to be a partner rather than the boss. It's what keeps our marriage healthy. He won't give me an inch of satisfaction. He won't acknowledge my superiority."

But it took them a long time and a lot of counseling to reach that place.

The first year her income exceeded her husband's—he was still in the real-estate business at that point—Barbara pretended it was an accounting error. "I explained it away as one good year," she remembers. "On some level, I was happy it was one good year. I explained away the second good year, too. By the time the third year hit and I was earning five times more than him, it was obvious we had to adjust to the reality."

Making things worse was the fact that Bill sold his company during that period and found himself adrift. "My mistake was I didn't have a plan," he says. "I'd sleep in. Resentment starts to build." "The real issue became social events," Corcoran says. "How do you introduce your husband and answer the New York question, 'What do you do?' I remember the day he said, 'I'm retired,' and I realized we were okay with it."

Corcoran also reports feeling less pressure among her fellow alpha earners after attending Fortune's annual "Most Powerful Women in Business Summit," where she said house husbands were the rule. "I don't think any of them are married to really successful men," she says of her peers. "All these men wrap themselves around their wives' schedules much like a trophy wife would."

Emily, a senior sales executive, admits she enjoys the control she has over Mark, a struggling photographer. But sex has become an issue.

"I can't give up the position of empress," she says. "Everything is in my name. When I've gotten really bratty, I've said, 'Well fine, leave,' knowing he can't leave. I've never had such security in a relationship. There's no risk of flight. But it's only giving me a short-term gain. Ultimately, it's emasculating for him.

"Mark," she adds, "was the best sex I ever had." But that was long ago. "We fight instead," she says. "We're embroiled in some weird combat. It's like *Lysistrata*. I tell him, 'Your business is going to have to get better faster.' Until then, I'm withholding."

When Emily comes home, she doesn't always want to be the boss. But she says her husband no longer has the authority to take over. "I want somebody to take that power role away from me," she explains. "Ultimately, it gets down to pretty basic stuff. It's hard to be the power broker every day and then be the femme fatale. I'm not going to pay the bills—I feel like his mother—and then come home and suck his d—k."

Among the more tantalizing facts scientists at the Center for Research on Families at the University of Washington have uncovered is that the more money the wife makes, the more housework she does in proportion to her husband, and it's not nearly as equitable as when both partners are working. "There's an association with housework being woman's work," says the center's associate director, Julie Brines. "They're not going to compound the difficulty by the husband doing more housework."

Or making them cook dinner. Betsy recalls the first and last time her husband did. "Tom made dinner one night," she says. "I came to the table and there was spaghetti, in the pot, right on the table. No salad, no bread, no napkin folded at your place. Why didn't he know about the rest of it? He does know about the rest of it. He's been eating all his life!"

Once Anna sought a divorce—"You know what my lawyer called him? A parasite"—she, like many other women in her position, was in for a shock. Divorce lawyer Harriet Newman Cohen explains, "The law is supposed to be gender-blind. Therefore, when a marriage is breaking up at the insistence of either the breadwinning wife or the supported husband, the lawyer has to apprise the client that when a big-earner wife comes in, the court bends over backward to be gender-neutral, and it is possible the bum is going to be rewarded for sitting on his hands. You do a flip-flop and make believe she is a guy."

More often than not, this doesn't involve alimony. "A lot of men, I've noticed, feel embarrassed to ask for alimony," says Ken Neumann, since they already know their partner's reaction. "The wife's idea is, 'You're not going to ask for alimony, are you? It's bad enough I was making more than you.'"

The wife's sense of being the victim of a scam can intensify when children are involved. Even though some freeloaders are excellent fathers, responsibilities for arranging playdates, setting the table for dinner, and soothing children with nightmares inevitably falls to the mother, whether she has a PowerPoint presentation to deliver at eight the next morning or not. "Once you add a child into the equation, the likelihood of resentment is much higher," observes Barbara Corcoran.

"I wouldn't mind as much if he'd really been 'Mommy' and I'd really been 'Daddy,'" says Anna, referring to the fact that she was forced to cut her husband a check for $100,000 when they divorced—half the amount of the appreciation over the course of their marriage of a house she owned. "But he wasn't really Mommy. We had full-time babysitting."

What she remembers with special bitterness was having to return to work two weeks after the arrival of their second child because she was freelancing. As the family's sole earner, she couldn't afford to take maternity leave.

Yet even in the best of marriages, where the husbands stay home while the wives go off to work, the women seem unable to avoid doubt over their decision.

"Every day, I ask myself, 'Will I regret it when I'm lying in my grave?'" Jami Floyd admits. The question is exacerbated in the Disneyland atmosphere of Manhattan, where legions of wealthy mothers seem to have carved out quasi-idyllic existences (at least it looks that way from the outside) centered on the rhythms of child-rearing, wraparound babysitting, and frequent lunches and dinners with friends.

"In our circle, there are so many mothers who either work part-time or don't work," says Jeff. "When Laura was on maternity leave, I could see her eyes opening.

"She can be a little envious of the relationship I have with our son," he adds. "There were times he'd say, 'I don't want Mommy, I want Daddy to tuck me in.' It was difficult for her. She felt she was not being a good mother.

"We've always made a rule: If we argue, we don't do it in front of the kids. We had more arguments this year where we have not been able to stop raising our voices in front of them. There were times when I said, 'I really hope we can make it through this year.'"

"It's hard," Laura acknowledges from her cab on the way to the airport for a Sunday-afternoon flight to Dallas. "I'd like to spend more time with the kids, but I'm in this crazy, nutso, high-paid job and I'd better go for it. There's no job security anymore. It's a struggle with two kids—you can't take your foot off the gas."

The combat resulted in an epiphany of sorts for Jeff. "It was a great eye-opener for me to think, Damn! Why doesn't my wife come home and tell me she appreciates the way I'm unpacking the moving boxes? I probably don't praise her in a way that she needs it—to say, 'I really appreciate what you're doing for the family.'"

After four years, the stay-at-home experience is starting to wear thin for Kurt Flehinger, too. "He's a highly intellectual person, and at the park, people want to talk about poop consistency and the shape of the pacifier," Jami explains. "I think he's ready to move on from that."

She also balks each time someone tells her how lucky she is to be married to "a saint." "While I applaud Kurt's forward-thinking and out-of-the-box approach to his life, no one ever comes up to a woman who has two children and says, 'You're a saint.' She's just a mom doing what's expected of her."

"It can be mind-numbing," admits Kurt, who's thinking of going back to work, much to his wife's regret. "I love my children, but in terms of stimulating my intellect, it doesn't do it for me."

Ken Neumann recently conducted a divorce mediation in which one of the sticking points involved the stay-at-home husband's wish to have his wealthy real-estate-professional wife continue to rent him an office even though he doesn't work. "He left his house in the morning with his kid pretending to go to work," Neumann recalls. "The wife said, 'You don't need the office,' and he said, 'I really want our daughter to see me as going to work.' So she said, 'Why don't you just get a job like everybody else?' Children do pick up when the father is a freeloader."

Anna says that after she and her spouse split and sold their apartment, her 8-year-old asked her why her new apartment was larger and more luxurious than her dad's. "I said, 'Because I pay the rent here,'" she recalls. "And she said, 'You do work harder than Daddy, don't you?' Kids are not stupid. I work way harder than Daddy."

Betsy isn't sure how being the child of a marriage where the mother is all-powerful will affect her college-age son. "I'm curious myself how it will play out," she says. "He says to me, 'I'm 70 percent my father, and the 30 percent that's you is working real hard.'"

For her part, Anna has promised to be more tough-minded in her choice of mate if and when she slips back into the dating scene. "I didn't ask the right questions," she laments. " 'What have you done? Where have you come from, and how much have you made?' It's not the kind of thing one talks about. You believe what you want to believe. When you're madly in love, you don't really care about that kind of thing. But I will the next time."

Behind Every Great Woman

By Carol Hymowitz
Bloomberg Businessweek, January 4, 2012

Among the 80 or so customers crammed into Bare Escentuals, it's easy to spot Leslie Blodgett. It's not merely her six-inch platform heels and bright magenta-and-blue dress that set her apart in the Thousand Oaks (Calif.) mall boutique, but her confidence. To the woman concerned she's too old for shimmery eye shadow, Blodgett swoops in and encourages her to wear whatever she wants. With a deft sweep of a brush, she demonstrates a new shade of blush on another customer's cheek. And when she isn't helping anyone, she pivots on her heels for admirers gushing about her dress, made by the breakout designer Erdem.

Blodgett, 49, has spent the past 18 years nurturing Bare Escentuals from a startup into a global cosmetics empire. She sold the company for $1.7 billion to Shiseido in March 2010 but still pitches products in stores around the world and chats incessantly with customers online. Scores of fans post daily messages on Blodgett's Facebook page, confessing details about their personal lives and offering opinions on her additive-free makeup. She only wishes her 19-year-old son, Trent, were in touch with her as frequently as he is with her husband, Keith. In 1995, at 38, Keith quit making television commercials to raise Trent, freeing up Leslie to build her business. She'd do it all again, but she's jealous of her husband's relationship with her son. Trent, a college sophomore, texts his father almost every day; he often goes a week without texting her.

"Once I knew my role was providing for the family, I took that very seriously. But there was envy knowing I wasn't there for our son during the day," says Blodgett. "Keith does everything at home—the cooking, repairs, finances, vacation planning—and I could work long hours and travel a lot, knowing he took such good care of Trent. I love my work, but I would have liked to have a little more balance or even understand what that means."

Blodgett's lament is becoming more familiar as a generation of female breadwinners look back on the sacrifices—some little, some profound—required to have the careers they wanted. Like hundreds of thousands of women who have advanced into management roles in the past two decades—and, in particular, the hundreds who've become senior corporate officers—she figured out early what every man with a corner office has long known: To make it to the top, you need a wife. If that wife happens to be a husband, and increasingly it is, so be it.

When Carly Fiorina became Hewlett-Packard's (HPQ) first female chief executive officer, the existence of her househusband, Frank Fiorina, who had retired early from AT&T (T) to support her career, was a mini-sensation; now this arrangement isn't at all unusual. Seven of the 18 women who are currently CEOs of Fortune 500 companies—including Xerox's (XRX) Ursula Burns, PepsiCo's (PEP) Indra Nooyi, and WellPoint's (WLP) Angela Braly—have, or at some point have had, a stay-at-home husband. So do scores of female CEOs of smaller companies and women in other senior executive jobs. Others, like IBM's (IBM) new CEO, Ginni Rometty, have spouses who dialed back their careers to become their powerful wives' chief domestic officers.

This role reversal is occurring more and more as women edge past men at work. Women now fill a majority of jobs in the U.S., including 51.4 percent of managerial and professional positions, according to U.S. Census Bureau data. Some 23 percent of wives now out-earn their husbands, according to a 2010 study by the Pew Research Center. And this earnings trend is more dramatic among younger people. Women 30 and under make more money, on average, than their male counterparts in all but three of the largest cities in the U.S.

During the recent recession, three men lost their jobs for every woman. Many unemployed fathers, casualties of layoffs in manufacturing and finance, have ended up caring for their children full-time while their wives are the primary wage earners. The number of men in the U.S. who regularly care for children under age five increased to 32 percent in 2010 from 19 percent in 1988, according to Census figures. Among those fathers with preschool-age children, one in five served as the main caregiver.

Even as the trend becomes more widespread, stigmas persist. At-home dads are sometimes perceived as freeloaders, even if they've lost jobs. Or they're considered frivolous kept men—gentlemen who golf. The househusbands of highly successful women, after all, live in luxurious homes, take nice vacations, and can afford nannies and housekeepers, which many employ at least part-time. In reaction, at-home dads have launched a spate of support groups and daddy blogs to defend themselves.

"Men are suddenly seeing what it's been like for women throughout history," says Linda R. Hirshman, a lawyer and the author of *Get to Work*, a book that challenges at-home moms to secure paying jobs and insist that their husbands do at least half the housework. Caring for children all day and doing housework is tiring, unappreciated work that few are cut out for—and it leaves men and women alike feeling isolated and diminished.

There's some good news about the at-home dads trend. "By going against the grain, men get to stretch their parenting abilities and women can advance," notes Stephanie Coontz, a family studies professor at Evergreen State College in Olympia, Wash., and author of *Marriage: A History*. And yet the trend underscores something else: When jobs are scarce or one partner is aiming high, a two-career partnership is next to impossible. "Top power jobs are so time-consuming and difficult, you can't have two spouses doing them and maintain a marriage and family," says Coontz. This explains why, even as women make up more of the workforce, they're still a small minority (14 percent, according to New York-based Catalyst) in senior executive jobs. When they reach the always-on, all-consuming executive level, "it's still women who more often put family ahead of their careers," says Ken Matos, a senior director at Families and Work Institute in New York. It may explain, too, why bookstore shelves and e-book catalogs are jammed with self-help books for ambitious women, of which *I'd Rather Be in Charge*, by former Ogilvy-Mather Worldwide CEO Charlotte Beers, is merely the latest. Some, such as Hirshman's top-selling *Get to Work*, recommend that women "marry down"—find husbands who won't mind staying at home—or wed older men who are ready to retire as their careers take off. What's indisputable is that couples increasingly are negotiating whose career will take precedence before they start a family.

"Your wife's career is about to soar, and you need to get out of her way." That's what Ken Gladden says his boss told him shortly before his wife, Dawn Lepore, was named the first female CIO at Charles Schwab (SCHW) in 1994. He was a vice-president at Schwab in computer systems. Lepore's promotion meant she'd become his top boss. "I married above my station," Gladden jokes.

Gladden moved to a job at Visa (V). When their son, Andrew, was born four years later in 1998, Gladden quit working altogether. He and Lepore had tried for years to have a child and didn't want him raised by a nanny. Being a full-time dad wasn't the biggest adjustment Gladden made for Lepore's career. That came later, when Seattle-based drugstore.com recruited Lepore to become its CEO in 2004.

Gladden had lived in the San Francisco Bay Area for 25 years and wasn't keen to move to a city where it rains a lot and he didn't know anyone. He rejected Lepore's suggestion that she commute between Seattle and San Francisco, and after some long discussions he agreed to relocate—on the condition that they kept their Bay Area home. They still return for holidays and some vacations. "To do what I'm doing, you've got to be able to say 'my wife's the breadwinner, the more powerful one,' and be O.K. with that. But you also need your own interests," says Gladden, who has used his computing skills to launch a home-based business developing software for schools.

The couple's five-bedroom Seattle home overlooks Lake Washington. Gladden, 63, is chief administrator of it and their children, who now are 9 and 13. While they're in school, he works on his software. From 3 p.m. until bedtime, he carpools to and from sports and music lessons, warms up dinners prepared by a part-time housekeeper, and supervises homework. Lepore, 57, is often out of town. She oversaw the sale of drugstore.com to Walgreens (WAG) last year, for $429 million. As CEO, she was rarely home before 8 or 9 p.m. and traveled several days a week. Now, as a consultant to several startups and a director at EBay (EBAY), she still travels frequently. If Gladden envies anything, it's the ease with which his wife can walk into a room filled with well-known executives like Bill Gates and "go right up to them and start talking. I don't feel like I can participate," he says.

Lepore wishes her "biggest supporter" would get more recognition for everything he does at home. When an executive recently told her "having an at-home husband makes it easy for you to be a CEO," she responded, "no, not easy. He makes it possible." Lepore advises younger women to "choose your spouse carefully. If you want a top job, you need a husband who isn't self-involved and will support your success," even if you go further than him. There are tradeoffs, she warns: "I've missed so much with my kids—school plays, recitals, just seeing them every day."

For Lepore and Gladden, the role reversal paid off, and, as one of the few couples willing to go public about their domestic arrangement, they're a rare source of inspiration for those who are still figuring it out. Like Gladden, Matt Schneider, 36, is an at-home dad. A former technology company manager and then a sixth grade teacher, he cares for his sons Max and Sam, 6 and 3, while his wife, Priyanka, also 36, puts in 10-hour days as chief operating officer at a Manhattan real estate management startup. He feels "privileged," he says, to be with his sons full-time "and see them change every day," while allowing that child care and housework can be mind-numbing. He uses every minute of the 2.5 hours each weekday when Sam is in preschool to expand the NYC DADS Group he co-founded, 450 members strong. Members meet for play dates with their kids, discuss parenting, and stand up for at-home dads. "We're still portrayed as bumbling idiots," Schneider says. He rails against a prejudice that moms would do a better job—if only they were there. "Everyone is learning from scratch how to change diapers and toilet-train," he says, "and there's no reason to think this is woman's work."

Schneider and his wife, who met as undergraduates at University of Pennsylvania's Wharton School of Business, decided before they wed that she'd have the big career and he'd be the primary parent. "It's her name on the paycheck, and sure, we've thought about the precariousness of having just one breadwinner. But she wouldn't earn what she does if I wasn't doing what I do," he says. Which is not to say that he doesn't wonder "whether I can get back to a career when I want to and build on what I've done before."

At-home moms have snubbed him at arts and crafts classes and on playgrounds. "Men, even those of us pushing strollers, are perceived as dangerous," Schneider says. He was rejected when he wanted to join an at-home neighborhood moms' group, which prompted him to blog more about the similarities among moms and dads. "I've met moms and dads who are happy to give a screaming kid a candy bar to get him to settle down, and moms and dads who show up at play dates with containers filled with organic fruit," he says. "The differences aren't gender-specific."

It's no different for gay couples. Brad Kleinerman and Flint Gehre have taken turns being at-home dads for their three sons, now 19, 18, and 10. When their sons—biological siblings they adopted through the Los Angeles County foster care system—were young, Kleinerman and Gehre relied first on a weekday nanny and then a live-in one while both worked full-time. Kleinerman, 50, was an executive in human resources at Walt Disney (DIS) and NASA. Gehre, 46, was a teacher and then director of global learning and communications at Disney. Five years ago, they decided they no longer wanted to outsource parenting. "We always wanted to have dinner together as a family, but by the time we got home, the nanny had fed our kids," says Gehre. "Our kids were at pivotal ages—the two oldest about to go to high school and the youngest to first grade. We wanted to be the ones instilling our values and be there when they needed help with homework or had to get to a doctor."

In 2007 the couple moved from Los Angeles to Avon, Conn., where they were able to get married legally and find better schools for their kids. Kleinerman became the full-time dad and Gehre kept his Disney job, working partly from home and traveling frequently to Los Angeles. A year later they switched: Gehre quit Disney to parent full-time and Kleinerman found a new job as a human resources director at Cigna Healthcare (CI). Gehre says he's never felt discriminated against as a gay dad or a stay-at-home dad. "No one has ever said to me, 'Why would you stay home with the kids?' Where we're discriminated is when we pay taxes. We don't qualify for the marriage deduction, we have to file as single people," he says. If he has one regret about being at home, it's the lack of adult conversation and stimulation: "I worked in a very high-intensity atmosphere with very intelligent and hard-driving people, and that keeps you sharp." Any dullness doesn't make Gehre doubt his decision. Having consciously chosen to have a family, he and Kleinerman felt they had not only to provide the essentials, but also to be present.

Is there an alternate universe where both parents can pursue careers without outsourcing child care? The five Nordic countries—Iceland, Norway, Sweden, Finland, and Denmark—are noted leaders in keeping moms, in particular, on the job. "These countries have made it possible to have a better division of labor both at work and at home through policies that both encourage the participation of women in the labor force and men in their families," says Saadia Zahidi, co-author of the World Economic Forum's *Global Gender Gap Report*. The policies Zahidi refers to include mandatory paternal leave in combination with maternity leave; generous, federally mandated parental leave benefits; gender-neutral tax incentives; and post-maternity reentry programs.

There were no such programs or precedents for Jennifer Granholm and Dan Mulhern. When the two met at Harvard Law School, she grilled him about what he expected from a wife. Mulhern accepted that Granholm would never be a homemaker like his mother, but he never expected her to run for political office. "When I was young," he says, "I thought I'd be the governor"—not married to the governor. Granholm was governor of Michigan from 2003 through 2010, and her election forced Mulhern to walk away from the Detroit-based consulting business he founded, which had numerous contracts with state-licensed health insurance companies, municipalities, and school districts. Once that happened, he felt "in a backroom somewhere" and in a marriage that was "a lot more give than take."

Mulhern understood that his wife faced "extraordinary pressure" during her two terms, including a $1.7 billion budget deficit and the bankruptcies of General Motors (GM) and Chrysler. She had limited time for their three children, who were 6, 11, and 14 when she was elected, and even less for him. "I didn't want to say, 'hey, you missed my birthday' or 'you haven't even noticed what happened with the kids,' but I sometimes felt resentful," he says.

Mulhern says he complained to his wife that they spent 95 percent of the little time they had together talking about her work. He missed the attention she used to give him but felt humiliated asking for it. He gradually changed his expectations. He stopped waiting for Granholm to call him in the middle of the day to share what had happened at meetings they'd spent time talking about the prior evening. And he realized he couldn't recreate for her all the memorable or awkward moments he had with their children—like the time he found his daughter and her high school friends in the outdoor shower, "ostensibly with their clothes on. I had to call all the parents and tell them, as a courtesy, 'I want you to know this happened at the Governor's mansion,'" he says. "While my wife was battling the Republican head of the State Senate, I had a teenage daughter who was a more formidable opponent."

When Granholm left office and was asked, "What's next?," she said, "It's Dan's turn." As a former governor, though, she's the one with more obvious opportunities. Later this month, Granholm launches a daily political commentary show on Current TV. She's also teaching at the University of California at Berkeley, where Dan has a part-time gig thanks to his wife.

"The employment opportunities that come my way—and my salary potential—aren't what my wife's are now," says Mulhern. He plans to continue to teach, write, and do some consulting, while also taking care of their 14-year-old son. "Someone has to be focused on him every day," he says.

The experiences and reflections of powerful women and their at-home husbands could lead to changes at work so that neither women nor men have to sacrifice their careers or families. "There's no reason women should feel guilty about achieving great success, but there should be a way for success to include professional and personal happiness for everyone," says *Get to Work* author Hirshman. "If you have to kill yourself at work, that's bad for everyone."

Kathleen Christensen agrees. As program director at the Alfred P. Sloan Foundation, she has focused on work and family issues and says we're back to the 1950s, only "instead of Jane at home, it's John. But it's still one person doing 100 percent of work outside the home and the other doing 100 percent at home." Just as we saw the Feminine Mystique in the 1960s among frustrated housewives, Christensen predicts, "we may see the Masculine Mystique in 2020."

The children of couples who have reversed roles know the stakes better than anyone. One morning last year, when Dawn Lepore was packing for a business trip to New York, her nine-year-old daughter burst into tears. "I don't want you to travel so much," Elizabeth told her mother. Lepore hugged her, called her school, and said her daughter would be staying home that morning. Then she rescheduled her flight until much later that day. "There have been times when what Elizabeth wants most is a mom who stays home and bakes cookies," she says.

Lepore is sometimes concerned that her children won't be ambitious because they've often heard her complain about how exhausted she is after work. But they're much closer to their father than kids whose dads work full-time, and they have a different perspective about men's and women's potential. When a friend of her daughter's said that fathers go to offices every day, Lepore recalls, "Elizabeth replied, 'Don't be silly, dads are at home.'"

Who Does More at Home: Men or Women?

By Belinda Luscombe
Time, March 19, 2013

A new study suggests men and women are getting closer to 50-50 at home. But is it measuring the right thing?

In the recent slew of coverage of What's Holding Women Back from the Highest Echelons of Leadership, a recurring theme is the revolution at home. Or lack thereof.

Men, as I wrote in *Time*'s recent cover story on Sheryl Sandberg's book *Leaning In*, have generally made room for women in the workplace. But the home front remains more of a battleground. Most studies suggest that women are carrying the heavy end of the domestic load. Men are catching up. But they're beginning to stagger a bit under the weight.

According to an interesting new Pew study, men have taken on vastly more of the domestic workload than they did in 1965—about two and a half times as much. No surprises there. But a very small percentage of fathers bear the brunt of the housework and childcare in their home. Moms still spend about twice as much time with their children as dads do (13.5 hours per week for mothers in 2011, compared with 7.3 hours for fathers, according to Pew).

What has changed is the attitudes these men have about the shift. They are quickly becoming O.K. with the idea that the mothers of their children will be working outside the home too. This trend has been quite dramatic: "In 2009, 54% of fathers with children under age 17 said the ideal situation for young children was to have a mother who did not work at all outside the home," Pew reports. "Today only 37% of fathers say that—a drop of 17 percentage points." This could well have something to do with the economy. The number of households who can survive on the income of only one of the two potential breadwinners has dwindled since the recent recession.

Perhaps as a result, men and women are beginning to feel that old work-life-balance anxiety almost equally. Half the men Pew surveyed expressed difficulty juggling the demands of work and home, as did 56% of women. And more fathers than mothers worried that they weren't spending enough time with the kids (46% vs. 23%). Obviously, this is largely because women actually do spend more time with the kids. But it raises an interesting question. If you're the primary breadwinner, are you cut some slack at home? Does bringing home the bacon count as a home chore?

How does your home stack up? Pew has a nifty tool with which you can compare your division of household labor with those it surveyed. Note that the biggest chunk of males feel that they do as much housework and child care as their female partners. The biggest share of women feel they do more than the men in their lives. It's unlikely they can both be right. Perhaps this gap is partly explained by the insufficiency of a time-usage study. Men may do as much around the house and with the kids. But women feel that this arena is still more their responsibility. They have to think about it more. (If you're the person who remembers its pajama day at school, does that count as time spent?)

It boils down to this: there's a difference between spending time and paying attention. Women, in my long years of observation of this phenomenon, say more of their mental energy or bandwidth has to be set aside for matters of the hearth. They can't silo their attention in the way men can. Until somebody figures out a way to do a bandwidth study, the gap between who thinks they do more and who actually does more is still going to be fertile ground for many a domestic tiff.

Race? No, Millennials Care Most About Gender Equality

By Morley Winograd and Michael D. Hais
The National Journal, October 25, 2013

The purview of next-gen leaders is that "there are no inherently male or female roles in society."

The attitude of the millennial generation (those born from 1982 to 2003) that will have the most impact on the daily lives of Americans is the distinctive and historically unprecedented belief that there are no inherently male or female roles in society. This belief stems directly from millennials' experience growing up in families in which the mother and father took on roughly equal responsibilities for raising their offspring. As men and women enter the workforce on an equal footing, this generation's belief in gender neutrality will force major changes in our laws governing the work place and its relationship to family life.

Historically, "civic" generations like millennials have tended to emphasize distinctions between the sexes, while "idealist" generations, such as today's boomers, have advanced the cause of women's rights. This includes the transcendental generation that founded the feminist movement in the 1840s, the missionary-generation suffragists in the early 20th century, and of course the boomers who revitalized the women's movement in the 1960s.

By comparison, as Neil Howe and William Strauss, the founders of generational theory point out, the 18th-century civic republican generation, which included many of our founders, "associated 'effeminacy' with corruption and disruptive passion, 'manliness' with reason and disinterested virtue." During World War II, as the men in the civic-minded 20th-century GI generation joined the military, many women went to work in America's factories, assuming jobs traditionally held by males. But at war's end, willingly or unwillingly, most of Rosie the Riveter's sisters returned to their traditional roles as wives and mothers.

By contrast, today's millennial women are refusing to accept any restrictions, based on their gender or color, on what they might be allowed to do and what they may be able to achieve. The result has been vastly improved educational and income opportunities for women and a greater demand for the ability to blend work with the rest of life's responsibilities and pleasures from both sexes.

Although the civically oriented GI generation was notable for providing equal opportunities for women and men to attend high school, the millennial generation is the first in U.S. history in which women are more likely to attend and graduate from college and professional school than are men. In 2006, nearly 58 percent of college students were women. By 2016, women are projected to earn 64 percent of associate's degrees, 60 percent of bachelor's, 63 percent of master's, and 56 percent of doctorates. These achievements have produced a generation of self-confident women who, unlike many of their boomer mothers and grandmothers, do not see themselves in conflict or competition with men.

All of this has led some male millennials to rethink the entire concept of masculinity. It's becoming increasingly clear, for instance, that male millennials will take greater advantage of paternity-leave opportunities to bond with their newborn children and support the mothers of those children. Remarkably, in sharp distinction to the usual partisan rancor these days, polls show that majorities of Republicans (62 percent), Democrats (92 percent), and independents (71 percent) now support the idea of paid paternity leave. The federal budget already includes money to help states start paternity-leave programs. Under pressure from the growing presence of millennials in the electorate, a paid paternity- and maternity-leave program is likely to become an employee-funded federal insurance program, similar to Social Security, which could be financed by a small payroll tax increase of about three-tenths of 1 percent.

The biggest changes for American men will come as millennials become the predominant generation in the workplace. Economic necessity will force young men to train for and work in a range of careers, such as nursing and teaching, that previously have been considered women's work. As the blurring of occupational gender distinctions becomes commonplace, millennials will demand that employers provide opportunities for more work-life blending. With both parents equally involved in career and family, employers who wish to attract top talent will have no other choice but to accommodate the generation's demand for such things as telecommuting, flexible hours, and child care. Politicians who support policies designed to encourage the provision of such benefits will receive a positive reception from their millennial constituents.

The result will be a new national consensus on what it means to be a man or a woman, and a new respect for the full participation of both sexes in all aspects of American family life.

The Gender Gap

Changing Roles in Education and Economy, Love and Marriage

By Julia Perla Huisman
NWI Times, November 16, 2013

For the past couple of decades, more women have been attending college than men, and the gap is projected to continue growing. This trend is reflected in Northwest Indiana's three largest universities: Valparaiso University has 52 percent women, Purduc Calumet is at 57 percent, and Indiana University Northwest brings in a whopping 67 percent of female students.

There are many reasons behind the statistics. For one, "there's a greater economic benefit of a college education for women," said Cynthia O'Dell, Associate Vice Chancellor of Academic Affairs and a member of the Women and Gender Studies Program at IUN.

O'Dell said the college wage premium is higher for women than for men, which means, "going to college pays off in terms of wages for women at a higher rate, even if the overall salaries for women might not be as high as for men."

Cultural perception plays another factor. According to a recent survey by the Student Research Center, women rate the importance of a college education higher than men do.

"The population at large believes that a college education is more important for women than for men," said O'Dell.

But why? "For men, there is still work that doesn't require a college education," O'Dell said. Many young men are able to find a suitable job straight out of high school at a steel mill or in a trade vocation, though that trend is changing too, as there is a national move toward more white-collar jobs.

The growing gender gap in education could affect more than the economy, however. Some researchers project it might also impact dating, marriage and the overall family unit.

"Educated women who want to marry a man with comparable or more education have a dwindling pool of eligible mates," said Scott Hall, Ph.D., Associate Professor of Family Studies at Ball State University. "Thus, if the education trends continue, fewer women will marry, fewer women will marry someone with a college education, and more women will have a higher education than their husbands."

Eryn MacNeil, 20, a junior at Valparaiso University, echoes Hall's assessment that women still prefer a man with an education. "I'm pretty ambitious, and I don't think I could be with someone who didn't share that ambition, or at least support me in it," MacNeil said. "Part of being in a successful relationship is sharing the same goals, and I don't think I could be with someone who didn't value education the same way I do."

O'Dell, however, said she believes that our definition of what makes an ideal partnership will catch up to the reality of the situation over time. "As more and more women have moved into the workforce and our definitions of family have changed quite a bit, there will be some continual changes in society in how we define those kinds of things," she said.

"Today, men and women may be defining marriage in traditional ways, but as the actual reality of individuals' employment continues to evolve, eventually our definitions will evolve with them."

In other words, 20 years from now, it may be the norm for women to pursue college and a career while the men stay at home with the kids. And everyone just might be okay with that.

On the other hand, Hall said this shift could lead to more divorce, pointing out that divorce rates are high among couples that face this educational gender gap already.

O'Dell agrees that this is a potential problem. "If individuals are going to have traditional feelings about who should earn the most money, who should stay home, etc., if that doesn't match with the other individual's definition, it could lead to conflict and eventually something more severe like divorce," she said.

Though, O'Dell said, definitions change with the reality. "If people know going into a marriage that they have the same ideas, there's going to be less conflict."

Military Gender Issue Reignites as 45 Percent of Female Marines Fail Pull-up Test

By Bob Adelmann
The New American, January 6, 2014

A brief announcement on the U.S. Marine Corps' social networking site was enough to set off another round in the gender wars: "Corps postpones pull-ups for women & female Marines."

The reason was simple: Despite being given more than a year's warning that pull-ups would be the only option for testing females' upper body strength in the Corps' Physical Fitness Test (PFT) starting January 1, only 45 percent of those tested at Paris Island, South Carolina, met the bare minimum of three. In the wisdom of the Marine Corps, this was the minimum "muscular strength required to perform common military tasks such a scaling a wall, climbing up a rope or lifting and carrying heavy munitions."

The delay is for an undetermined period of time because its implementation ran "the risk of losing recruits and hurting retention of women already in the service," according to the Associated Press.

This is part of the plan to gradually install females into combat positions in the U.S. armed forces, starting in 2016. Said Marine Corps Commandant General James Amos, the Corps wants to "continue to gather data and ensure that female Marines are provided with the best opportunity to succeed." In the interim, they may continue to opt out of the pull-up requirement in favor of the much less demanding "flexed-arm hang," which requires only that the soldier hang with her chin above the bar for a minimum of 15 seconds.

This isn't the first time that females have been unable to complete tasks assigned to males in the Corps. In September, 15 female and 266 male Marines took the Corps' grueling two-month infantry course, carrying 85-pound packs and rifles and engaging in various obstacle courses while at the same time learning how to shoot, launch grenades, conduct patrols, and avoid IEDs (roadside bombs). Of the men, 221 made it through the course, while just three women finished. Earlier 20 female Marines attempted to complete the even more difficult officers' training course, and none passed.

Differences in gender have been reflected in PFTs for years. At present a perfect score for a male requires 20 pull-ups, 100 crunches in less than two minutes, and a three-mile run in 18 minutes or less. For a female a perfect score requires only the flexed arm hang for 70 seconds, 100 crunches, and a 21-minute three-mile run.

The only way "equality" on the PFTs can be achieved will be to lower the bar for women, according to James Joyner, writing for *Outside the Beltway*:

> It's pretty clear that very few women are cut out for the infantry. Thus far, in tests conducted with the most highly motivated and physically fit women the Marine Corps can find, zero women have made it through [the] infantry officer training and only a handful have made it through the enlisted course . . . .
>
> We're never going to be able to produce female grunts in large [numbers] without lowering standards.

This was confirmed in a statement by Captain Maureen Krebs, acting as a spokeswoman for the Marine commandant: "The commandant has no intent to introduce a standard that would negatively affect the current status of female Marines or their ability to continue serving in the Marine Corps."

The founder of the Center for Military Readiness, Elaine Donnelly, said that some allowances can be made for female Marines serving behind the lines, but they cannot be made for those intending to serve at the front:

> Gender-specific allowances to improve fitness can be justified in basic and entry-level exercises. [But] they are not acceptable in training for infantry combat, where lives and missions depend upon individual strength, endurance, team cohesion and trust for survival. . . .
>
> Thirty years of studies and reports . . . have confirmed that in the close combat environment, women do not have the equal opportunity to survive, or to help fellow soldiers survive.

The Marine Corps no doubt will find a way to soften the requirements while keeping them "equal." According to Donnelly, one may soon expect to read about how new "gender-neutral" standards will include fitness testing standards that are measured using "gender-normed" scores: a distinction intending to hide the difference.

Fitness experts think that the real difference in performance is because of genetic makeup and that training approaches may only help close the gap a little. As Richard Liegy noted wryly in the *Washington Post*: "Putting physiology, social policy, behavioral theory and military doctrine aside, it appears that for reasons known only to the Maker, men and women are different."

Is it too much to ask that such a revelation inform the commandant and his superiors who at present think there should be no difference between genders, and that any apparent difference can be erased by changing the numbers?

When Mom Comes Home from War

By Champ Clark and Susan Keating
People, May 7, 2012

After six months in Afghanistan, Air Force Surgeon Major Dolly Skeete returned to her husband, three sons and a cherished life—but also to some unexpected adjustments.

> I am on a plane. My six months at Bagram Air Base are coming to a close. . . . Home is just a mirage in this barren desert. . . . [Later] flying over New York City, I can make out the Statue of Liberty. I still remember showing my boys the video clips of 9/11 before I left in an attempt to explain why we were at war. Why their mommy had to leave them for six months.

It wasn't her little boy running with a Nerf gun that disturbed Maj. Dolly Skeete. As a mother of three sons, she is used to chaos in the house. But her 5-year-old's game of make-believe irked her. "Austin was talking about blowing people up," says Skeete. "I got angry. I said to him, 'Do you know what happens when you blow up someone? To their skin and bones and body?' Then I told him what happens, and that it was my job to fix people who got blown up."

Before her deployment, it might never have occurred to Skeete, an Air Force hand surgeon, to explain the carnage of war to a preschooler. But she isn't the same woman who left her family to serve her country, and the family she returned to has also evolved. "It's wonderful to come home. But it's hard too," she says, navigating the large, well-organized kitchen in her home near Eglin AFB in Florida. "You can't just plop into life and return where you left off."

While the pain of separation and the thrill of reunion are well documented, the more subtle stresses of reentry to family life are rarely discussed publicly. Skeete, 38, is one of more than 100,000 moms who left kids to serve in the Afghanistan and Iraq wars since 2001. (Currently some 6,300 are serving.) She agreed to open her private journals and let *People* capture some of her early days at home.

May 5, 2011, the day Skeete deployed:

> As I walked through the terminal, random civilians paused to thank me for my service. I wanted to grab them and scream, "I just left my husband and three sons! I left a baby! I'm going to the edge of a war zone!" But I just nodded in thanks.

Skeete knows she is one of the luckier ones. "I'm not the only parent who left—there are so many mothers and fathers who go for longer," she acknowledges. And,

---

of course, some never come home. When she walked gratefully through the same airport six months later, "I was overjoyed to be with my husband and little gentlemen. I held them all."

Gabriel, 8, had been the first to spot her by the baggage claim, and Austin too was thrilled. But baby Neil, who was just 5 months old when his mother went away, didn't respond. "Part of me expected him not to recognize me. But that was hard to take."

From pictures e-mailed to her in Afghanistan, Skeete knew she had missed a lot. But it is rough to see Neil run around the house, knowing that his time as a wobbly toddler is over. "Dolly left strict instructions that if Neil were to start walking before she came back, we were to knock him down on his butt," says husband of 10 years Larry Skeete, 40, an ER doctor whom she met when she was a med student in Chicago. They kept in e-mail touch while she was gone and are visibly still close, snuggling and eating off each other's plates at a dinner out. But time didn't stop for the kids. "At 9 months, Neil grabbed my mom's finger and took his first steps. It was bittersweet sharing that with someone besides my wife." His mom, Jackie Skeete, moved up from Jamaica to help out, and Dolly's mom also visited. All three took it easy on the boys, who were missing their mother. "During the day they were big and brave," says Jackie. "At night they got small. They wanted to be cuddled." Adds Larry: "My mother and Dolly's mother are wonderful, but grandmothers do not discipline the way a parent does."

One result? "Things are very different," says Skeete. "I trained them to make their beds, put dishes away, pick up their towels. When I was gone, they stopped doing some of those things. There has been a change in going from one authority figure to two."

Skeete reimposed familiar military order. The kids do calisthenics in the morning with the regularity of "brushing their teeth." There is now a chart with her schedule, Larry's and both the kids' school and swimming plans back on the kitchen wall. Slowly the beds started getting made again. The towels found their racks. Says Larry, who had surrendered some control to his mom and her more relaxed methods: "It was great to get back on track."

On a recent Sunday afternoon, Skeete, with Neil on her hip—he's been a little clingy since she returned—prepares dinner: panini and homemade salsa. "Before, Austin didn't like tomatoes," she reports, operating a blender with one hand. But recently, "I made him a sandwich, and he wanted tomato in it. It struck me: It was something I wasn't used to." It is a little thing, but those details—Larry also switched their brand of diapers—gently underscore her outsider status. "I've had to relearn their schedules, their wants. In Afghanistan I just had myself: one moving part. Here I have many moving parts."

Skeete served in southwest Afghanistan, a hotbed of Taliban activity. In 180 days she performed 400 surgeries, including multiple amputations, on U.S. and NATO soldiers and Afghan civilians of all ages.

June 2011:

> The Afghan kids look like my kids. My own children are half Indian, half African-American. These brown little children look like my sons. . . . Every morning I expect to be in my own bed. To roll over and feel the warm body of my husband. I expect to hear my baby cooing for his milk. I expect to kiss the necks of my little boys and smell the sleep hiding under their covers. And, again, I wake up and am in my B-hut.

Now, some days, she wakes from a dream next to her husband and thinks she is still in Afghanistan. She likes her work and is proud of what she did there. "I'm good at taking care of people; I love my patients," says Skeete, who entered the Air Force Academy in order to have her education expenses paid. But her tour of duty has left a lasting mark. "I've seen guys lose their legs. Now I don't take running for granted. I've seen kids die. I don't take healthy kids for granted." The children she treated are still in her memory, even as she is surrounded by her own. "Afghan kids have no toys." When Christmas came, "my kids didn't get as many toys; we donated a lot [to needy children]." She says they didn't mind. "Kids don't want as much as we think."

As she pulls into the driveway after hospital work at the Eglin base and a fast trip through the market, she sees Austin and Gabriel battling with plastic light sabers. They don't rush to her as they did in the airport, perhaps a sign that having mom home is starting to feel normal. They are unaware of it now, but the threat of a redeployment looms over the family. "If I get recalled, I will have to go," says Skeete, who has three years left to serve. "Would it wreak havoc on my family? Probably. Would I have guilt? Yes, I have guilt."

After dinner the boys run through the house. Mom joins in, tackling Austin, until they are both laughing on the floor. Later Skeete pores over photos of them on her computer, just as she did in Bagram, even though they are right outside. "It's so good to be home," she says. "It's so good to be home."

Bibliography

❖

Armstrong, Cory L. *Media Disparity: A Gender Battleground*. Lanham: Lexington, 2013. Print.

Campus, Donatella. *Women Political Leaders and the Media*. New York: Palgrave, 2013. Print.

Carreiras, Helena. *Gender and the Military: Women in the Armed Forces of Western Democracies*. New York: Routledge, 2006. Print.

Chambers, Deborah, Linda Steiner, and Carole Fleming. *Women and Journalism*. London: Routledge, 2004. Print.

Chuang, Susan S, and Catherine S. Tamis-LeMonda. *Gender Roles in Immigrant Families*. New York: Springer, 2013. Print.

DiPrete, Thomas A, and Claudia Buchmann. *The Rise of Women: The Growing Gender Gap in Education and What It Means for American Schools*. New York: Russell, 2013. Print.

Fox, Suzy, and Terri R. Lituchy. *Gender and the Dysfunctional Workplace*. Cheltenham: Elgar, 2012. Print.

Gender Roles: A Cross-Cultural Perspective. Boston: Wadsworth, 2013. Print.

Heppner, Rebekah S. *The Lost Leaders: How Corporate America Loses Women Leaders*. New York: Palgrave, 2013. Print.

Kariv, Dafna. *Female Entrepreneurship and the New Venture Creation: An International Overview*. New York: Routledge, 2013. Print.

Kosut, Mary. *Encyclopedia of Gender in Media*. Thousand Oaks: SAGE, 2012. Print.

Leman, Patrick, and Harriet Tenenbaum. *Gender and Development*. Hoboken: Taylor, 2013. Print.

Milestone, Katie, and Anneke Meyer. *Gender and Popular Culture*. Cambridge: Polity, 2012. Print.

Nkwake, Apollo M. *Changing Gender Roles?: A Study on Fathers' Involvement in Childcare*. Mustang: Tate, 2013. Print.

Palmer, Barbara, and Dennis Simon. *Breaking the Political Glass Ceiling: Women and Congressional Elections*, 2nd ed. New York: Routledge, 2008. Print.

Raftery, Deirdre, and Maryann G. Valiulis. *Gender Balance and Gender Bias in Education: International Perspectives*. London: Routledge, 2011. Print.

Ranson, Gillian. *Against the Grain: Couples, Gender, and the Reframing of Parenting*. Toronto: U of Toronto P, 2010. Print.

Smith, Jeremy A. *The Daddy Shift: How Stay-at-Home Dads, Breadwinning Moms, and Shared Parenting Are Transforming the American Family*. Boston: Beacon, 2009. Print.

Stryker, Susan, and Aren Z. Aizura. *The Transgender Studies Reader 2*. New York: Routledge , 2013. Print.

Websites

❖

Geena Davis Institute on Gender in Media
www.seejane.org/

The Geena Davis Institute on Gender in Media offers a three-pronged approach— research, education and advocacy—to address gender stereotypes and the portrayal of gender roles in the national media and entertainment industry. The institute operates a programming arm, called See Jane, and the website delivers a wealth of research pertaining to gender imbalance in the media.

Gender Spectrum
www.genderspectrum.org

A nonprofit organization, Gender Spectrum is devoted to providing support and educational resources related to gender nonconforming and transgender youth. Education and training resources are also offered for families and institutions. Program resources provided on the website are divided into many different sections, including school-based training resources, medical and mental health resources, and legal and social services resources.

National At-Home Dad Network
athomedad.org

The National At-Home Dad Network is committed to unifying and supporting stay-at-home fathers through education and advocacy. Among the services provided through the organization and its website are information about local gatherings and groups, statistics and other research, and resources pertaining to fatherhood in general.

National Center for Transgender Equality (NCTE)
transequality.org

A nonprofit, the NCTE works toward advancing the rights and visibility of transgendered people. Its advocacy covers a broad spectrum of social justice issues, from fair housing and school bullying to military service and privacy issues. Extensive resources for advancing the transgender equality movement are found on the organization's website.

National Center for Women & Information Technology (NCWIT)

www.ncwit.org

This nonprofit alliance of institutions and organizations is committed to empowering women in technology and computing. The website offers a broad collection of information, news, and resources to support the participation of girls and women in information technology fields, including a portal for Spanish speakers.

National Council for Research on Women (NCRW)

www.ncrw.org

The National Council for Research on Women is dedicated to ending gender discrimination and inequality and is built from a network that encompasses academia, government, labor, and business interests. The website provides research on a broad range of issues, from the effect of environmental degradation on women to the misinformation concerning female representation in the media.

Women's Media Center (WMC)

www.womensmediacenter.com

Founded in 2005 as a nonprofit media organization, the Women's Media Center specializes in the advocacy, promotion, and research of women in the media. The website offers a wealth of information related to the visibility of women in the media, including extensive research through statistics and media monitoring, as well as training portals and resources for working in the media and other organizations such as webinars and leadership training programs.

WomenWatch

www.un.org/womenwatch

An online portal of the United Nations, WomenWatch functions as an international resource for gender equality. Through this site, the organization provides a directory of resources and relevant and real-time news feeds related to gender equality, as well as information pertaining to gender mainstreaming practices within the UN itself. It is managed by the Inter-Agency Network on Women and Gender Equality (IANWGE).

Index

❖